Extra practice problems to help you succeed at

Math 31
Alberta

Problem

Solved

CASTLE ROCK
RESEARCH CORP

Canadian Cataloguing in Publication Data

Rao, Gautam, 1961 –
Problem Solved – Math 31 Alberta

1. Mathematics – Juvenile Literature. I. Title

Published by
Castle Rock Research Corp.
2340 Manulife Place
10180 – 101 Street
Edmonton, AB T5J 3S4

1 2 3 FP 13 12 11

Publisher
Gautam Rao

Contributor
Nadine Molnar
Ken Kulka
Bob Frizzell

Dedicated to the memory of Dr. V. S. Rao

CONTENTS

Extreme Values and Curve Sketching

Applications of Derivatives

Andtiderivatives and Area

Methods of Integration and Applications

Answers and Solutions

PRE-CALCULUS

FACTORING

Factor each of the following expressions using an appropriate method.

1. $8x^3 - 125y^3$

2. $64x^3 + 1$

3. $2a^{\frac{5}{2}} + a^{\frac{3}{2}} - 3a^{\frac{1}{2}}$

4. $5a^{\frac{3}{2}} - 20a^{\frac{-1}{2}}$

5. $(x+2)^{\frac{5}{2}} - 3(x+2)^{\frac{3}{2}}$

6. $(x+4)^{\frac{7}{2}} - 4(x+4)^{\frac{-1}{2}}$

7. $\dfrac{(2x-5)^{\frac{1}{2}} + 4(2x-5)^{\frac{-1}{2}}}{2x-1}$

8. $x^2 - 20$

RATIONALIZING NUMERATORS AND DENOMINATORS

1. Rationalize the denominator in each of the following expressions and then simplify each.

    a) $\dfrac{1}{x - 2\sqrt{x}}$

    b) $\dfrac{x - 5}{\sqrt{x} + \sqrt{5}}$

    c) $\dfrac{4x}{\sqrt{2 - x} + \sqrt{2}}$

2. Rationalize the numerator in each of the following expressions and then simplify each.

    a) $\dfrac{\sqrt{2x - 5} - \sqrt{7}}{x - 6}$

    b) $\left(\sqrt{x^2 + x - 11}\right) - 1$

    c) $\dfrac{\dfrac{1}{\sqrt{x}} - 4\sqrt{x}}{4x - 1}$

OPERATIONS WITH FUNCTIONS AND COMPOSITION OF FUNCTIONS

1. Given $g(x) = x^2 - 2x - 8$ and $h(x) = x - 4$, find and sketch the graph for each of the following equations.

   a) $f(x) = g(x) - h(x)$

   b) $f(x) = \dfrac{g(x)}{h(x)}$

   c) $g(h(x))$

2. Given $g(x) = \sin x$ and $h(x) = x^2$, evaluate each of the following expressions.

   a) $\dfrac{h(x)}{g(x)}$

   b) $g(h(x))$

   c) $h(g(x))$

3. Given $g(x) = \dfrac{1}{\sqrt{x}}$ and $h(x) = x^2 - 1$, rationalize the denominators of the resulting functions of each of the following equations.

a) $f(x) = g(x) + h(x)$

b) $g(x)h(x)$

c) $h(g(x))$

TRANSFORMATIONS OF FUNCTIONS

1. Complete the following chart to describe the effect of each of the given transformations to the graph of $y = f(x)$.

	Equation of Transformation	Line that the Graph is Reflected In	Vertical Stretch Factor about the x-axis	Horizontal Stretch Factor about the y-axis	Vertical Translation	Horizontal Translation
a)	$y = -5f(2x) + 1$					
b)	$y = f(3x - 6)$					
c)	$y = -f(-x) - 2$					
d)	$y = f^{-1}(x) - 7$					
e)	$y = -7f\left(-\frac{1}{3}x - 3\right) + 8$					

2. Complete the chart below for the graph of each of the given functions.

		Amplitude	Period	Phase Shift	Vertical Displacement
a)	$y = 3\sin(2x)$				
b)	$y = -5\cos(x + \pi)$				
c)	$y = -\cos\left(3x - \frac{\pi}{2}\right) - 11$				
d)	$y = 10\sin(4x - 3\pi) + 6$				

3. Write the equation of the transformation that was applied to each of the graphs on the left to produce the graphs on the right.

a)

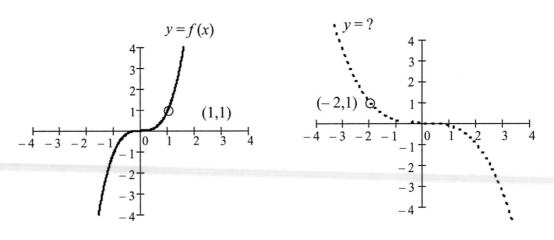

b)

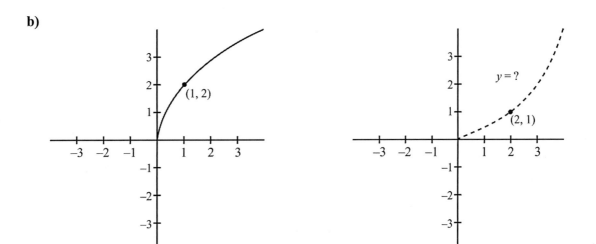

c)

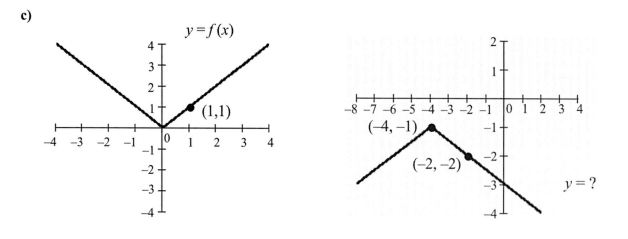

$y = f(x)$

(1,1)

$(-4, -1)$

$(-2, -2)$

$y = ?$

d)

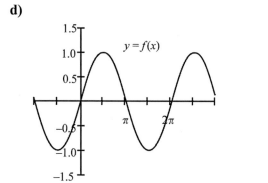

$y = f(x)$

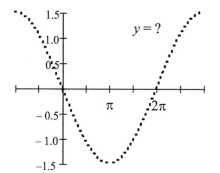

$y = ?$

e)

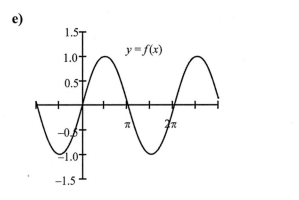

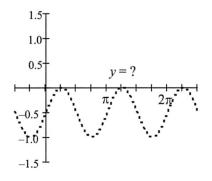

TOPIC PRACTICE QUESTIONS 1

1. Factor each of the following expressions.

   a) $x^3 - 125$

   b) $(x-7)^{\frac{3}{2}} + 3(x-7)^{-\frac{1}{2}}$

2. Rationalize the numerator of the expression $\dfrac{\sqrt{x+6} + \sqrt{10}}{x^2 - 16}$.

3. Describe the transformations that are applied to $y = f(x)$ in order to get the function $y = -5f(2x-6) + 1$.

4. Given $g(x) = 2x^2$ and $h(x) = 6x - 4$, solve each of the following equations.

a) $f(x) = \dfrac{h(x)}{g(x)}$

b) $f(x) = g(x) - h(x)$

c) $f(x) = g(h(x))$

INTERVAL NOTATION

1. Write each of the following inequality statements in interval notation.

   a) $-5 < x < 8$

   b) $x \geq 2$

   c) $x < 1$ or $x \geq 10$

   d) $x < -1$ or $0 \leq x \leq 10$

   e) $x \leq 7$ or $12 < x \leq 15$

   f) $x \neq 0$

2. Write and expression that represents the values of the following number lines.

a)

-3

b)

c)

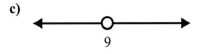

QUADRATIC INEQUALITIES

1. Solve each of the following quadratic inequalities. State the solution using interval notation.

   a) $2x+5<7$

   b) $2x<2$

   c) $x^2-9\le 0$

   d) $x^2-6>0$

   e) $x\ge -\dfrac{5}{2}$

   f) $x<1$

RATIONAL INEQUALITIES

1. Solve the following rational inequalities. State the solutions using interval notation.

a) $\dfrac{x-2}{x} < 0$

b) $\dfrac{x}{x+5} > 0$

c) $\dfrac{x^2}{x-3} \le 0$

d) $\dfrac{x^2 - x - 6}{x+1} \ge 0$

e) $\dfrac{3}{x^2 + 4} > 0$

f) $\dfrac{x}{x^2 - x - 5} > 0$

ABSOLUTE VALUE INEQUALITIES

1. Solve each of the following inequalities. State solutions using interval notation.

   a) $|x+1| < 5$

   b) $|x+2| > 6$

   c) $|x-4| - 3 \le 0$

   d) $|5x-2| < 6$

   e) $\left| \dfrac{x-5}{x} \right| \ge 0$

USING TRIGONOMETRIC IDENTITIES

1. Simplify the following expressions.

   a) $\cos^2 x - \sin^2 x - \cos(2x)$

   b) $(\sin x + \cos x)^2 - \sin(2x)$

2. Prove the following identities.

   a) $\cos\left(\dfrac{\pi}{2} + x\right) = -\sin x$

   b) $\dfrac{\sin^2 x \cos x + \cos^3 x - \cos x \tan^2 x}{2\sin x} = \dfrac{1 - \tan^2 x}{2\tan x}$

   c) $\dfrac{1 + \sin x}{\cos x} = \dfrac{\cos x}{1 - \sin x}$

   d) $\dfrac{1}{1 + \sin x} + \dfrac{1}{1 - \sin x} = 2\sec^2 x$

TOPIC PRACTICE QUESTIONS 2

1. Factor the following expressions.

a) $8x^3 + 1$

b) $(x+1)^{\frac{3}{2}} + 5(x+1)^{\frac{1}{2}} + 6(x+1)^{-\frac{1}{2}}$

2. Rationalize the denominator in the following expression.

$$\frac{x-6}{\sqrt{x^2 - x - 25} + \sqrt{5}}$$

3. Given $g(x) = x^2 - x$ and $h(x) = 5x - 1$, solve each of the following functions.

a) $f(x) = g(x)h(x)$

b) $f(x) = g(h(x))$

4. Complete the following chart for the transformations of $y = f(x)$. Put "n/a" if an answer is not possible.

New Functions	Reflection about	Vertical Stretch Factor about x-axis	Horizontal Stretch Factor About y-axis	Vertical Translation	Horizontal Translation
$y = -5f(3x) + 2$					
$y = 2f(-3x + 12)$					
$y = f^{-1}(x) - 6$					
	x-axis	$\dfrac{1}{3}$	2	Up 1	Left 5

5. For the function $y = -3\sin(4x - \pi) + 6$, determine each of the following characteristics.

a) Amplitude _____

b) Period _____

c) Phase Shift _____

d) Vertical Displacement _____

6. Solve each of the following inequalities and express the answer using interval notation.

a) $x^2 - 9x - 22 > 0$

b) $2x^2 - 5x - 1 \le 0$

c) $\dfrac{x-5}{x+2} < 0$

d) $\dfrac{x^2 - 1}{x+5} \ge 0$

e) $|x - 4| > 5$

7. Show that $\csc(2x) + \csc(2x) = \csc x \sec x$.

LIMITS

INTRODUCTION TO LIMITS

1. Evaluate the limits for the following continuous functions.

   a) $\lim\limits_{x \to 2} 2x^2 - x$

   b) $\lim\limits_{x \to 10} x^2 - 10x$

2. Use the graph of $y = f(x)$ to answer the questions that follow.

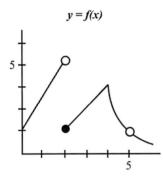

   y = f(x)

   a) Evaluate each of the following limits.

   i. $\lim\limits_{x \to 1} f(x)$

   ii. $\lim\limits_{x \to 2^-} f(x)$

   iii. $\lim\limits_{x \to 2^+} f(x)$

   iv. $\lim\limits_{x \to 2} f(x)$

   b) State two values of x for which the function is discontinuous.

3. Sketch the following function and evaluate the limits that follow.

$$f(x) = \begin{cases} 2x+4 & \text{if } x < -1 \\ x^2 & \text{if } -1 \le x < 2 \\ -x+6 & \text{if } x > 2 \end{cases}$$

a) $\lim\limits_{x \to -1^+} f(x)$

b) $\lim\limits_{x \to -1^-} f(x)$

c) $\lim\limits_{x \to -1} f(x)$

d) $\lim\limits_{x \to 2^-} f(x)$

e) $\lim\limits_{x \to 2^+} f(x)$

f) $\lim\limits_{x \to 2} f(x)$

LIMITS FOR RATIONAL EXPRESSIONS

1. Evaluate the following limits.

a) $\lim\limits_{x \to 0} \dfrac{x^2 + x}{x}$

b) $\lim\limits_{x \to 3} \dfrac{x^2 - 9}{2x^2 - x - 15}$

c) $\lim\limits_{x \to 5} \dfrac{\sqrt{x - 1} - 2}{x - 5}$

d) $\lim\limits_{x \to 2} \dfrac{x^2 + 2x - 8}{x^3 - 8}$

e) $\lim\limits_{x \to -3} \dfrac{\dfrac{1}{3} + \dfrac{1}{x}}{3 + x}$

2. Explain why the following limit does not exist.

$\lim\limits_{x \to 2} \dfrac{x^2 + 3x + 2}{x^2 - 4}$

USING LIMITS TO FIND SLOPES OF TANGENTS

1. Find the slope of the tangent to the function $f(x) = x^2 + 4$ at each of the following points.

   a) $x = 5$ **b)** $x = -3$

2. Find the slope of the tangent to the function $f(x) = 3x - 4$ at each of the following points.

   a) $x = 2$ **b)** $x = 5$

   c) What do you notice? Why is this?

3. Find the slope of the tangent to the function $f(x) = x^3 - 3$ at $x = 4$.

4. Find the slope of the tangent to the function $f(x) = \dfrac{x+1}{x-2}$ at $x = 5$.

TOPIC PRACTICE QUESTIONS

1. For the following function, determine the following limits.

$$f(x)\begin{cases} x^2 & \text{if} & x < 1 \\ x+1 & \text{if} & 1 \le x < 3 \\ -x+7 & \text{if} & x \ge 3 \end{cases}$$

   a) $\lim\limits_{x \to 1^+} f(x)$

   b) $\lim\limits_{x \to 1^-} f(x)$

   c) $\lim\limits_{x \to 1} f(x)$

   d) $\lim\limits_{x \to 3^+} f(x)$

   e) $\lim\limits_{x \to 3^-} f(x)$

   f) $\lim\limits_{x \to 3} f(x)$

   g) For what value(s) of x is the function discontinuous?

2. Evaluate the following limits.

   a) $\lim\limits_{x \to 9} x^2 - 3x - 5$

   b) $\lim\limits_{x \to 7} \dfrac{x^2 - 49}{x - 7}$

c) $\lim\limits_{x \to -1} \dfrac{x^2 - 1}{x^3 + 1}$

d) $\lim\limits_{x \to 9} \dfrac{\sqrt{x - 5} - 2}{9 - x}$

3. For the function $f(x) = x^2 - 5$, determine the slope of the tangent when

    a) $x = 4$ **b)** $x = 1$

4. For the function $f(x) = \dfrac{1}{2x}$, determine the slope of the function when $x = 7$.

DERIVATIVES AND DERIVATIVE THEOREMS

DERIVATIVES USING FIRST PRINCIPLES

1. Use first principles to find the derivative of each of the following functions.

   a) $f(x) = 4x^2 - 7$

   b) $y = 2x^3 - 6x$

   c) $y = \dfrac{1}{x}$

   d) $f(x) = \sqrt{3x + 1}$

2. Use first principles to find the derivative of each of the following functions. Use the derivative to find the slope of the tangent at the specified point, and then write the equation for each tangent.

a) $y = 5x^2 - x$ at $(1, 4)$

b) $f(x) = (x+3)^2$ at $(2, 25)$

c) $f(x) = \dfrac{1}{x^2 - 2}$ at $\left(2, \dfrac{1}{2}\right)$

d) $f(x) = \dfrac{x+2}{x^2}$ at $\left(3, \dfrac{5}{9}\right)$

e) $y = \sqrt{5x - 7}$ at $\left(2, \sqrt{3}\right)$

f) $y = \dfrac{3x}{\sqrt{x}}$ at $\left(2, 3\sqrt{2}\right)$

THE POWER RULE

1. Use the power rule to find the derivatives of the following functions.

    a) $f(x) = 6x^3$

    b) $y = \sqrt{x}$

    c) $f(x) = \dfrac{1}{x^4}$

    d) $y = 5\sqrt[3]{x^4}$

2. Use the sum and the difference rules to find the derivatives of the following functions.

    a) $f(x) = 5x^3 - 2x$

    b) $y = 4x^2 + x - 5$

    c) $y = 2\sqrt{x} - \dfrac{1}{2}$

    d) $f(t) = \dfrac{4}{t} - \dfrac{1}{t^2}$

e) $y = \dfrac{x^3 - x^2 - x}{x}$

f) $f(x) = \dfrac{x^2 - 2\sqrt{x}}{\sqrt{x}}$

3. Find the derivative of each of the following functions and write the equation of the tangent line at the given point.

a) $y = 7x^2$; (2, 28)

b) $f(x) = x - \dfrac{4}{x}$; (2, 0)

4. **a)** At which point does the curve $y = 3x^2 - 4x$ have a tangent with a slope of 2?

b) At which points does the curve $y = x^3 - 3x^2 - 24x$ have horizontal tangent lines?

THE PRODUCT RULE

1. Find the derivative of each of the following functions using the product rule.

   a) $y = \left(x^3\right)\left(15x^4\right)$

   b) $f(x) = \left(5x^7\right)\left(\dfrac{6}{x}\right)$

   c) $y = \left(5\sqrt{x^3}\right)\left(9x^4\right)$

   d) $f(x) = \left(7 - x^2\right)\left(\sqrt{x}\right)$

   e) $y = \left(5x^3 - x\right)\left(\dfrac{1}{2\sqrt{x}}\right)$

   f) $f(x) = \left(3x^2 - x + 18\right)\left(2x^3 - x\right)$

THE QUOTIENT RULE

1. Find the derivative of each of the following functions by using the quotient rule.

a) $y = \dfrac{1+x}{3x^2}$

b) $f(x) = \dfrac{5x^2 - 1}{2x + 4}$

c) $y = \dfrac{\sqrt[3]{x^2}}{2\sqrt{x}}$

2. Find the derivative of each of the following functions by using the product and the quotient rules.

a) $y = \dfrac{\left(x^4\right)(2x-1)}{4x^3}$

b) $f(x) = \dfrac{3x^3 - 12x}{(x+3)(2x-7)}$

THE CHAIN RULE

1. Differentiate the following problems.

a) $f(x) = (5x^3 - x)^9$

b) $y = \sqrt{x^2 - 2x}$

c) $f(x) = x^3(3x - 1)^2$

d) $y = \dfrac{\sqrt{5x}}{2x^2 - 3}$

e) $f(x) = \sqrt{2x\sqrt{x+3}}$

TOPIC PRACTICE QUESTIONS 1

1. Use first principles to find the derivative of the function $f(x) = 6x^2 - x$.

2. Differentiate the following functions.

    a) $y = 8x^4 - 6x^3 + x - 7$

    b) $f(x) = \sqrt{x}(x^2 - 6)$

    c) $y = \dfrac{3x^3}{x - 3}$

    d) $f(x) = (x^3 + 4)^6$

e) $f(x) = \dfrac{x\sqrt{x-1}}{x+2}$

f) $y = x^2\left(3x^2 - 7\right)^4$

3. Find the derivative and use it to determine the slope of the function $f(x) = \dfrac{1}{x^3}$ at the point $\left(2, \dfrac{1}{2}\right)$.

Then, write the equation of this tangent.

IMPLICIT DIFFERENTIATION

1. For each of the following equations, find the derivative with respect to x.

   a) $4x^2 + 4y^2 = 20$

   b) $4xy^2 + 2y = 3x$

   c) $3y - \dfrac{y^4}{x^2} = 2y$

2. For each of the following equations, find the slope of the tangent at the point indicated.

   a) $4x^3 - y^2 = y + 2$ at point $(2, 5)$

   b) $7xy = 21$ at point $\left(6, \dfrac{1}{2}\right)$

3. Write the equation of the line tangent to the curve at the point indicated.
   $3x - y^2 + 6y = x^2 - x$ at point $(5, 1)$

HIGHER DERIVATIVES

1. Find the second derivative of each of the following functions.

a) $f(x) = 3x^3 - 9x^2 + 16x - 5$

b) $f(x) = 10x$

c) $y = \dfrac{4x}{x-7}$

d) $y = (3x^2 - 5)^3$

2. For each of the following functions, find $f''(-1)$.

a) $f(x) = 7x^3 - 2x$

b) $f(x) = \dfrac{5x+1}{x^2}$

TOPIC PRACTICE QUESTIONS 2

1. Use first principles to find the derivative of the following function $f(x) = \dfrac{-5}{\sqrt{x}}$

2. Identify which rule(s) you should use to differentiate each function, and then use it (them) to find each derivative.

   a) $y = 16x^7 - x$

   b) $f(x) = \dfrac{-6}{x^3}$

   c) $y = 6x\sqrt{x}$

   d) $f(x) = \dfrac{2x}{5-x}$

   e) $f(x) = \sqrt{x^2 - 7}$

   f) $y = (x-3)^2(4x+1)$

3. Find the slope and equation of the tangent of $y = \dfrac{6x^2}{x+1}$ at the point (1, 3).

4. At what point is the slope of the tangent to the function $f(x) = \dfrac{4}{x^2}$ equal to –1?

5. Use implicit differentiation to find $\dfrac{dy}{dx}$ given the following function.

$3xy = 2x^2 - 6y^3$

6. Find the first and second derivative of each of the following equations.

a) $y = 2x^4 - 3x^2 + 1$

b) $f(x) = \dfrac{2}{\sqrt{x}}$

7. The following function represents the displacement (s) in metres of a particle as a function of time (t) in seconds.

$$s = t^3 - 6t^2 - 8 \qquad \text{Recall} \quad v = \frac{ds}{dt} \text{ and } a = \frac{dv}{dt}$$

a) Find the velocity and acceleration functions with respect to t.

b) Determine the acceleration after 35 seconds.

DERIVATIVES OF TRIGONOMETRIC, LOGARITHMIC, AND EXPONENTIAL FUNCTIONS

LIMITS OF TRIGONOMETRIC FUNCTIONS

1. Evaluate the following limits.

a) $\displaystyle\lim_{x \to 0} \frac{\sin(4x)}{4x}$

b) $\displaystyle\lim_{x \to 0} \frac{2 - 2\cos x}{x}$

c) $\displaystyle\lim_{\theta \to 0} \frac{\sin(4\theta)}{\sin(3\theta)}$

d) $\displaystyle\lim_{x \to 0} \frac{\sin(3x)}{3x^2 + x}$

e) $\displaystyle\lim_{\theta \to 0} \frac{1 - \cos(2\theta)}{\theta}$

f) $\displaystyle\lim_{x \to 0} \frac{5\tan x - 5\sin x}{x \cos x}$

DERIVATIVES OF TRIGONOMETRIC FUNCTIONS
PART 1: SINE AND COSINE

1. Differentiate each of the following trigonometric functions.

   a) $y = 4\cos x$

   b) $f(x) = 3\sin(5x^2)$

   c) $y = \dfrac{\sin^2 x}{\cos(2x)}$

   d) $f(x) = -2\cos^3(7x)$

   e) $y = x\sin x$

2. Find the slope of the tangent to the function $y = \cos^2(2x)$ at the point $x = \dfrac{\pi}{2}$.

DERIVATIVES OF TRIGONOMETRIC FUNCTIONS
PART 2: TANGENT, COTANGENT, SECANT, AND COSECANT

1. Differentiate the following functions.

a) $f(x) = 2\cot(2x)$

b) $y = \sin x \sec(2x)$

c) $f(x) = \dfrac{\tan(5x - 4)}{\cos x^3}$

d) $y = \csc^3(3x^2)$

TOPIC PRACTICE QUESTIONS 1

1. Evaluate the following limits.

   a) $\displaystyle\lim_{x\to 0}\frac{\sin^2(4x)}{2x^2}$

   b) $\displaystyle\lim_{x\to 0}\frac{\cos x - 1}{3x}$

2. Differentiate the following trigonometric functions.

   a) $y = 4\sin^2 x$

   b) $f(x) = \tan^3(5x)$

   c) $y = x\cos(4x)$

   d) $f(x) = \dfrac{\sec x}{\tan x}$

e) $y = \csc^3\left(x^2 - 1\right)$ **f)** $y\sin x = 3x - \cos y$

3. Find the slope of the tangent to the function $y = 4\tan^2 x$ at the point $x = \dfrac{\pi}{4}$.

DERIVATIVES OF FUNCTIONS WITH NATURAL LOGARITHMS

Differentiate each of the following functions.

1. $y = \ln x^2$ **2.** $f(x) = 3x^2 \ln(x+1)$

3. $y = \dfrac{\ln x}{x^3}$ **4.** $y = \ln(3x^2 - 1)$

5. $xy = \ln y$

DERIVATIVES OF EXPONENTIAL AND LOGARITHMIC FUNCTIONS

1. Differentiate the following exponential functions.

   a) $y = 2^x$
                                               b) $y = 4\left(5^{x^2}\right)$

   c) $y = 7^{x^3 - x}$

2. Find the derivatives of the following logarithmic functions.

   a) $y = \log_7 x$
                                               b) $y = 2\log_3 (x - 6)$

3. Using the methods used in this chapter combined with the rules for differentiating, differentiate the following complex functions.

a) $f(x) = 2^{\sin x}$

b) $y = 4x^2 \ln x$

c) $f(x) = 2^x x^2$

d) $y = x \ln \cos(2x)^2$

TOPIC PRACTICE QUESTIONS 2

1. Evaluate the following limit.

$$\lim_{x \to 0} \frac{5 \sin 5x}{2x}$$

2. Differentiate the following trigonometric functions.

   a) $y = \csc x$

   b) $y = \sin(3x) \cos x^2$

   c) $y = 2 \tan^2 (2x - 5)$

   d) $f(x) = 4x^3 \sec(7x)$

3. Find the slope of the tangent to the curve $f(x) = 3 \cos^2 (2x)$, when $x = \dfrac{\pi}{3}$.

4. Differentiate the following logarithmic and exponential functions.

a) $f(x) = 5\ln 3x$

b) $y = 5^{2x^2}(4x)$

c) $y = \log_2(3x - 9)$

d) $y = 2^{xy}$

5. Find the derivative of the following functions.

a) $f(x) = \sin^2(\ln(2x))$

b) $y = 5^{x\sin x}$

EXTREME VALUES AND CURVE SKETCHING

INTERCEPTS AND ZEROS

1. Find the *x*- and *y*-intercepts of the following functions.

a) $y = 2x - 6$

b) $y = x^2 - x$

c) $y = 3x^2 + 10x - 8$

d) $y = 3\sin x$, where $0 \le x \le \pi$

e) $y = \dfrac{4x^2 - x}{3x - 7}$

f) $y = 2x^2 - 3x - 7$

SYMMETRY OF FUNCTIONS

1. Determine whether or not the following functions are even.

   a) $y = 4x^2 - 3$

   b) $f(x) = 2x^3 + 3x - 1$

   c) $y = 4x^4 + 2x^2 - 1$

   d) $y = 2\cos x + 3$

2. Determine whether or not the following functions are odd.

   a) $y = 3x^3$

   b) $y = 4x^2 - x$

c) $f(x) = 2x^3 - 5x$

d) $y = \dfrac{1}{2}\sin(2x)$

3. Determine what type of symmetry if any, each of the following functions has.

a) $y = 3x^2 - 5$

b) $y = 2x^3 - 7x$

c) $y = x^3 - x^2$

d) $y = 4\sin x \cos x$

INTERVALS OF INCREASE AND DECREASE AND MAXIMUM AND MINIMUM VALUES

1. For each of the following functions, state the intervals of increase and decrease, and determine the local maximum and minimum values.

   a) $y = 2x^2 - 16x + 39$

   b) $f(x) = \dfrac{2}{x-3}$

   c) $f(x) = 3\sin(x) + 2$, where $0 \le x \le 2\pi$

   d) $y = 2\cos^2(2x)$, where $0 < x < \dfrac{3\pi}{4}$

CONCAVITY AND POINTS OF INFLECTION

1. Use the following diagram to fill in the blanks below.

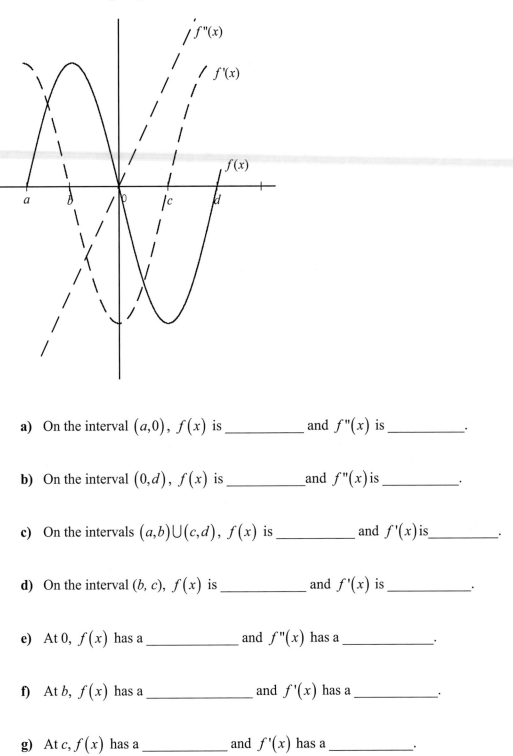

a) On the interval $(a,0)$, $f(x)$ is _____ and $f''(x)$ is _____.

b) On the interval $(0,d)$, $f(x)$ is _____ and $f''(x)$ is _____.

c) On the intervals $(a,b) \cup (c,d)$, $f(x)$ is _____ and $f'(x)$ is _____.

d) On the interval (b, c), $f(x)$ is _____ and $f'(x)$ is _____.

e) At 0, $f(x)$ has a _____ and $f''(x)$ has a _____.

f) At b, $f(x)$ has a _____ and $f'(x)$ has a _____.

g) At c, $f(x)$ has a _____ and $f'(x)$ has a _____.

2. Find the concavity intervals and inflection points for each of the following functions.

   a) $f(x) = x^2 - 8x$

   b) $f(x) = 5x^3 - 5x^2 + 8$

   c) $f(x) = \dfrac{x^2 - 1}{x}$

   d) $f(x) = 5\cos(2x) - x$, where $0 < x < \pi$

3. Using the x values of a, b, c, d, and 0 shown on the following graph, state the interval(s) over which each statement below is true.

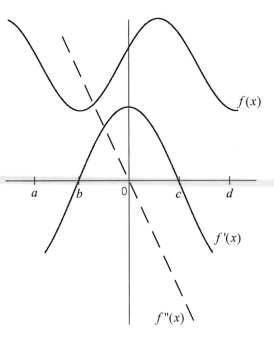

a) $f'(x)$ is positive _____

b) $f(x)$ is concave down _____

c) $f''(x)$ is positive _____

d) $f(x)$ is decreasing _____

4. Using first and second derivatives, sketch the graph of the given function by examining intervals of increase/decrease, local extrema, intervals of concavity, inflection points, and y-intercept.
   $f(x) = 4x^3 - 3x^2 - 36x + 12$

5. For each derivative function, f', draw a possible sketch of function f.

a)

b)

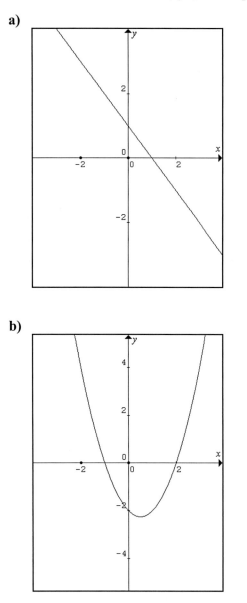

OPTIMIZATION PROBLEMS

1. Find 2 positive numbers whose product is 100 and whose sum is a minimum.

2. Find the dimensions of a rectangle whose area is 8 000 cm^2 and whose perimeter is as small as possible.

3. Find the maximum area of a triangle inscribed in a semicircle of diameter 40 cm. Use the diagram below to help you.

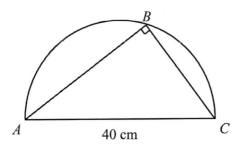

Recall that an angle inscribed in a semicircle is always a right angle.

4. A farmer wishes to build a fence around a rectangular pasture and divide it into 2 rectangular areas as shown in the diagram below:

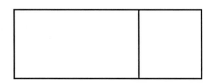

The farmer has 600 m of fencing. Find the maximum *total* area that he can fence.

5. A piece of wire 20 cm long is to be cut into two pieces. One piece will be bent into a square and the other will be bent into an equilateral triangle. How should the wire be cut to enclose a minimum total area?

TOPIC PRACTICE QUESTIONS 1

1. Determine what symmetry, if any, the following function has.

$$f(x) = \frac{4x^4 - 1}{x^2}$$

2. Determine the intervals of increase and decrease, as well as any maximum and minimum values for the following functions.

a) $f(x) = x^2 - 4x + 1$

b) $y = \frac{x^2 + 1}{x}$

3. Determine the concavity intervals and inflection points for the following functions.

   a) $y = x^3 + 2x^2 - x + 4$ **b)** $f(x) = 2\sin x$, where $0 < x < 2\pi$

4. A manufacturer wants to make a can that will hold 355 mL of soup. What should the dimensions of the can be so that the cost required (materials) to make the can is a minimum? Recall that $355 \text{ mL} = 355 \text{ cm}^3$.

VERTICAL ASYMPTOTES

1. Determine the location of any vertical asymptotes, and sketch the function near these asymptotes.

a) $f(x) = \dfrac{1}{x+1}$

b) $f(x) = \dfrac{2}{x^2 + 2x - 3}$

c) $f(x) = \sec x$ on interval $(0, 2\pi)$

d) $y = \dfrac{x+5}{x+4}$

HORIZONTAL ASYMPTOTES

1. Determine the equations of the horizontal asymptotes for each of the following functions, if they exist, by evaluating the $\lim\limits_{x \to \pm\infty} f(x)$.

a) $f(x) = \dfrac{x^2}{x^3 - 4}$

b) $f(x) = \dfrac{2x^2 - x}{4x^2 - 3}$

c) $f(x) = \dfrac{-5x^3 - 4x^2}{3x^2 + x}$

d) $f(x) = \dfrac{-4x^3 + 2x^2 - 1}{6x^3 - x + 5}$

2. Find the equations of the vertical and horizontal asymptotes for each of the following functions and draw a rough sketch of each graph.

a) $f(x) = \dfrac{2x + 1}{x - 3}$

b) $f(x) = \dfrac{-4x^2 - x}{x^2 - 2x - 15}$

OBLIQUE ASYMPTOTES

1. Which of the following functions will have an oblique asymptote?

   a) $f(x) = \dfrac{3x^2 - x}{x + 7}$

   b) $f(x) = \dfrac{-5x + 2}{x - 3}$

   c) $f(x) = \dfrac{3x^2 + 4}{x}$

   d) $f(x) = \dfrac{3x^3 - x^2}{x^2 + 5}$

   e) $f(x) = \dfrac{6x^3 + 2x^2 + 3x + 1}{-7x^3 + x}$

   f) $f(x) = \dfrac{4x^4 + 6}{2x^2 - 1}$

2. Find the equation of the oblique asymptotes for each of the following functions.

   a) $f(x) = \dfrac{2x^2 + 3}{x}$

   b) $f(x) = \dfrac{3x^2 - 7x}{x - 2}$

   c) $f(x) = \dfrac{6x^3 - 5x}{x^2 + 1}$

   d) $f(x) = \dfrac{-4x^3 + 2x^2 + x - 4}{x^2 - 2x}$

TOPIC PRACTICE QUESTIONS 2

1. Use the following graph to answer the questions below.

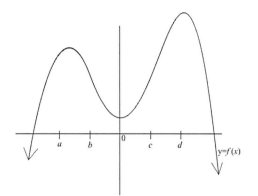

The function graphed above is a degree 4 polynomial function. Using $\pm\infty$, a, b, and 0, state the interval(s) or x-values when each of the following situations is true.

a) $f(x)$ is increasing _____

b) $f'(x)$ is negative _____

c) $f''(x)$ is positive _____

d) $f'(x) = 0$ _____

2. For the following functions, determine
    a) the intervals of increase and decrease
    b) any local maximum and minimum values
    c) the concavity intervals
    d) any inflection points

i) $f(x) = 5x^3 - 5x^2 - 15$

ii) $f(x) = 2x^3 + 3x^2 - 120x + 48$

3. For the function $f(x) = \dfrac{x+2}{x^2-9}$,

   a) determine the x- and y-intercepts

   b) determine the equation of any vertical asymptotes and the left- and right-hand limits as the function approaches the asymptote

   c) determine the equation of any horizontal asymptotes

   d) determine the intervals of increase/decrease and any maximum or minimum values

   e) determine the intervals of concavity and any points of inflection

   f) use the information from parts a), b), c), d) and e) above to sketch a graph of the function

4. For the function $f(x) = \dfrac{x^2 + 4x + 4}{x+1}$,

   a) determine the x- and y-intercepts

   b) determine the equation of any vertical asymptotes and the left- and right-hand limits, as the function approaches the asymptote

   c) determine the equation of the oblique asymptote

   d) determine the intervals of increase/decrease and any maximum or minimum values

   e) determine the intervals of concavity and any points of inflection

   f) use the information from parts a), b), c), d) and e) above to sketch a graph of the function

5. A new square-bottomed juice box needs to be designed to hold 1 litre of juice. What should the dimensions of the box be so that it has a minimum surface area. Recall that $1L = 1\ 000\ cm^3$.

6. What is the maximum possible area of an isosceles triangle whose equal sides each measure 10 cm?

7. Using first and second derivatives, sketch the graph of the given function by examining intervals of increase/decrease, local extrema, intervals of concavity, inflection points, and the y-intercept.
$f(x) = -x^3 + 4x^2 + 3x + 5$

APPLICATIONS OF DERIVATIVES

DISTANCE, VELOCITY, AND ACCELERATION

1. A bullet is fired straight up in the air at a speed of 900 m/s. The equation relating its height as a function of time is $h = -4.9t^2 + 900t + 2.4$.

    a) How long does it take the bullet to hit the ground?

    b) What are the maximum and minimum values of the velocity of the bullet?

    c) What is the velocity of the bullet after 60 seconds? Which direction is the bullet traveling?

2. On the moon, an object is dropped straight down into a crater 150 m deep. The height of the object from the bottom of the crater, as it falls, is given by $h = -0.8t^2 + 150$.

    a) What is the falling object's maximum speed?

    b) What is the acceleration due to gravity on the moon?

3. On three different planets, the following functions express the height of an object that is thrown downward and is falling 200 m.

Neptune: $h = -5.88t^2 - 8t + 200$

Mars: $h = -1.85t^2 - 8t + 200$

Venus: $h = -4.45t^2 - 8t + 200$

a) What is the acceleration due to gravity on each planet?

b) What is the maximum speed of the falling object on Venus?

c) How much faster is the maximum speed of the falling object on Neptune than the maximum speed of the falling object on Mars?

RATES OF CHANGE INVOLVING AREA AND VOLUME

1. For each of the following problems, find the desired rate.

    a) $V = s^3$

    $\dfrac{ds}{dt} = 3$ m/s

    Find $\dfrac{dV}{dt}$ when $s = 10$ m.

    b) $A = \pi r^2$

    $\dfrac{dA}{dt} = -1.2$ m²/s

    Find $\dfrac{dr}{dt}$ when $A = 15$ m².

2. The area of a square is increasing at a rate of 20 cm²/s. At what rate is the side length increasing when the side length is 200 cm?

3. The volume of a melting spherical ball of snow is decreasing at a rate of 40 cm^3/s. If it is assumed that the ball of snow is melting uniformly, at what rate is the radius decreasing when the radius of the ball is 3.5 cm?

4. A landscaping company is pouring rock chips into a conical pile with a constant ratio of 2:5 between the radius and height. The volume of the rock chips is increasing at a rate of 1.8 m^3/min. At what rate is the height increasing when the radius is 3 m?

5. The volume of an expanding cube is increasing at a rate of 6 m^3/s. At what rate is the length of the side of the cube increasing when the surface area of the cube is 40 m^2?

RATES OF CHANGE INVOLVING TRIANGLES

1. A man and a woman walk away from the same location at the same time. The man travels east at a rate of 2 m/s. The woman travels south at a rate of 1.8 m/s. At what rate is the distance between them increasing 5 minutes later?

2. A spotlight set on the ground is shining on a wall 20 m away. A person 1.7 m tall walks away from the light toward the wall at a rate of 1.4 m/s. At what rate is the shadow cast on the wall decreasing in height when the person is 14 m from the light?

3. A child is flying a kite. When her arm is outstretched, her hand is 1.6 m off the ground. The kite is at a constant altitude of 16.6 m. The wind is blowing the kite horizontally at a rate of 4 m/s. At what rate is the length of string increasing when there is 30 m of string between the child's hand and the kite?

4. The length of the hypotenuse of a right triangle is constant at 64 cm. The vertical leg of the triangle is decreasing at a rate of 5 cm/s. At what rate is the angle opposite the vertical side changing when the horizontal side is 40 cm long?

5. A triangle's altitude is increasing at a rate of 3 cm/min and the triangle's area is increasing at a rate of 9 cm^2/min. At what rate is the base changing when the altitude is 20 cm and the area is 300 cm^2?

6. Two sides of a triangle have fixed lengths of 20 cm and 24 cm. The third side is increasing at a rate of 3.5 cm/s. When the third side is 15 cm in length, what is the rate of change for the angle between the fixed sides?

TOPIC PRACTICE QUESTIONS 1

1. The height in metres from the ground of a falling object after t seconds is found to be $h = -4.9t^2 + 5t + 85$.

   a) How long will it take the falling object to reach the ground?

   b) What is the maximum speed of the falling object?

   c) What is the velocity of the object after 2.5 s?

   d) What is the acceleration of the falling object?

2. Find the unknown rate.
   $$V = \frac{4}{3}\pi r^3 \; ; \; \frac{dV}{dt} = -6 \text{ m}^3 / \text{s}, \text{ when } r = 5 \text{ m}, \frac{dr}{dt} = ?$$

3. A drop of water creates a circular ripple that moves outward at a rate of 20 cm/s. At what rate is the circumference of the circle increasing when the area of the circle is 10 000 cm^2?

4. As the sun rises, the shadow cast by a 15 m tree is decreasing at a rate of 55 cm/h. At what rate is the angle of elevation from the shadow to the sun increasing when the shadow is 15 m in length?

APPLICATIONS IN ECONOMICS

1. A cost function, for cost in dollars, is represented as $C(x) = 3\,000 + 4.2x + 0.01x^2$.

   a) What is the marginal cost function?

   b) Determine the marginal cost when production is at 1 000 units.

   c) How many units need to be produced to give a marginal cost of $40?

2. A demand function is $p(x) = 6 - 0.008x$.

   a) What is the revenue function?

   b) What is the marginal revenue function?

   c) Determine the marginal revenue when 650 items are produced.

3. Using the demand function from question 2, and the cost function
$C(x) = 55 + 1.9x - 0.009x^2 + 0.000\ 08x^3$

a) What is the profit function?

b) How many items need to be produced in order to maximize profit?

APPLICATIONS IN BIOLOGICAL SCIENCES

1. Which of the following functions is a growth function and which is a decay function?

   a) $f(t) = 40e^{\frac{-\ln 3}{7}t}$

   b) $f(t) = 1\,000e^{\left(\frac{1}{4}\ln 2\right)t}$

2. The mass, in grams, of a radioactive substance remaining after t days is given by $f(t) = 35e^{\frac{-\ln 3}{40}t}$.

   a) Find the decay rate after t days.

   b) Find the decay rate after 20 days.

3. The number of bacteria after t hours is given by $f(t) = 1\,500e^{\frac{\ln 3}{7}t}$.

   a) Determine the growth rate after 5 hours.

   b) Determine the length of time it will take for the growth rate to reach 2 000 bacteria per hour.

---

4. A sample of a radioactive substance has a mass of 100 g. After 30 days, it has a mass of 25 g.

a) What is the mass after t days?

b) What is the decay rate after t days?

c) How long will it take the decay rate to reach -3 g/day?

NEWTON'S METHOD

Use Newton's method to find the desired approximation of the roots for the following equations.

1. $x^2 - 12 = 0$; $x_1 = 2$; $x_4 = ?$

2. $x^3 - 5x - 5 = 0$; $x_1 = 2$; $x_3 = ?$

3. $\sin x = 0$; $x_1 = 3$; $x_3 = ?$,
(where x is in radians)

4. $x^2 - 2 = \dfrac{x+4}{x}$; $x_1 = 2$; $x_3 = ?$

5. $4\sin^2 x - 3 = 0$; $x_1 = 1$; $x_3 = ?$
   (where x is in radians)

TOPIC PRACTICE QUESTIONS 2

1. The height in metres of a falling object as a function of time in seconds is defined by $h = -4.9t^2 - 6t + 9$.

   a) What is the object's maximum and minimum velocity, and its maximum speed?

   b) How long does it take the object to reach a velocity of -10 m/s?

2. Determine the unknown rate for each of the following questions.

   a) $A = 4\pi r^2$; $r = 12\,\text{m}$; $\dfrac{dr}{dt} = -1.5\,\text{m/s}$; $\dfrac{dA}{dt} = ?$

b) $A = 2\pi r^2 + 2\pi rh$; $h = 2r$; $r = 3\,\text{cm}$; $\dfrac{dA}{dt} = 50\,\text{cm}^2/\text{s}$; $\dfrac{dr}{dt} = ?$

3. A conical water tank has a height of 7 metres and a diameter of 6 metres. It is draining at a rate of $2\text{m}^3/\text{min}$. At what rate is the water level decreasing when

   a) the water level is 4 m?   **b)** the radius at the top of the water is 1 m?

4. A train is 100 km due east of a car at 4:00 P.M. The car travels due north at a rate of 60 km/h and the train travels due west at a rate of 70 km/h. At what rate is the distance between them changing at

   a) 5:00 P.M. ?   **b)** 6:30 P.M. ?

5. The cost of producing x items is defined by $C(x) = 400 + 3x + 0.013x^2$. The price (demand) function is $p(x) = 2 + 0.02x$.

a) Determine the marginal cost of producing 100 items.

b) Determine the marginal revenue if 800 items are produced.

c) How many items should be produced to maximize profit?

6. A bacterial culture has grown from 650 to 1 950 bacteria in 2 hours.

a) Determine the number of bacteria as a function of time.

b) What is the growth rate of the bacteria after 10 hours?

7. Use Newton's method to approximate a relevant root of the following functions:

a) x_3 for $x^3 + 2x - 1 = 0$, where $x_1 = 1$

b) x_3 for $x^2 - 4x - 5 = 0$, where $x_1 = 3$

ANTIDERIVATIVES AND AREA

THE ANTIDERIVATIVE

1. Solve the following differential equations.

   a) $\dfrac{dy}{dx} = -3x^2 - 2x + 1$

   b) $\dfrac{dp}{dz} = \dfrac{3}{z} - \dfrac{3}{z^2} + \dfrac{2}{z^3}, z \neq 0$

   c) $\dfrac{dy}{dx} = \sec^2 x$

   d) $\dfrac{du}{dy} = y - \cos y$

2. Evaluate each indefinite integral.

   a) $\displaystyle\int \left(x^5\right) dx$

   b) $\displaystyle\int \left(5^x\right)\left(\ln 5\right) dx$

   c) $\displaystyle\int \left(\sin^2 x + \cos^2 x\right) dx$

   d) $\displaystyle\int \left(27 e^x\right) dx$

3. Use the method of substitution to evaluate each of the following indefinite integrals.

a) $\int (5x-3)^{12}\, dx$

b) $\int \left(\sqrt{4x^2-10x} \right)(4x-5)\, dx$

c) $\int \left[\cos^4(8x) \right]\left[\sin(8x) \right] dx$

d) $\int \left(e^{\ln(4x)} \right)\left(\dfrac{1}{x} \right) dx$

DIFFERENTIAL EQUATIONS WITH INITIAL CONDITIONS

1. Solve the following differential equations using the initial conditions given.

   a) Given that an object accelerates according to the function $a(t) = t + 1$, what are the equations representing velocity and displacement given that initial velocity is 0 and initial displacement is also 0 where $t \geq 0$?

   b) Given $a = 3\sin t$ for $t \geq 0$ find s if $v(0) = 1$ and $s(0) = 1$.

   c) Find the equation of a function y given that $\dfrac{d^2 y}{dx^2} = x - 1$ and knowing that at the origin the rate of change of the function is 1. As well, the original function passed through the point (1, 2).

d) An object has a velocity defined as $v = 2t - 1$ in metres/second for all $t \geq 1$. Find the distance travelled by the object from $t = 3$ to $t = 5$.

e) Solve $y'' + 16y = 0$ given that when $x = \dfrac{\pi}{2}$, $y = 1$, and $y' = 1$.

f) A spring with a mass of 0.5 kg has a natural length of 0.1 m. A force of 10 N is required to stretch it to 0.2 m. If the spring is stretched to 3 times its normal length, held at rest and then released, what is the displacement of the mass at time t?

g) The rate at which a rabbit population grows is proportional to the number of rabbits present at any particular instant. If there are 100 rabbits present now and 900 rabbits present in 2 years then what number of rabbits will be present in 3 years?

TOPIC PRACTICE QUESTIONS 1

1. Evaluate $\int \left(2x^2 - 3\right)dx$.

2. Evaluate $\int \left(2e^{2x} - \sin x\right)dx$.

3. Find the antiderivative of $f'(x) = 3 - \dfrac{3}{x}$ where $x \neq 0$.

4. Solve the following differential equation with the given initial conditions given.

$\dfrac{ds}{dt} = t^2 - 1$ where $s = 1$ at $t = 0$.

5. Find $F(x)$ given that $F'(x) = x,$ and that the point $\left(1, -\dfrac{1}{2}\right)$ lies on $F(x)$.

6. If $y'' + ky = 0$ and a solution exists at $y = A\sin\left(\sqrt{k}\,x\right) + B\cos\left(\sqrt{k}\,x\right)$, solve $y'' + 100y = 0$ when $y = 0$, when $x = 0$, and when $y' = 2$ when $x = 0$.

7. Evaluate $\int\left(\cos^3 x\right) dx$

SIGNED AREA

1. Find the signed area under the curve for each of the following functions over the interval indicated.

   a) $f(x) = \dfrac{1}{x}$ $[1,3]$

   b) $f(x) = \sin x$ $[0, \pi]$

   c) $\dfrac{f(x)}{2} = x^2 - 1$ $[2,3]$

   d) $f(x) = \dfrac{2\sqrt{x}}{3}$ $[1,4]$

   e) $f(x) = x^2 - 4x$ $[0,3]$

   f) $f(x) = e^x$ $[0,1]$

THE DEFINITE INTEGRAL AND THE FUNDAMENTAL THEOREM OF CALCULUS

1. Approximate the signed area under the function $f(x) = 4 - x^2$ in the interval [0, 4] by using a left rectangular approximation with 4 rectangles.

2. Evaluate each definite integral algebraically. Verify your result with your graphing calculator.

a) $\int_{-4}^{3} (4 - x^2) dx$

b) $\int_{\frac{\pi}{2}}^{\frac{5\pi}{3}} (\sin t + \cos t) dt$

c) $\int_{2}^{3} \left(\frac{1}{x}\right) dx$

d) $\int_{-1}^{3} (e^{2p}) dp$

3.

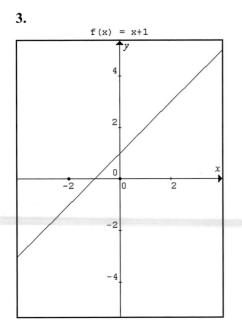

f(x) = x+1

Function p is defined as $p(x) = \int_{-2}^{x} \left[f(t) \right] dt$.

a) Evaluate $p(x)$

b) Determine the value of $p(-2)$, $p(3)$, and $p(-3)$

4. Determine the total area enclosed by the function $f(x) = \sin x$ and the x-axis in the interval $\left[\dfrac{\pi}{6}, \dfrac{4\pi}{3} \right]$.

5. Solve for x if $\int_2^x (2t-3)\,dt = 12$.

6. Determine the value of $\int_2^5 \left[f(x)\right]dx$ if $\int_2^4 \left[f(x)\right]dx = 10$ and $\int_4^5 \left[f(x)\right]dx = -17$

7. Determine the value of $\int_2^5 \left[f(x)\right]dx$ if $\int_4^2 \left[f(x)\right]dx = 10$ and $\int_5^4 \left[f(x)\right]dx = -17$

8. Determine the average value of the function $f(x) = 4 - x^2$. Where does the function take on this value?

AREA BETWEEN CURVES

1. Find the area of the enclosed region between the given curves over the indicated interval. If there are intersection points, indicate them.

   a) $f(x) = x^2$ and $g(x) = 1$ in quadrant I

   b) $f(x) = x^2$ and $g(x) = 1$, between both intersection points

   c) $y = -x^2 + 4$ and $y = -2x$ for any area bounded between the curves and the y-axis (as a right-hand boundary) i.e. only areas left of or touching the y-axis

d) $y = x^2 - 4$, above the x-axis and the line $x = 4$

e) $y = \sin x$ and $y = \cos x$ between the y-axis and $\dfrac{\pi}{4}$ radians along the positive x-axis

f) $y = x^3 - 3x^2 + x + 4$, $y = -x^2 + 4x + 4$, and the y-axis, in Cartesian Quadrant I

AREA USING NUMERICAL METHODS (REVISITED)

1. **a)** Use the Rectangular Rule to approximate the area under the curve of $f(x) = \cos x$ for the interval of $\left[0, \dfrac{\pi}{2}\right]$. Use six rectangles.

b) For the function in (a) solve for the area using the antiderivative and then compare answers.

2. Given $f(x) = \dfrac{1}{x}$, over the interval $[1,3]$ and using 4 rectangles

a) Find the width of each rectangle.

b) List the boundaries of each rectangle (sub-interval for each).

c) What would be the height of each rectangle to be used in a Reimann Sum for a lower sum (m) and an upper sum (M)?

3. a) Find the area under the curve $y = 2x^2 + 1$ from 0 to 2 using approximation with the Trapezoid Rule and using 4 trapezoids.

b) Find the area under the curve in **a)** using a definite integral and then compare answers.

TOPIC PRACTICE QUESTIONS 2

1. Evaluate each indefinite integral:

   a) $\int \left(-\dfrac{e^{-x}}{2} + 2\cos x \right) dx$

   b) $\int (\sin x - \pi) dx$

2. A stone falls from rest off a cliff that is 50 m tall. Using 9.8 m/s^2 for the acceleration due to gravity, calculate to one decimal place the time it takes the stone to reach the ground.

3. A spring hangs with a mass of 0.1 kg in its rest position. The spring and mass are stretched downward 0.02 m by a 1 force, and then released from rest. Use Hooke's Law to find an equation representing the displacement (s) of the mass at any time (t).

4. A triangular area is enclosed under the line $y = 3x + 1$ above the x-axis and bounded on the right by the line $x = 2$..

a) Where does the function $f(x) = 3x + 1$ touch the x-axis?

b) Calculate the area of the triangle formed using the geometric area formula.

c) Use a definite integral to calculate the area under the curve from the intersection point found in (a) to 2 (the line $x = 2$).

5. Find the area bounded by the curves of $f(x) = x + 1$ and $g(x) = \dfrac{x}{3}$ on the interval $[0,3]$ using the following two methods.

a) Use the difference of 2 definite integrals.

b) Use one definite integral involving a difference function.

6. Approximate the area under $f(x) = x^2 + 1$ over the interval $[0,4]$ using the Rectangular Rule with 4 rectangles. Compare your approximation with the actual area as found by using the antiderivative and   show all your work.

7. Approximate the area under $f(x) = x^2 + 1$ over the interval $[0,4]$ using the Trapezoidal Rule with 8 trapezoids. Compare this answer with the answers from question **6**.

8. Approximate the area under $f(x) = \dfrac{1}{2 + \sin^2 x}$ over the interval $[0, \pi]$ and use 4 trapezoids.

9. Evaluate each definite integral:

    a) $\displaystyle\int_{-2}^{4}\left(3x^2 + 2x - 1\right)dx$

b) $\int_0^\pi (\cos 10x)\,dx$

10. Given $p(x) = \int_{-1}^{x}(3t^2 - 4)\,dt$

    a) What is the value of $p(-1)$?

    b) What is the value of $p'(-1)$?

    c) Evaluate $p(x)$

    d) What is the value of $p(5)$?

11. Determine the average value of the function $f(x) = \cos x$ in the interval $\left[\dfrac{\pi}{6}, \dfrac{\pi}{3}\right]$.

12. Function f shown below is the **derivative** function of function g.

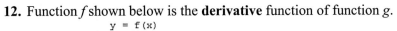

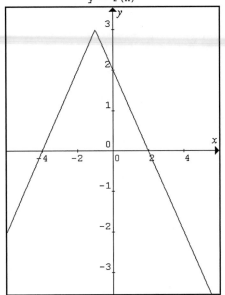

$g(x) = \displaystyle\int_{-4}^{x} [f(t)]\, dt$

a) Evaluate $g(2)$.

b) Evaluate $g'(2)$.

METHODS OF INTEGRATION AND APPLICATIONS

FUNDAMENTAL THEOREM OF CALCULUS (REVISITED)

1. Given $\int_{a}^{b} f(x)\,dx = F(3) - F(1)$, find a and b.

2. In order to apply the fundamental theorem of calculus, a function must be _____ over the region imposed by the limits of integration.

3. Given $f(x) = \dfrac{1}{x^2}$, and $F'(x) = f(x)$, find $F(x)$.

4. Find $\int \sin x\,dx$.

5. Evaluate $\displaystyle\int_0^\pi \sin x \, dx$.

6. Evaluate $\displaystyle\int_2^3 4\, dx$.

7. Complete the equation: $\displaystyle\int 2\cos x\, dx = \int \cos x\, dx + \int$

INTEGRATION BY SUBSTITUTION

1. Evaluate the following indefinite integrals.

   a) $\int \cot x \, dx$

   b) $\int \dfrac{2e^{\sqrt{x}}}{\sqrt{x}} \, dx$

2. Evaluate the following definite integrals using the substitution of variable u.

   a) $\int_0^2 \left[\dfrac{x}{\left(2 + x^2\right)^2} \right] dx$

3. Evaluate the integral $\int_3^4 \left(\dfrac{1}{x - 1} \right) dx$,

   a) Solve using substitution and evaluate the integral over the substitute variable.

   b) Solve without substitution and compare with the answer from (a).

INTEGRATION BY PARTIAL FRACTIONS

1. Use the method of partial fractions to solve the following indefinite integrals.

    a) $\displaystyle\int \frac{x+1}{x^2}\,dx$

    b) $\displaystyle\int \frac{x^3 - x^2 - 1}{x+1}\,dx$

    c) $\displaystyle\int \frac{1}{2x^2 - 2}\,dx$

    d) $\displaystyle\int \frac{x+2}{(x+1)^2}\,dx$

2. Solve the following integrals.

a) $\displaystyle\int_3^4 \left(\frac{-x-1}{x^2-3x+2} \right) dx$

b) $\displaystyle\int_3^4 \left(\frac{2x-4}{2(x-2)^2} \right) dx$

INTEGRATION BY PARTS

1. Solve the following integrals by using integration by parts.

a) $\int (2x+1)e^{-x}\,dx$

b) $\int x\cos(3x)\,dx$

c) $\int x\sec^2 x\,dx$, given that $\int \tan x = -\ln|\cos x|$

d) $\int \dfrac{xe^x}{2}\,dx$

e) $\int_0^{\pi} 2x\cos x\,dx$

f) $\int_0^{\frac{\pi}{2}} 2x\cos x\,dx$

TOPIC PRACTICE QUESTIONS 1

1. Evaluate the following definite integral.

$$\int_0^\pi (x + \cos x)\, dx$$

2. Solve the following indefinite integral using substitution.

$$\int 2 \tan x\, dx$$

3. Solve the following integral using partial fractions (Hint: look for a difference of squares).

$$\int \frac{(x^2 - 1)}{(x^2 - 1)^2 (x - 1)}\, dx$$

4. Solve the following integral using integration by parts.

$$\int 2x \cos x \, dx$$

5. Evaluate the following definite integral.

$$\int_1^2 \left(\frac{e^x}{1-e^x} \right) dx$$

6. Determine the following indefinite integral

$$\int \left(4 - x^2 \right) dx \quad - \quad \int \left(x - x^2 \right) dx$$

VOLUMES OF REVOLUTION

1. For each of the following functions, we will be rotating the section about the *x*-axis. Find the volume of the solid created over the given interval.

    a) $f(x) = x^2$ in the interval [2, 3].

    b) Find the interval in radians and apply the interval that corresponds to $\left[0,\, 45^0\right]$.

    c) $y = 2$ in the interval [0, 3] (Confirm answer through the use of a geometric formula)

    d) $y = (x-1)^2$ in the interval [0, 1].

    e) $y = (x-1)^2$ in the interval [1, 2]. Then compare with question d.

    f) $y = \sqrt{x}$ in the interval [0, *a*]. Then evaluate where $a = 2$.

TOPIC PRACTICE QUESTIONS 2

1. The Fundamental Theorem of Calculus states that:

    $\int_a^b f(x)\,dx =$ _____ , given that _____ is an antiderivative of f.

    Also f is _____ on the interval $(a \to b)$.

2. Find $\int (6x^2 - \sin x)\,dx$.

3. Find $\int \left[\sqrt{3x^2 - 5}\,(12x) \right] dx$.

4. Find $\int (3\sin^5 x \cos x)\,dx$.

5. Find $\int 5x\sin x\,dx$.

6. Find $\int x^2 e^x\,dx$ (Hint: the solution requires two steps).

7. Choose any two of the above indefinite integrals from question 6 and evaluate them over the interval [0, 1], i.e., $\int_0^1$. Indicate what method of integration was used initially.

8. Resolve $\dfrac{x+2}{(x+4)^2}$ into partial fractions. If this were an integral, what conditions would be placed on the values of the variable (limits of integration)?

9. Illustrate the form that the partial fraction decomposition will take for the following functions. Do not set up the system or solve.

   a) $\dfrac{2x}{\left(x^2 - x - 1\right)\left(x - 3\right)}$

   b) $\dfrac{x^2 - x + 1}{\left(x - 2\right)^3\left(x^2 + x + 1\right)}$

10. Find the volume of revolution for the following function, revolved about the x-axis: $y = x^2 - 6x + 9$ in the interval [3, 5]. Describe the original function.

NOTES

Answers and
Solutions

Problem
Solved

PRE-CALCULUS
Factoring

ANSWERS AND SOLUTIONS

1. $= (2x-5y)(4x^2+10xy+25y^2)$

$8x^3 - 125y^3$
$= (2x-5y)\left((2x)^2 + (2x)(5y) + (5y)^2\right)$
$= (2x-5y)(4x^2+10xy+25y^2)$

2. $= (4x+1)(16x^2-4x+1)$

$64x^3 + 1$
$= (4x+1)\left((4x)^2 - (4x)(1) + (1)^2\right)$
$= (4x+1)(16x^2-4x+1)$

3. $= a^{\frac{1}{2}}(2a+3)(a-1)$

$2a^{\frac{5}{2}} + a^{\frac{3}{2}} - 3a^{\frac{1}{2}}$
$= a^{\frac{1}{2}}\left(2a^{\frac{4}{2}} + a^{\frac{2}{2}} - 3\right)$
$= a^{\frac{1}{2}}\left(2a^2 + a - 3\right)$
$= a^{\frac{1}{2}}(2a+3)(a-1)$

4. $= 5a^{\frac{-1}{2}}(a-2)(a+2)$

$5a^{\frac{3}{2}} - 20a^{\frac{-1}{2}}$
$= 5a^{\frac{-1}{2}}\left(a^{\frac{4}{2}} - 4\right)$
$= 5a^{\frac{-1}{2}}\left(a^2 - 4\right)$
$= 5a^{\frac{-1}{2}}(a-2)(a+2)$
$= \dfrac{5(a-2)(a+2)}{a^{\frac{1}{2}}}$
$= \dfrac{5(a-2)(a+2)}{\sqrt{a}}$

5. $= (x+2)^{\frac{3}{2}}(x-1)$

$(x+2)^{\frac{5}{2}} - 3(x+2)^{\frac{3}{2}}$
$= (x+2)^{\frac{3}{2}}\left[(x+2)^{\frac{2}{2}} - 3\right]$
$= (x+2)^{\frac{3}{2}}\left[(x+2)^{1} - 3\right]$
$= (x+2)^{\frac{3}{2}}(x-1)$

6. $= \dfrac{\left[(x+4)^2 - 2\right]\left[(x+4)^2 + 2\right]}{x+4^{\frac{1}{2}}}$

$(x+4)^{\frac{7}{2}} - 4(x+4)^{\frac{-1}{2}}$
$= (x+4)^{\frac{-1}{2}}\left[(x+4)^{\frac{8}{2}} - 4\right]$
$= (x+4)^{\frac{-1}{2}}\left[(x+4)^4 - 4\right]$
$= (x+4)^{\frac{-1}{2}}\left[(x+4)^2 - 2\right]\left[(x+4)^2 + 2\right]$
$= \dfrac{\left[(x+4)^2 - 2\right]\left[(x+4)^2 + 2\right]}{(x+4)^{\frac{1}{2}}}$
$= \dfrac{\left(x+4+\sqrt{2}\right)\left(x+4-\sqrt{2}\right)\left[(x+4)^2 + 2\right]}{(x+4)^{\frac{1}{2}}}$

7. $= \dfrac{1}{\sqrt{2x-5}}$

$\dfrac{(2x-5)^{\frac{1}{2}} + 4(2x-5)^{\frac{-1}{2}}}{2x-1}$
$= \dfrac{(2x-5)^{\frac{-1}{2}}\left[(2x-5)^{\frac{2}{2}} + 4\right]}{2x-1}$
$= \dfrac{(2x-5)^{\frac{-1}{2}}(2x-5+4)}{2x-1}$
$= \dfrac{(2x-5)^{\frac{-1}{2}}(2x-1)}{2x-1}$
$= \dfrac{1}{\sqrt{2x-5}}$

8. $= \left(x - 2\sqrt{5}\right)\left(x + 2\sqrt{5}\right)$

$= x^2 - 20$

$= \left(x - \sqrt{20}\right)\left(x + \sqrt{20}\right)$

$= \left(x - 2\sqrt{5}\right)\left(x + 2\sqrt{5}\right)$

Rationalizing Numerators and Denominators

ANSWERS AND SOLUTIONS

1. a) $= \dfrac{x + 2\sqrt{x}}{x^2 - 4x}$

$\dfrac{1}{\left(x - 2\sqrt{x}\right)} \times \dfrac{\left(x + 2\sqrt{x}\right)}{\left(x + 2\sqrt{x}\right)}$

$= \dfrac{x + 2\sqrt{x}}{x^2 - 4x}$

b) $= \left(\sqrt{x} - \sqrt{5}\right)$

$\dfrac{(x - 5)}{\left(\sqrt{x} + \sqrt{5}\right)} \times \dfrac{\left(\sqrt{x} - \sqrt{5}\right)}{\left(\sqrt{x} - \sqrt{5}\right)}$

$= \dfrac{(x - 5)\left(\sqrt{x} - \sqrt{5}\right)}{x - 5}$

$= \left(\sqrt{x} - \sqrt{5}\right)$

c) $\dfrac{4x}{\sqrt{2 - x} + \sqrt{2}}$

$= \dfrac{4x}{\left(\sqrt{2 - x} + \sqrt{2}\right)} \times \dfrac{\left(\sqrt{2 - x} - \sqrt{2}\right)}{\left(\sqrt{2 - x} - \sqrt{2}\right)}$

$= \dfrac{4x\left(\left(\sqrt{2 - x} - \sqrt{2}\right)\right)}{2 - x - 2}$

$= \dfrac{4\cancel{x}\left(\sqrt{2 - x} - \sqrt{2}\right)}{-\cancel{x}}$

$= -4\left(\sqrt{2 - x} - \sqrt{2}\right)$

2. a) $= \dfrac{2}{\left(\sqrt{2x - 5} + \sqrt{7}\right)}$

$\dfrac{\left(\sqrt{2x - 5} - \sqrt{7}\right)}{(x - 6)} \times \dfrac{\left(\sqrt{2x - 5} + \sqrt{7}\right)}{\left(\sqrt{2x - 5} + \sqrt{7}\right)}$

$= \dfrac{(2x - 5) - 7}{(x - 6)\left(\sqrt{2x - 5} + \sqrt{7}\right)}$

$= \dfrac{2x - 12}{(x - 6)\left(\sqrt{2x - 5} + \sqrt{7}\right)}$

$= \dfrac{2(x - 6)}{(x - 6)\left(\sqrt{2x - 5} + \sqrt{7}\right)}$

$= \dfrac{2}{\left(\sqrt{2x - 5} + \sqrt{7}\right)}$

b) $= \dfrac{x^2 + x - 12}{\sqrt{x^2 + x - 11} + 1}$

$\dfrac{\left(\sqrt{x^2 + x - 11} - 1\right)}{1} \times \dfrac{\left(\sqrt{x^2 + x - 11} + 1\right)}{\left(\sqrt{x^2 + x - 11} + 1\right)}$

$= \dfrac{x^2 + x - 11 - 1}{\sqrt{x^2 + x - 11} + 1}$

$= \dfrac{x^2 + x - 12}{\sqrt{x^2 + x - 11} + 1}$

c) $= \dfrac{-1}{\sqrt{x}}$

$\dfrac{\dfrac{1}{\sqrt{x}} - 4\sqrt{x} \times \dfrac{\sqrt{x}}{\sqrt{x}}}{4x - 1}$

$\dfrac{\dfrac{1 - 4x}{\sqrt{x}}}{4x - 1}$

$= \dfrac{1 - 4x}{\sqrt{x}(4x - 1)}$

$= \dfrac{-(4x - 1)}{\sqrt{x}(4x - 1)}$

$= \dfrac{-1}{\sqrt{x}}$

Operations with Functions and Composition of Functions

ANSWERS AND SOLUTIONS

1. a)

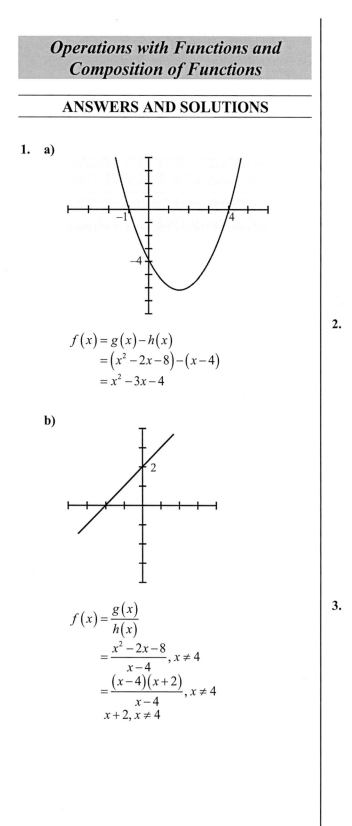

$$f(x) = g(x) - h(x)$$
$$= (x^2 - 2x - 8) - (x - 4)$$
$$= x^2 - 3x - 4$$

b)

$$f(x) = \frac{g(x)}{h(x)}$$
$$= \frac{x^2 - 2x - 8}{x - 4}, x \neq 4$$
$$= \frac{(x-4)(x+2)}{x-4}, x \neq 4$$
$$x + 2, x \neq 4$$

c)

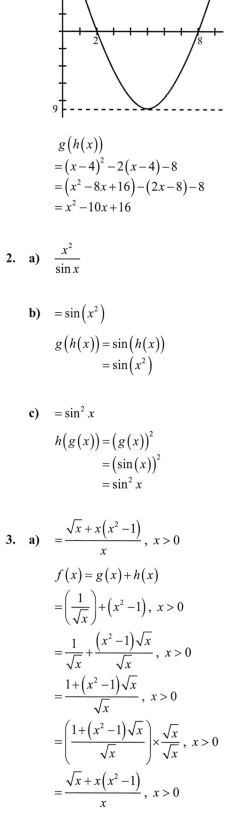

$$g(h(x))$$
$$= (x-4)^2 - 2(x-4) - 8$$
$$= (x^2 - 8x + 16) - (2x - 8) - 8$$
$$= x^2 - 10x + 16$$

2. a) $\dfrac{x^2}{\sin x}$

b) $= \sin(x^2)$

$$g(h(x)) = \sin(h(x))$$
$$= \sin(x^2)$$

c) $= \sin^2 x$

$$h(g(x)) = (g(x))^2$$
$$= (\sin(x))^2$$
$$= \sin^2 x$$

3. a) $= \dfrac{\sqrt{x} + x(x^2 - 1)}{x}, x > 0$

$$f(x) = g(x) + h(x)$$
$$= \left(\frac{1}{\sqrt{x}}\right) + (x^2 - 1), x > 0$$
$$= \frac{1}{\sqrt{x}} + \frac{(x^2 - 1)\sqrt{x}}{\sqrt{x}}, x > 0$$
$$= \frac{1 + (x^2 - 1)\sqrt{x}}{\sqrt{x}}, x > 0$$
$$= \left(\frac{1 + (x^2 - 1)\sqrt{x}}{\sqrt{x}}\right) \times \frac{\sqrt{x}}{\sqrt{x}}, x > 0$$
$$= \frac{\sqrt{x} + x(x^2 - 1)}{x}, x > 0$$

b) $= \dfrac{(x^2-1)\sqrt{x}}{x}$, $x > 0$

$g(x)h(x)$

$= \left(\dfrac{1}{\sqrt{x}}\right)(x^2-1)$, $x > 0$

$= \dfrac{x^2-1}{\sqrt{x}}$, $x > 0$

$= \dfrac{(x^2-1)\sqrt{x}}{x}$, $x > 0$

c) $= \dfrac{1-x}{x}$, $x > 0$

$h(g(x))$

$= (g(x))^2 - 1$

$= \left(\dfrac{1}{\sqrt{x}}\right)^2 - 1$, $x > 0$

$= \dfrac{1}{x} - 1$, $x > 0$

$= \dfrac{1-x}{x}$, $x > 0$

ANSWERS AND SOLUTIONS

1.

	Equation of Transformation	Line that the Graph is Reflected In	Vertical Stretch Factor about the x-axis	Horizontal Stretch Factor about the y-axis	Vertical Translation	Horizontal Translation
a)	$y = -5f(2x) + 1$	x-axis	5	$\frac{1}{2}$	1 up	n/a
b)	$y = f(3x-6)$	n/a	1	$\frac{1}{3}$	n/a	2 right
c)	$y = -f(-x) - 2$	x-axis, y-axis	1	1	2 down	n/a
d)	$y = f^{-1}(x) - 7$	$y = x$	1	1	7 down	n/a
e)	$y = -7f\left(-\frac{1}{3}x - 3\right) + 8$	x-axis, y-axis	7	3	8 up	9 left

2.

		Amplitude	Period	Phase Shift	Vertical Displacement
a)	$y = 3\sin(2x)$	3	π	n/a	n/a
b)	$y = -5\cos(x+\pi)$	5	2π	left π	n/a
c)	$y = -\cos\left(3x - \dfrac{\pi}{2}\right) - 11$	1	$\dfrac{2\pi}{3}$	right $\dfrac{\pi}{6}$	down 11
d)	$y = 10\sin(4x - 3\pi) + 6$	10	$\dfrac{\pi}{2}$	right $\dfrac{3\pi}{4}$	up 6

3. **a)** $y = f\left(-\dfrac{1}{2}x\right)$

   b) $y = f^{-1}(x)$

   c) $y = -f\left(\dfrac{1}{2}(x+4)\right) - 1$

   d) $y = -1.5f\left(\dfrac{1}{2}x\right)$

   e) $y = \dfrac{1}{2}f\left(2\left(x - \dfrac{\pi}{4}\right)\right) - \dfrac{1}{2}$

Topic Practice Questions 1

ANSWERS AND SOLUTIONS

1. **a)** $(x-5)(x^2 + 5x + 25)$

   b) $= \dfrac{x^2 - 14x + 52}{(x-7)^{\frac{1}{2}}}$

   $\dfrac{(x-7)^{-\frac{1}{2}}\left((x-7)^2 + 3\right)}{}$
   $= \dfrac{x^2 - 14x + 52}{(x-7)^{\frac{1}{2}}}$

2. $\dfrac{1}{(x+4)\left(\sqrt{x+6} - \sqrt{10}\right)}$

$\dfrac{\left(\sqrt{x+6} + \sqrt{10}\right)}{(x^2 - 16)} \times \dfrac{\left(\sqrt{x+6} - \sqrt{10}\right)}{\left(\sqrt{x+6} - \sqrt{10}\right)}$

$\dfrac{x + 6 - 10}{(x^2 - 16)\left(\sqrt{x+6} - 10\right)}$

$\dfrac{x - 4}{(x+4)(x-4)\left(\sqrt{x+6} - \sqrt{10}\right)}$

$\dfrac{1}{(x+4)\left(\sqrt{x+6} - \sqrt{10}\right)}$

3. $y = -5f\left(2(x-3)\right) + 1$

- vertical expansion in the x-axis by a factor of 5
- horizontal compression in the y-axis by a factor of $\dfrac{1}{2}$
- vertical reflection in the x-axis
- horizontal translation of 3 units to the right
- vertical translation of 1 unit up

4. **a)** $= \dfrac{3x - 2}{x^2}$

   $f(x) = \dfrac{6x - 4}{2x^2}$
   $= \dfrac{3x - 2}{x^2}$

   b) $= 2x^2 - 6x + 4$

   $f(x) = 2x^2 - (6x - 4)$
   $= 2x^2 - 6x + 4$

   c) $= 72x^2 - 96x + 32$

   $f(x) = 2\left(h(x)\right)^2$
   $= 2(6x - 4)^2$
   $= 2\left(36x^2 - 48x + 16\right)$
   $= 72x^2 - 96x + 32$

Interval Notation

ANSWERS AND SOLUTIONS

1. a) $(-5, 8)$

   b) $[2, \infty)$

   c) $(-\infty, 1) \cup [10, \infty)$

   d) $(-\infty, -1) \cup [0, 10]$

   e) $(-\infty, 7] \cup (12, 15]$

   f) $(-\infty, 0) \cup (0, \infty)$

2. a) $[-3, \infty)$

   b) $(-\infty, 0] \cup (5, \infty)$

   c) $(-\infty, -9) \cup (-9, \infty)$

Quadratic Inequalities

ANSWERS AND SOLUTIONS

1. a) $(-3, 5)$

   $x^2 - 2x - 15 = 0$
   $(x - 5)(x + 3) = 0$
   $x = 5 \quad x = -3$

   Test values: $x = -4, 0, 6$
   Check:
   $(-4)^2 - 2(-4) - 15 = 9$
   $\qquad 9 \not< 0$
   $(0)^2 - 2(0) - 15 = -15$
   $\qquad -15 < 0$
   $(6)^2 - 2(6) - 15 = 9$
   $\qquad 9 \not< 0$
   $= (-3, 5)$

b) $(-\infty, -7] \cup \left[\dfrac{1}{2}, \infty\right)$

   $2x^2 + 13x - 7 = 0$
   $(2x - 1)(x + 7) = 0$
   $x = \dfrac{1}{2} \quad x = -7$

   Test values: $x = -8, 0, 1$
   Check:
   $2(-8)^2 + 13(-8) - 7 = 17$
   $\qquad 17 \geq 0$
   $(0)^2 + 13(0) - 7 = -7$
   $\qquad -7 \not\geq 0$
   $2(1) + 13(1) - 7 = 8$
   $\qquad 8 \geq 0$
   $= (-\infty, -7] \cup \left[\dfrac{1}{2}, \infty\right)$

c) $[-3, 3]$

   $x^2 - 9 = 0$
   $\qquad x = \pm 3$

   Test values: $x = -4, 0, 4$
   Check:
   $(-4)^2 - 9 = 7$
   $\qquad 7 \not\leq 0$
   $(0)^2 - 9 = -9$
   $\qquad -9 \leq 0$
   $(4)^2 - 9 = 7$
   $\qquad 7 \not\leq 0$
   $= [-3, 3]$

d) $\left(-\infty,-\sqrt{6}\right)\cup\left(\sqrt{6},\infty\right)$

$x^2-6=0$
$\qquad x=\pm\sqrt{6}$

Test values: $x=-3,0,3$
Check:
$(-3)^2-6=3$
$\qquad 3>0$
$(0)^2-6=-6$
$\qquad -6\not>0$
$(3)^2-6=3$
$\qquad 3>0$
$=\left(-\infty,-\sqrt{6}\right)\cup\left(\sqrt{6},\infty\right)$

e) $\left(-\infty,-2\right]\cup\left[5,\infty\right)$

$-x^2+3x+10=0$
$-(x-5)(x+2)=0$
$x=5\quad x=-2$

Test values: $x=-3,0,6$
Check:
$-(-3)^2+3(-3)+10=-8$
$\qquad -8\le 0$
$-(0)^2+(0)+10=10$
$\qquad 10\not\le 0$
$-(6)^2+3(6)+10=-8$
$\qquad -8\le 0$
$\left(-\infty,-2\right]\cup\left[5,\infty\right)$

f) $\left(-\infty,-2-\sqrt{11}\right]\cup\left[-2+\sqrt{11},\infty\right)$

$x^2+4x-7=0$
$\qquad x=\dfrac{-4\pm\sqrt{(4)^2-4(1)(-7)}}{2(1)}$
$\qquad x=-2\pm\sqrt{11}$

Test values: $x=-6,0,2$
Check:
$(-6)^2+4(-6)-7=5$
$\qquad 5\ge 0$
$(0)^2+4(0)-7=-7$
$\qquad -7\not\ge 0$
$(2)^2+4(2)-7=5$
$\qquad 5\ge 0$
$=\left(-\infty,-2-\sqrt{11}\right]\cup\left[-2+\sqrt{11},\infty\right)$

Rational Inequalities

ANSWERS AND SOLUTIONS

1. a) $(0,2)$

Undefined value
$x=0$
Solve equality
$\dfrac{x-2}{x}=0$
$\qquad x=2$
Test values $x=-1,1,3$
Check
$\dfrac{-1-2}{-1}=3$
$\qquad 3\not< 0$
$\dfrac{1-2}{1}=-1$
$\qquad -1<0$
$\dfrac{3-2}{3}=\dfrac{1}{3}$
$\qquad \dfrac{1}{3}\not< 0$
$=(0,2)$

b) $\left(-\infty,-5\right)\cup\left(0,\infty\right)$

Undefined values
$x+5=0$
$\qquad x=-5$
Solve equality
$\dfrac{x}{x+5}=0$
$\qquad x=0$
Test values $x=-6,-1,1$
Check
$\dfrac{-6}{-6+5}=6$
$\qquad 6>0$
$\dfrac{-1}{-1+5}=\dfrac{-1}{4}$
$\qquad \dfrac{-1}{4}\not> 0$
$\dfrac{1}{1+5}=\dfrac{1}{6}$
$\qquad \dfrac{1}{6}>0$
$=\left(-\infty,-5\right)\cup\left(0,\infty\right)$

c) $(-\infty, 3)$

Undefined values
$$x - 3 = 0$$
$$x = 3$$

Solve equality
$$\frac{x^2}{x-3} = 0$$
$$x = 0$$

Test values $x = -1, 1, 4$

Check
$$\frac{(-1)^2}{(-1)-3} = \frac{-1}{4}$$
$$\frac{-1}{4} \leq 0$$
$$\frac{1^2}{1-3} = \frac{-1}{2}$$
$$\frac{-1}{2} \leq 0$$
$$\frac{(4)^2}{4-3} = 16$$
$$16 \not\leq 0$$
$$= (-\infty, 3)$$

d) $[-2, -1) \cup [3, \infty)$

Undefined values
$$x + 1 = 0$$
$$x = -1$$

Solve equality
$$\frac{x^2 - x - 6}{x+1} = 0$$
$$x^2 - x - 6 = 0$$
$$(x-3)(x+2) = 0$$
$$x = 3 \qquad x = -2$$

Test values $x = -3, \dfrac{-3}{2}, 0, 4$

Check
$$\frac{(-3)^2 - (-3) - 6}{-3+1} = -3$$
$$-3 \not\geq 0$$
$$\frac{\left(\frac{-3}{2}\right)^2 - \left(\frac{-3}{2}\right) - 6}{\frac{-3}{2}+1} = \frac{9}{2}$$
$$\frac{9}{2} \geq 0$$
$$\frac{(0)^2 - (0) - 6}{0+1} = -6$$
$$-6 \not\geq 0$$
$$\frac{(4)^2 - (4) - 6}{4+1} = \frac{6}{5}$$
$$\frac{6}{5} \geq 0$$
$$= [-2, -1) \cup [3, \infty)$$

e) $(-\infty, \infty)$

Undefined values
$$x^2 + 4 = 0$$
$$x = \sqrt{-4}$$

No real solution, so no undefined values.

Solve equality
$$\frac{3}{x^2 + 4} = 0$$

No solution
Test value $x = 0$
$$\frac{3}{0^2 + 4} = \frac{3}{4}$$
$$\frac{3}{4} > 0$$

So all values of x satisfy the inequality:
$$(-\infty, \infty)$$

f) $\left(\dfrac{1-\sqrt{21}}{2},0\right)\cup\left(\dfrac{1+\sqrt{21}}{2},\infty\right)$

Undefined values
$$x^2 - x - 5 = 0$$
$$x = \frac{-(-1)\pm\sqrt{(-1)^2 - 4(1)(-5)}}{2(1)}$$
$$= \frac{1\pm\sqrt{21}}{2}$$

Solve the equality
$$\frac{x}{x^2 - x - 5} = 0$$
$$x = 0$$

Test values $x = -2,\ -1,\ 1,\ 3$

Check
$$\frac{-2}{(-2)^2 - (-2) - 5} = -2$$
$$-2 \not> 0$$
$$\frac{-1}{(-1)^2 - (-1) - 5} = \frac{1}{3}$$
$$\frac{1}{3} > 0$$
$$\frac{1}{1^2 - 1 - 5} = \frac{-1}{5}$$
$$\frac{-1}{5} \not> 0$$
$$\frac{3}{3^2 - 3 - 5} = 3$$
$$3 > 0$$
$$= \left(\frac{1-\sqrt{21}}{2},0\right)\cup\left(\frac{1+\sqrt{21}}{2},\infty\right)$$

Absolute Value Inequalities

ANSWERS AND SOLUTIONS

1. a) $(-6,4)$

Case 1	Case 2
$x + 1 < 5$	$-(x+1) < 5$
$x < 4$	$x + 1 > -5$
$=(-6,4)$	$x > -6$

b) $(-\infty,-8)\cup(4,\infty)$

Case 1	Case 2
$x + 2 > 6$	$-(x+2) > 6$
$x > 4$	$x + 2 < -6$
$=(-\infty,-8)\cup(4,\infty)$	$x < -8$

c) $[1,7]$

Case 1	Case 2
$(x-4) - 3 \le 0$	$-(x-4) - 3 \le 0$
$x - 4 \le 3$	$x - 4 \ge -3$
$x \le 7$	$x \ge 1$
$=[1,7]$	

d) $\left(-\dfrac{4}{5},\dfrac{8}{5}\right)$

Case 1	Case 2
$5x - 2 < 6$	$-(5x-2) < 6$
$x < \dfrac{8}{5}$	$5x - 2 > -6$
	$5x > -4$
$=\left(-\dfrac{4}{5},\dfrac{8}{5}\right)$	$x > \dfrac{-4}{5}$
	$5x - 2 > -6$

e) $(-\infty,0)\cup(0,\infty)$

Case 1	Case 2
$\dfrac{x-5}{x} \ge 0$	$-\left(\dfrac{x-5}{x}\right) \ge 0$
$x - 5 \ge 0$	$\dfrac{x-5}{x} \le 0$
$x \ge 5$	$x - 5 \le 0$
Undefined values: $x = 0$	$x \le 5$
$=(-\infty,0)\cup(0,\infty)$	

Using Trigonometric Identities

ANSWERS AND SOLUTIONS

1. **a)** $= 0$

$$\cos^2 x - \sin^2 x - \cos(2x)$$
$$= \cos^2 x - (1 - \cos^2 x) - (2\cos^2 x - 1)$$
$$= \cos^2 x - 1 + \cos^2 x - 2\cos^2 x + 1$$
$$= 0$$

b) $= 1$

$$(\sin x + \cos x)^2 - \sin(2x)$$
$$= \sin^2 x + 2\sin x \cos x + \cos^2 x - 2\sin x \cos x$$
$$= \sin^2 x + \cos^2 x$$
$$= 1$$

2. **a)**

LS	RS
$\cos\left(\dfrac{\pi}{2} + x\right)$ $= \cos\dfrac{\pi}{2}\cos x - \sin\dfrac{\pi}{2}\sin x$ $= (0)\cos x - (1)\sin x$ $= -\sin x$	$= -\sin x$
LS = RS	

b)

LS	RS
$\dfrac{\sin^2 x \cos x + \cos^3 x - \cos x \tan^2 x}{2\sin x}$ $= \dfrac{\cos x (\sin^2 x + \cos^2 x - \tan^2 x)}{2\sin x}$ $= \dfrac{\cot x (1 - \tan^2 x)}{2}$ $= \dfrac{1 - \tan^2 x}{2\tan x}$	$= \dfrac{1 - \tan^2 x}{2\tan x}$
LS = RS	

c)

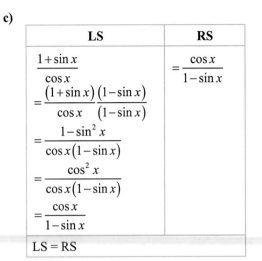

LS	RS
$\dfrac{1 + \sin x}{\cos x}$ $= \dfrac{(1 + \sin x)}{\cos x}\dfrac{(1 - \sin x)}{(1 - \sin x)}$ $= \dfrac{1 - \sin^2 x}{\cos x(1 - \sin x)}$ $= \dfrac{\cos^2 x}{\cos x(1 - \sin x)}$ $= \dfrac{\cos x}{1 - \sin x}$	$= \dfrac{\cos x}{1 - \sin x}$
LS = RS	

d)

LS	RS
$\dfrac{1}{1 + \sin x} + \dfrac{1}{1 - \sin x}$ $= \dfrac{(1 - \sin x) + (1 + \sin x)}{1 - \sin^2 x}$ $= \dfrac{1 + 1 - \sin x + \sin x}{\cos^2 x}$ $= \dfrac{2}{\cos^2 x}$ $= 2\sec^2 x$	$= 2\sec^2 x$
LS = RS	

Topic Practice Questions 2

ANSWERS AND SOLUTIONS

1. **a)** $(2x + 1)(4x^2 - 2x + 1)$

b) $\dfrac{(x + 3)(x + 4)}{(x + 1)^{\frac{1}{2}}}$

$$(x + 1)^{\frac{3}{2}} + 5(x + 1)^{\frac{1}{2}} + 6(x + 1)^{-\frac{1}{2}}$$
$$= (x + 1)^{-\frac{1}{2}}\left((x + 1)^2 + 5(x + 1) + 6\right)$$
$$= (x + 1)^{-\frac{1}{2}}\left((x + 1) + 2\right)\left((x + 1) + 3\right)$$
$$= \dfrac{(x + 3)(x + 4)}{(x + 1)^{\frac{1}{2}}}$$

2.
$$= \frac{\sqrt{x^2 - x - 25} - \sqrt{5}}{x + 5}$$

$$\frac{x - 6}{\sqrt{x^2 - x - 25} + \sqrt{5}}$$

$$= \frac{(x - 6)}{\left(\sqrt{x^2 - x - 25} + \sqrt{5}\right)} \times \frac{\left(\sqrt{x^2 - x - 25} - \sqrt{5}\right)}{\left(\sqrt{x^2 - x - 25} - \sqrt{5}\right)}$$

$$= \frac{(x - 6)\left(\sqrt{x^2 - x - 25} - \sqrt{5}\right)}{\left(x^2 - x - 25 - 5\right)}$$

$$= \frac{(x - 6)\left(\sqrt{x^2 - x - 25} - \sqrt{5}\right)}{x^2 - x - 30}$$

$$= \frac{(x - 6)\left(\sqrt{x^2 - x - 25} - \sqrt{5}\right)}{(x - 6)(x + 5)}$$

$$= \frac{\sqrt{x^2 - x - 25} - \sqrt{5}}{x + 5}$$

3. **a)** $= 5x^3 - 6x^2 + x$

$$f(x) = (x^2 - x)(5x - 1)$$
$$= 5x^3 - x^2 - 5x^2 + x$$
$$= 5x^3 - 6x^2 + x$$

b) $= 25x^2 - 15x + 2$

$$f(x) = (5x - 1)^2 - (5x - 1)$$
$$= 25x^2 - 15x + 2$$

4.

New Function	Reflection about	Vertical Stretch Factor about x-axis	Horizontal Stretch Factor about y-axis	Vertical Translation	Horizontal Translation
$y = -5f(3x) + 2$	x-axis	5	$\frac{1}{3}$	Up 2	n/a
$y = 2f(-3x + 12)$	y-axis	2	$\frac{1}{3}$	n/a	Right 4
$y = f^{-1}(x) - 6$	y = x	n/a	n/a	Down 6	n/a
$y = -\frac{1}{3}f\left(\frac{1}{2}(x+5)\right) + 1$	x-axis	$\frac{1}{3}$	2	Up 1	Left 5

5. **a)** Amplitude: 3

b) Period: $\frac{\pi}{2}$

c) Phase Shift: right $\frac{\pi}{4}$

d) Vertical Displacement: 6

6. **a)** $(-\infty, -2) \cup (11, \infty)$

$$x^2 - 9x - 22 = 0$$
$$(x - 11)(x + 2) = 0$$
$$x = 11 \quad x = -2$$

Test values $x = -3, 0, 12$

$$(-3)^2 - 9(-3) - 22 = 14$$
$$14 > 0$$
$$0^2 - 9(0) - 22 = -22$$
$$-22 \not> 0$$
$$12^2 - 9(12) - 22 = 14$$
$$14 > 0$$
$$= (-\infty, -2) \cup (11, \infty)$$

b) $\left[\dfrac{5 - \sqrt{33}}{4}, \dfrac{5 + \sqrt{33}}{4}\right]$

$$2x^2 - 5x - 1 \le 0$$

Solve equation:

$$2x^2 - 5x - 1 = 0$$
$$x = \frac{5 \pm \sqrt{25 - 4(2)(-1)}}{4}$$
$$x = \frac{5 \pm \sqrt{33}}{4}$$

Test values: $x = -1, 0, 3$

$$2(-1)^2 - 5(-1) - 1 = 6$$
$$6 \not\le 0$$
$$2(0)^2 - 5(0) - 1 = -1$$
$$-1 \le 0$$
$$2(3)^2 - 5(3) - 1 = 2$$
$$2 \not\le 0$$
$$= \left[\frac{5 - \sqrt{33}}{4}, \frac{5 + \sqrt{33}}{4}\right]$$

c) $(-2, 5)$

$$\frac{x-5}{x+2} < 0$$

Undefined values:

$x = -2$

Solve equation:

$$\frac{x-5}{x+2} = 0$$

$$x - 5 = 0$$

$$x = 5$$

Test values: $x = -3, \ -1, \ 6$

$$\frac{-3-5}{-3+2} = 8$$

$$8 \not< 0$$

$$\frac{-1-5}{-1+2} = -6$$

$$-6 < 0$$

$$\frac{6-5}{6+2} = \frac{1}{8}$$

$$\frac{1}{8} \not< 0$$

$$= (-2, 5)$$

d) $(-5, -1] \cup [1, \infty)$

$$\frac{x^2-1}{x+5} \geq 0$$

Undefined value:

$x = -5$

Solve equation:

$$\frac{x^2-1}{x+5} = 0$$

$$x^2 - 1 = 0$$

$$x = \pm 1$$

Test values: $x = -6, \ -2, \ 0, \ 2$

$$\frac{(-6)^2-1}{-6+5} = -35$$

$$-35 \not\geq 0$$

$$\frac{(-2)^2-1}{-2+5} = 1$$

$$1 \geq 0$$

$$\frac{(0)^2-1}{0+5} = \frac{-1}{5}$$

$$\frac{-1}{5} \not\geq 0$$

$$\frac{(2)^2-1}{2+5} = \frac{3}{7}$$

$$\frac{3}{7} \geq 0$$

$$= (-5, -1] \cup [1, \infty)$$

e) $(-\infty, -1) \cup (9, \infty)$

$$|x-4| > 5$$

Case 1	Case 2
$(x-4) > 5$	$-(x-4) > 5$
$x > 9$	$x - 4 < -5$
$= (-\infty, -1) \cup (9, \infty)$	$x < -1$

7. $\csc(2x) + \csc(2x) = \csc x \sec x$

LS	RS
$\csc(2x) + \csc(2x)$ $= 2\csc(2x)$ $= \dfrac{2}{\sin(2x)}$ $= \dfrac{2}{2\sin x \cos x}$ $= \dfrac{1}{\sin x \cos x}$ $= \csc x \sec x$	$= \csc x \sec x$
LS = RS	

LIMITS

Introduction to Limits

ANSWERS AND SOLUTIONS

1. **a)** 6

$$\lim_{x \to 2} 2(x)^2 - x$$
$$= 2(2)^2 - 2$$
$$= 6$$

b) 0

$$\lim_{x \to 10} x^2 - 10x$$
$$= 10^2 - 10(10)$$
$$= 0$$

2. **a)** **i.** 2
ii. 4
iii. 1
iv. Does not exist because $\lim_{x \to 2^-} \neq \lim_{x \to 2^+}$

b) $x = 2$ and $x = 5$

3.

a) 1

b) 2

c) Does not exist

d) 4

e) 4

f) 4

Limits for Rational Expressions

ANSWERS AND SOLUTIONS

1. **a)** 1

$$\lim_{x \to 0} \frac{x(x+1)}{x}$$
$$= \lim_{x \to 0} x + 1$$
$$= (0) + 1$$
$$= 1$$

b) $\frac{6}{11}$

$$\lim_{x \to 3} \frac{(x+3)(x-3)}{(2x+5)(x-3)}$$
$$= \lim_{x \to 3} \frac{x+3}{2x+5}$$
$$= \frac{(3)+3}{2(3)+5}$$
$$= \frac{6}{11}$$

c) $\frac{1}{4}$

$$\lim_{x \to 5} \frac{(\sqrt{x-1}-2)(\sqrt{x-1}+2)}{(x-5)(\sqrt{x-1}+2)}$$
$$= \lim_{x \to 5} \frac{x-1-4}{(x-5)(\sqrt{x-1}+2)}$$
$$= \lim_{x \to 5} \frac{x-5}{(x-5)(\sqrt{x-1}+2)}$$
$$= \lim_{x \to 5} \frac{1}{\sqrt{x-1}+2}$$
$$= \frac{1}{\sqrt{5-1}+2}$$
$$= \frac{1}{4}$$

d) $\dfrac{1}{2}$

$$\lim_{x\to 2}\frac{(x-2)(x+4)}{(x-2)(x^2+2x+4)}$$

$$=\lim_{x\to 2}\frac{(x+4)}{x^2+2x+4}$$

$$=\frac{2+4}{2^2+2(2)+4}$$

$$=\frac{6}{12}$$

$$=\frac{1}{2}$$

e) $-\dfrac{1}{9}$

$$\lim_{x\to -3}\frac{\dfrac{x+3}{3x}}{3+x}$$

$$=\lim_{x\to -3}\frac{x+3}{3x(x+3)}$$

$$=\lim_{x\to -3}\frac{1}{3x}$$

$$=-\frac{1}{9}$$

2. When simplified, the limit becomes

$$\lim_{x\to 2}\frac{(x+1)(x+2)}{(x+2)(x-2)}$$

$$=\lim_{x\to 2}\frac{(x+1)}{(x-2)}$$

which still cannot be evaluated.

By inspection of the graph,

$$\lim_{x\to 2^+}f(x)=\infty$$

and

$$\lim_{x\to 2^-}f(x)=-\infty$$

Since the left- and right-hand limits are not equal, the limit does not exist.

Using Limits to Find Slopes of Tangents

ANSWERS AND SOLUTIONS

1. a) $=10$

$$m=\lim_{h\to 0}\frac{f(x+h)-f(x)}{h}$$

$$=\lim_{h\to 0}\frac{(x+h)^2+4-(x^2+4)}{h}$$

$$=\lim_{h\to 0}\frac{(5+h)^2+4-(5^2+4)}{h}$$

$$=\lim_{h\to 0}\frac{25+10h+h^2+4-25-4}{h}$$

$$=\lim_{h\to 0}\frac{10h+h^2}{h}$$

$$=\lim_{h\to 0}\frac{\cancel{h}(10+h)}{\cancel{h}}$$

$$=\lim_{h\to 0}10+h$$

$$=10+(0)$$

$$=10$$

b) $=-6$

$$m=\lim_{h\to 0}\frac{f(x+h)-f(x)}{h}$$

$$m=\lim_{h\to 0}\frac{(x+h)^2+4-(x^2+4)}{h}$$

$$=\lim_{h\to 0}\frac{(-3+h)^2+4-\left((-3)^2+4\right)}{h}$$

$$=\lim_{h\to 0}\frac{9-6h+h^2+4-9-4}{h}$$

$$=\lim_{h\to 0}\frac{-6h+h^2}{h}$$

$$=\lim_{h\to 0}\frac{\cancel{h}(-6+h)}{\cancel{h}}$$

$$=\lim_{h\to 0}-6+h$$

$$=-6+0$$

$$=-6$$

2. a) $= 3$

$$m = \lim_{h \to 0} \frac{f(x+h) - f(x)}{h}$$
$$= \lim_{h \to 0} \frac{3(x+h) - 4 - (3x-4)}{h}$$
$$= \lim_{h \to 0} \frac{3(2+h) - 4 - (3(2)-4)}{h}$$
$$= \lim_{h \to 0} \frac{6 + 3h - 4 - 2}{h}$$
$$= \lim_{h \to 0} \frac{3\cancel{h}}{\cancel{h}}$$
$$= \lim_{h \to 0} 3$$
$$= 3$$

b) $= 3$

$$m = \lim_{h \to 0} \frac{f(x+h) - f(x)}{h}$$
$$= \lim_{h \to 0} \frac{3(x+h) - 4 - (3x-4)}{h}$$
$$= \lim_{h \to 0} \frac{3(5+h) - 4 - (3(5)-4)}{h}$$
$$= \lim_{h \to 0} \frac{15 + 3h - 4 - 11}{h}$$
$$= \lim_{h \to 0} \frac{3\cancel{h}}{\cancel{h}}$$
$$= \lim_{h \to 0} 3$$
$$= 3$$

c) The slopes are the same. This is because the function is linear and, therefore, has a constant slope that is the sameat all points in the domain.

3. $= 48$

$$m = \lim_{h \to 0} \frac{f(x+h) - f(x)}{h}$$
$$m = \lim_{h \to 0} \frac{(x+h)^3 - 3 - (x^3 - 3)}{h}$$
$$= \lim_{h \to 0} \frac{(4+h)^3 - 3 - (4^3 - 3)}{h}$$
$$= \lim_{h \to 0} \frac{64 + 48h + 12h^2 + h^3 - 3 - 64 + 3}{h}$$
$$= \lim_{h \to 0} \frac{48h + 12h^2 + h^3}{h}$$
$$= \lim_{h \to 0} \frac{\cancel{h}(48 + 12h + h^2)}{\cancel{h}}$$
$$= \lim_{h \to 0} 48 + 12h + h^2$$
$$= 48 + 12(0) + (0)^2$$
$$= 48$$

4. $= -\dfrac{1}{3}$

$$m = \lim_{h \to 0} \frac{f(x+h) - f(x)}{h}$$
$$m = \lim_{h \to 0} \frac{\dfrac{x+h+1}{x+h-2} - \dfrac{x+1}{x-2}}{h}$$
$$= \lim_{h \to 0} \frac{(x+h+1)(x-2) - (x+1)(x+h-2)}{h(x+h-2)(x-2)}$$
$$= \lim_{h \to 0} \frac{(5+h+1)(5-2) - (5+1)(5+h-2)}{h(5+h-2)(5-2)}$$
$$= \lim_{h \to 0} \frac{(6+h)(3) - 6(3+h)}{h(3+h)(3)}$$
$$= \lim_{h \to 0} \frac{-3h}{3h(3+h)}$$
$$= \lim_{h \to 0} -\frac{1}{3+h}$$
$$= -\frac{1}{3}$$

ANSWERS AND SOLUTIONS

1. a) 2

b) 1

c) Does not exist

d) 4

e) 4

f) 4

g) The function is discontinuous for $x = 1$ because $\lim\limits_{x \to 1^+} f(x) \neq \lim\limits_{x \to 1^-} f(x)$.

2. a) $= 49$

$$\lim_{x \to 9} x^2 - 3x - 5$$
$$= (9)^2 - 3(9) - 5$$
$$= 81 - 27 - 5$$
$$= 49$$

b) $= 14$

$$\lim_{x \to 7} \frac{(x+7)(x-7)}{(x-7)}$$
$$= \lim_{x \to 7} x + 7$$
$$= 7 + 7$$
$$= 14$$

c) $= -\dfrac{2}{3}$

$$\lim_{x \to -1} \frac{(x-1)(x+1)}{(x+1)(x^2-x+1)}$$
$$= \lim_{x \to -1} \frac{x-1}{x^2-x+1}$$
$$= \frac{-1-1}{(-1)^2-(-1)+1}$$
$$= -\frac{2}{3}.$$

d) $= -\dfrac{1}{4}$

$$\lim_{x \to 9} \frac{\left(\sqrt{x-5}-2\right)\left(\sqrt{x-5}+2\right)}{(9-x)\left(\sqrt{x-5}+2\right)}$$
$$= \lim_{x \to 9} \frac{x-5-4}{-(x-9)\left(\sqrt{x-5}+2\right)}$$
$$= \lim_{x \to 9} \frac{x-9}{-(x-9)\left(\sqrt{x-5}+2\right)}$$
$$= \frac{1}{-\left(\sqrt{9-5}+2\right)}$$
$$= -\frac{1}{4}$$

3. a) $= 8$

$$m = \lim_{h \to 0} \frac{f(x+h)-f(x)}{h}$$
$$= \lim_{h \to 0} \frac{(4+h)^2-5-(4^2-5)}{h}$$
$$= \lim_{h \to 0} \frac{16+8h+h^2-5-16+5}{h}$$
$$= \lim_{h \to 0} \frac{8h+h^2}{h}$$
$$= \lim_{h \to 0} \frac{\cancel{h}(8+h)}{\cancel{h}}$$
$$= \lim_{h \to 0} 8 + h$$
$$= 8 + 0$$
$$= 8$$

b) $= 2$

$$m = \lim_{h \to 0} \frac{f(x+h)-f(x)}{h}$$
$$m = \lim_{h \to 0} \frac{(1+h)^2-5-(1^2-5)}{h}$$
$$= \lim_{h \to 0} \frac{1+2h+h^2-5-1+5}{h}$$
$$= \lim_{h \to 0} \frac{2h+h^2}{h}$$
$$= \lim_{h \to 0} \frac{\cancel{h}(2+h)}{\cancel{h}}$$
$$= \lim_{h \to 0} 2 + h$$
$$= 2 + 0$$
$$= 2$$

4. $= -\dfrac{1}{98}$

$$m = \lim_{h \to 0} \frac{f(x+h) - f(x)}{h}$$

$$m = \lim_{h \to 0} \frac{\dfrac{1}{2(x+h)} - \dfrac{1}{2x}}{h}$$

$$= \lim_{h \to 0} \frac{\dfrac{1}{2(7+h)} - \dfrac{1}{2(7)}}{h}$$

$$= \lim_{h \to 0} \frac{\dfrac{14 - (14 + 2h)}{14(14 + 2h)}}{h}$$

$$= \lim_{h \to 0} \frac{-2h}{14h(14 + 2h)}$$

$$= \frac{-1}{7(14 + 2(0))}$$

$$= -\frac{1}{98}$$

DERIVATIVES AND DERIVATIVE THEOREMS

Derivatives Using First Principles

ANSWERS AND SOLUTIONS

1. a) $= 8x$

$$f'(x) = \lim_{h \to 0} \frac{f(x+h) - f(x)}{h}$$

$$= \lim_{h \to 0} \frac{4(x+h)^2 - 7 - (4x^2 - 7)}{h}$$

$$= \lim_{h \to 0} \frac{4(x^2 + 2xh + h^2) - 7 - 4x^2 + 7}{h}$$

$$= \lim_{h \to 0} \frac{4x^2 + 8xh + 4h^2 - 7 - 4x^2 + 7}{h}$$

$$= \lim_{h \to 0} \frac{8xh + 4h^2}{h}$$

$$= \lim_{h \to 0} \frac{h(8x + 4h)}{h}$$

$$= \lim_{h \to 0} 8x + 4h$$

$$= 8x$$

b) $= 6x^2 - 6$

$$y' = \lim_{h \to 0} \frac{f(x+h) - f(x)}{h}$$

$$= \lim_{h \to 0} \frac{2(x+h)^3 - 6(x+h) - (2x^3 - 6x)}{h}$$

$$= \lim_{h \to 0} \frac{2\left(x^3 + 3x^2 h + 3xh^2 + h^3\right) - 6x - 6h - 2x^3 + 6x}{h}$$

$$= \lim_{h \to 0} \frac{2x^3 + 6x^2 h + 6xh^2 + 2h^3 - 6x - 6h - 2x^3 + 6x}{h}$$

$$= \lim_{h \to 0} \frac{6x^2 h + 6xh^2 + 2h^3 - 6h}{h}$$

$$= \lim_{h \to 0} \frac{h\left(6x^2 + 6xh + 2h^2 - 6\right)}{h}$$

$$= \lim_{h \to 0} 6x^2 + 6xh + 2h^2 - 6$$

$$= 6x^2 - 6$$

c) $= -\dfrac{1}{x^2}$

$$y' = \lim_{h \to 0} \frac{f(x+h)-f(x)}{h}$$

$$= \lim_{h \to 0} \frac{\dfrac{1}{x+h}-\dfrac{1}{x}}{h}$$

$$= \lim_{h \to 0} \frac{x-(x+h)}{x(x+h)h}$$

$$= \lim_{h \to 0} \frac{-h}{x(x+h)h}$$

$$= \lim_{h \to 0} \frac{-1}{x(x+h)}$$

$$= -\frac{1}{x^2}$$

d) $= \dfrac{3}{2\sqrt{3x+1}}$

$$f'(x) = \lim_{h \to 0} \frac{f(x+h)-f(x)}{h}$$

$$= \lim_{h \to 0} \frac{\sqrt{3(x+h)+1}-\sqrt{3x+1}}{h}$$

$$= \lim_{h \to 0} \frac{\left(\sqrt{3(x+h)+1}-\sqrt{3x+1}\right)}{h}$$

$$\times \frac{\left(\sqrt{3(x+h)+1}+\sqrt{3x+1}\right)}{\left(\sqrt{3(x+h)+1}+\sqrt{3x+1}\right)}$$

$$= \lim_{h \to 0} \frac{3(x+h)+1-(3x+1)}{h\left(\sqrt{3x+h+1}+\sqrt{3x+1}\right)}$$

$$= \lim_{h \to 0} \frac{3h}{h\left(\sqrt{3x+h+1}\right)+\sqrt{3x+1}}$$

$$= \lim_{h \to 0} \frac{3}{\sqrt{3x+h+1}+\sqrt{3x+1}}$$

$$= \frac{3}{\sqrt{3x+1}+\sqrt{3x+1}}$$

$$= \frac{3}{2\sqrt{3x+1}}$$

2. a) $9x-y=5$

$$y' = \lim_{h \to 0} \frac{f(x+h)-f(x)}{h}$$

$$= \lim_{h \to 0} \frac{5(x+h)^2-(x+h)-5x^2+x}{h}$$

$$= \lim_{h \to 0} \frac{5(x^2+2xh+h^2)-x-h-5x^2+x}{h}$$

$$= \lim_{h \to 0} \frac{5x^2+10xh+5h^2-x-h-5x^2+x}{h}$$

$$= \lim_{h \to 0} \frac{10xh+5h^2-h}{h}$$

$$= \lim_{h \to 0} \frac{h(10x+5h-1)}{h}$$

$$= \lim_{h \to 0} 10x+5h-1$$

$$= 10x-1$$

So the slope at (1, 4) is
$$y = 10(1)-1$$
$$= 9$$
and the equation of the tangent is
$$9 = \frac{y-4}{x-1}$$
$$9x-9 = y-4$$
$$9x-y = 5$$

b) $10x-y=-5$

$$f'(x) = \lim_{h \to 0} \frac{f(x+h)-f(x)}{h}$$

$$= \lim_{h \to 0} \frac{(x+h+3)^2-(x+3)^2}{h}$$

$$= \lim_{h \to 0} \frac{\begin{array}{c}x^2+2xh+6x+6h+h^2\\+9-x^2-6x-9\end{array}}{h}$$

$$= \lim_{h \to 0} \frac{2xh+6h+h^2}{h}$$

$$= \lim_{h \to 0} 2x+6+h$$

$$= 2x+6$$

So, the slope at (2, 25) is
$$f'(2) = 2(2)+6$$
$$= 10$$
and the equation of the tangent is
$$10 = \frac{y-25}{x-2}$$
$$10x-20 = y-25$$
$$10x-y = -5$$

c) $2x+2y=5$

$$f'(x) = \lim_{h \to 0} \frac{f(x+h) - f(x)}{h}$$

$$= \lim_{h \to 0} \frac{\dfrac{1}{(x+h)^2 - 2} - \dfrac{1}{x^2 - 2}}{h}$$

$$= \lim_{h \to 0} \frac{x^2 - 2 - \left((x+h)^2 - 2\right)}{\left((x+h^2) - 2\right)(x^2 - 2)h}$$

$$= \lim_{h \to 0} \frac{x^2 - 2 - x^2 - 2xh - h^2 + 2}{\left((x+h)^2 - 2\right)(x^2 - 2)h}$$

$$= \lim_{h \to 0} \frac{-2xh - h^2}{\left((x+h)^2 - 2\right)(x^2 - 2)h}$$

$$= \lim_{h \to 0} \frac{h(-2x - h)}{\left((x+h)^2 - 2\right)(x^2 - 2)h}$$

$$= \lim_{h \to 0} \frac{-2x - h}{\left((x+h)^2 - 2\right)(x^2 - 2)}$$

$$= \frac{-2x}{(x^2 - 2)^2}$$

So, the slope at $\left(2, \dfrac{1}{2}\right)$ is

$$f'(x) = \frac{-2(2)}{\left((2)^2 - 2\right)^2}$$

$$= \frac{-4}{4}$$

$$= -1$$

and the equation of the tangent is

$$-1 = \frac{y - \dfrac{1}{2}}{x - 2}$$

$$-x + 2 = y - \frac{1}{2}$$

$$-2x + 4 = 2y - 1$$

$$2x + 2y = 5$$

d) $7x + 27y = 36$

$$\frac{dy}{dx} = \lim_{h \to 0} \frac{f(x+h) - f(x)}{h}$$

$$= \lim_{h \to 0} \frac{\dfrac{x+h+2}{(x+h)^2} - \dfrac{x+2}{x^2}}{h}$$

$$= \lim_{h \to 0} \frac{x^2(x+h+2) - (x+2)(x+h)^2}{x^2(x+h)^2 h}$$

$$= \lim_{h \to 0} \frac{\begin{array}{c} x^3 + x^2h + 2x^2 \\ -\left(x^3 + 2x^2h + xh^2 + 2x^2 + 4xh + 2h^2\right) \end{array}}{x^2(x+h)^2 h}$$

$$= \lim_{h \to 0} \frac{-x^2h - xh^2 - 4xh - 2h^2}{x^2(x+h)^2 h}$$

$$= \lim_{h \to 0} \frac{h(-x^2 - xh - 4x - 2h)}{x^2(x+h)^2 h}$$

$$= \frac{-x^2 - 4x}{x^4}$$

$$= \frac{-x - 4}{x^3}$$

$$\frac{dy}{dx}\Big|_{x=3} = \frac{-(3) - 4}{(3)^3}$$

$$= \frac{-7}{27}$$

The equation of the tangent is

$$\frac{-7}{27} = \frac{y - \dfrac{5}{9}}{x - 3}$$

$$-7x + 21 = 27y - 27\left(\frac{5}{9}\right)$$

$$7x + 27y = 36$$

e) $5x - 2\sqrt{3}y = 4$

$$y' = \lim_{h \to 0} \frac{f(x+h) - f(x)}{h}$$

$$= \lim_{h \to 0} \frac{\sqrt{5(x+h) - 7} - \sqrt{5x - 7}}{h}$$

$$= \lim_{h \to 0} \frac{\left(\sqrt{5(x+h) - 7} - \sqrt{5x - 7}\right)}{h}$$
$$\times \frac{\left(\sqrt{5(x+h) - 7} + \sqrt{5x - 7}\right)}{\left(\sqrt{5(x+h) - 7} + \sqrt{5x - 7}\right)}$$

$$= \lim_{h \to 0} \frac{5h}{h\left(\sqrt{5(x+h) - 7} + \sqrt{5x - 7}\right)}$$

$$= \lim_{h \to 0} \frac{5}{\sqrt{5(x+h) - 7} + \sqrt{5x - 7}}$$

$$= \lim_{h \to 0} \frac{5}{2\sqrt{5x - 7}}$$

So the slope is

$$y' = \frac{5}{2\sqrt{5(2)-7}}$$

$$= \frac{5}{2\sqrt{3}}$$

The equation of the tangent is

$$\frac{5}{2\sqrt{3}} = \frac{y-\sqrt{3}}{x-2}$$

$$5x-10 = 2\sqrt{3}y - 2(3)$$

$$5x-10 = 2\sqrt{3}y - 6$$

$$5x - 2\sqrt{3}y = 4$$

f) $3x - 2\sqrt{2}y = -6$

$$y' = \lim_{h\to 0}\frac{f(x+h)-f(x)}{h}$$

$$= \lim_{h\to 0}\frac{\dfrac{3(x+h)}{\sqrt{x+h}}-\dfrac{3x}{\sqrt{x}}}{h}$$

$$= \lim_{h\to 0}\frac{\sqrt{x}(3x+3h)-3x\sqrt{x+h}}{\left(\sqrt{x+h}\right)\left(\sqrt{x}\right)h}$$

$$= \lim_{h\to 0}\frac{\left(\sqrt{x}(3x+3h)-3x\sqrt{x+h}\right)}{\left(\sqrt{x+h}\right)\left(\sqrt{x}\right)h}$$

$$\times \frac{\left(\sqrt{x}(3x+3h)+3x\sqrt{x+h}\right)}{\left(\sqrt{x}(3x+3h)+3x\sqrt{x+h}\right)}$$

$$= \lim_{h\to 0}\frac{\left(\sqrt{x}(3x+3h)\right)^2-\left(3x\sqrt{x+h}\right)^2}{\left(\sqrt{x+h}\right)\left(\sqrt{x}\right)h\left(\sqrt{x}(3x+3h)+3x\sqrt{x+h}\right)}$$

$$= \lim_{h\to 0}\frac{x(9x^2+18xh+9h^2)-9x^2(x+h)}{\left(\sqrt{x+h}\right)\left(\sqrt{x}\right)h\left(\sqrt{x}(3x+3h)+3x\sqrt{x+h}\right)}$$

$$= \lim_{h\to 0}\frac{9x^3+18x^2h+9xh^2-9x^3-9x^2h}{\left(\sqrt{x+h}\right)\left(\sqrt{x}\right)h\left(\sqrt{x}(3x+3h)+3x\sqrt{x+h}\right)}$$

$$= \lim_{h\to 0}\frac{h(18x^2+9xh-9x^2)}{\left(\sqrt{x+h}\right)\left(\sqrt{x}\right)h\left(\sqrt{x}(3x+3h)+3x\sqrt{x+h}\right)}$$

$$= \frac{9x^2}{x\left(3x\sqrt{x}+3x\sqrt{x}\right)}$$

$$= \frac{9x^2}{x\left(6x\sqrt{x}\right)}$$

$$= \frac{3}{2\sqrt{x}}$$

So the slope at $\left(2,3\sqrt{2}\right)$ is

$$\frac{dy}{dx}\Big|_{x=2} = \frac{3}{2\sqrt{2}}$$

$$= \frac{3}{2\sqrt{2}}\times\frac{\sqrt{2}}{\sqrt{2}}$$

$$= \frac{3\sqrt{2}}{4}$$

and the equation of the tangent is

$$\frac{3}{2\sqrt{2}} = \frac{y-3\sqrt{2}}{x-2}$$

$$3x-6 = 2\sqrt{2}y - 12$$

$$3x - 2\sqrt{2}y = -6$$

The Power Rule

ANSWERS AND SOLUTIONS

1. a) $f'(x) = 18x^2$

b) $\dfrac{1}{2\sqrt{x}}$

$$y = \sqrt{x}$$

$$y = x^{\frac{1}{2}}$$

$$\frac{dy}{dx} = \frac{1}{2}x^{\frac{-1}{2}}$$

$$= \frac{1}{2\sqrt{x}}$$

c) $f'(x) = -\dfrac{4}{x^5}$

$$f(x) = x^{-4}$$

$$f'(x) = -4x^{-5}$$

$$f'(x) = -\frac{4}{x^5}$$

d) $\dfrac{dy}{dx} = \dfrac{20}{3}\sqrt[3]{x}$

$y = 5x^{\frac{4}{3}}$

$\dfrac{dy}{dx} = 5\left(\dfrac{4}{3}x^{\frac{4}{3}-1}\right)$

$\dfrac{dy}{dx} = \dfrac{20}{3}x^{\frac{1}{3}}$

$\dfrac{dy}{dx} = \dfrac{20}{3}\sqrt[3]{x}$

2. a) $f'(x) = 15x^2 - 2$

b) $\dfrac{dy}{dx} = 8x + 1$

c) $\dfrac{dy}{dx} = \dfrac{1}{\sqrt{x}}$

$y = 2x^{\frac{1}{2}} - \dfrac{1}{2}$

$\dfrac{dy}{dx} = x^{\frac{-1}{2}}$

$\dfrac{dy}{dx} = \dfrac{1}{\sqrt{x}}$

d) $f'(t) = \dfrac{-4}{t^2} + \dfrac{2}{t^3}$

$f(t) = 4t^{-1} - t^{-2}$

$f'(t) = -4t^{-2} - \left(-2t^{-3}\right)$

$f'(t) = \dfrac{-4}{t^2} + \dfrac{2}{t^3}$

e) $\dfrac{dy}{dx} = 2x - 1$

$y = \dfrac{x^3}{x} - \dfrac{x^2}{x} - \dfrac{x}{x}$

$y = x^2 - x - 1$

$\dfrac{dy}{dx} = 2x - 1$

f) $f'(x) = \dfrac{3\sqrt{x}}{2}$

$f(x) = \dfrac{x^2 - 2x^{\frac{1}{2}}}{x^{\frac{1}{2}}}$

$f(x) = \dfrac{x^2}{x^{\frac{1}{2}}} - \dfrac{2x^{\frac{1}{2}}}{x^{\frac{1}{2}}}$

$f(x) = x^{\frac{3}{2}} - 2$

$f'(x) = \dfrac{3}{2}x^{\frac{1}{2}} - 0$

$f'(x) = \dfrac{3\sqrt{x}}{2}$

3. a) $28x - y = 28$

$y' = 14x$ Slope at $(2, 28)$

$m = 14(2)$

$m = 28$

Equation of tangent

$28 = \dfrac{y - 28}{x - 2}$

$28x - 56 = y - 28$

$28x - y = 28$

b) $2x - y = 4$

$f(x) = x - 4x^{-1}$

$f'(x) = 1 + 4x^{-2}$

$f'(x) = 1 + \dfrac{4}{x^2}$

Slope at $(2, 0)$

$m = 1 + \dfrac{4}{2^2}$

$m = 1 + 1$

$m = 2$

Equation of tangent

$2 = \dfrac{y - 0}{x - 2}$

$2x - 4 = y$

$2x - y = 4$

142

4. **a)** At point $(1, -1)$

$y' = 6x - 4$

When slope $= 2$

$2 = 6x - 4$

$6 = 6x$

$x = 1$

To find the y-coordinate,

$y = 3(1)^2 - 4(1)$

$y = 3 - 4$

$y = -1$

At point $(1, -1)$

b) At points $(4, -80)$ and $(-2, 28)$

$y' = 3x^2 - 6x - 24$

When slope $= 0$

$0 = 3x^2 - 6x - 24$

$0 = x^2 - 2x - 8$

$0 = (x - 4)(x + 2)$

$x = 4, -2$

y-coordinates for $x = 4$ and for $x = -2$

$y = 4^3 - 3(4)^2 - 24(4)$

$y = 64 - 48 - 96$

$y = -80$

$\quad (4, -80)$

$y = (-2)^3 - 3(-2)^2 - 24(-2)$

$y = -8 - 12 + 48$

$y = 28$

At point $(-2, 28)$

The Product Rule

ANSWERS AND SOLUTIONS

1. **a)** $\dfrac{dy}{dx} = 105x^6$

$g(x) = x^3$

$g'(x) = 3x^2$

$h(x) = 15x^4$

$h'(x) = 60x^3$

$\dfrac{dy}{dx} = g(x)h'(x) + h(x)g'(x)$

$\dfrac{dy}{dx} = (x^3)(60x^3) + (15x^4)(3x^2)$

$\dfrac{dy}{dx} = 60x^6 + 45x^6$

$\dfrac{dy}{dx} = 105x^6$

b) $f'(x) = 180x^5$

$f(x) = (5x^7)(6x^{-1})$

$g(x) = 5x^7$

$g'(x) = 35x^6$

$h(x) = 6x^{-1}$

$h'(x) = -6x^{-2}$

$f'(x) = g(x)h'(x) + h(x)g'(x)$

$f'(x) = 5x^7(-6x^{-2}) + (6x^{-1})(35x^6)$

$f'(x) = -30x^5 + 210x^5$

$f'(x) = 180x^5$

---

c) $\dfrac{dy}{dx} = \dfrac{495}{2}\sqrt{x^9}$

$$y = \left(5\sqrt{x^3}\right)\left(9x^4\right)$$

$$y = 5x^{\frac{3}{2}}\left(9x^4\right)$$

$$g(x) = 5x^{\frac{3}{2}}$$

$$g'(x) = \dfrac{15}{2}x^{\frac{1}{2}}$$

$$h(x) = 9x^4$$

$$h'(x) = 36x^3$$

$$\dfrac{dy}{dx} = g(x)h'(x) + h(x)g'(x)$$

$$\dfrac{dy}{dx} = \left(5x^{\frac{3}{2}}\right)\left(36x^3\right) + \left(9x^4\right)\left(\dfrac{15}{2}x^{\frac{1}{2}}\right)$$

$$\dfrac{dy}{dx} = 180x^{\frac{9}{2}} + \dfrac{135}{2}x^{\frac{9}{2}}$$

$$\dfrac{dy}{dx} = \dfrac{495}{2}\sqrt{x^9}$$

d) $f'(x) = \dfrac{7 - 5x^2}{2\sqrt{x}}$

$$g(x) = \left(7 - x^2\right)$$

$$g'(x) = -2x$$

$$h(x) = \left(\sqrt{x}\right) = \left(x^{\frac{1}{2}}\right)$$

$$h'(x) = \dfrac{1}{2}x^{-\frac{1}{2}}$$

$$f'(x) = g(x)h'(x) + h(x)g'(x)$$

$$f'(x) = \left(7 - x^2\right)\left(\dfrac{1}{2}x^{-\frac{1}{2}}\right) + \left(x^{\frac{1}{2}}\right)(-2x)$$

$$f'(x) = \dfrac{7}{2}x^{-\frac{1}{2}} - \dfrac{1}{2}x^{\frac{3}{2}} - 2x^{\frac{3}{2}}$$

$$f'(x) = \dfrac{1}{2}x^{-\frac{1}{2}}\left(7 - x^2 - 4x^2\right)$$

$$f'(x) = \dfrac{7 - 5x^2}{2\sqrt{x}}$$

e) $\dfrac{dy}{dx} = \dfrac{25x^2 - 1}{4\sqrt{x}}$

$$g(x) = 5x^3 - x$$

$$g'(x) = 15x^2 - 1$$

$$h(x) = \dfrac{1}{2}x^{-\frac{1}{2}}$$

$$h'(x) = -\dfrac{1}{4}x^{-\frac{3}{2}}$$

$$\dfrac{dy}{dx} = g(x)h'(x) + h(x)g'(x)$$

$$\dfrac{dy}{dx} = \left(5x^3 - x\right)\left(-\dfrac{1}{4}x^{-\frac{3}{2}}\right)$$

$$+ \left(\dfrac{1}{2}x^{-\frac{1}{2}}\right)\left(15x^2 - 1\right)$$

$$\dfrac{dy}{dx} = -\dfrac{5}{4}x^{\frac{3}{2}} + \dfrac{1}{4}x^{-\frac{1}{2}} + \dfrac{15}{2}x^{\frac{3}{2}} - \dfrac{1}{2}x^{-\frac{1}{2}}$$

$$\dfrac{dy}{dx} = \dfrac{1}{4}x^{-\frac{1}{2}}\left(-5x^2 + 1 + 30x^2 - 2\right)$$

$$\dfrac{dy}{dx} = \dfrac{25x^2 - 1}{4\sqrt{x}}$$

f) $f'(x) = 30x^4 - 8x^3 + 99x^2 + 2x - 18$

$$g(x) = 3x^2 - x + 18$$

$$g'(x) = 6x - 1$$

$$h(x) = 2x^3 - x$$

$$h'(x) = 6x^2 - 1$$

$$f'(x) = g(x)h'(x) + h(x)g'(x)$$

$$f'(x) = \left(3x^2 - x + 18\right)\left(6x^2 - 1\right)$$

$$+ \left(2x^3 - x\right)(6x - 1)$$

$$f'(x) = 18x^4 - 3x^2 - 6x^3 + x + 108x^2 - 18$$

$$+ 12x^4 - 2x^3 - 6x^2 + x$$

$$f'(x) = 30x^4 - 8x^3 + 99x^2 + 2x - 18$$

The Quotient Rule

ANSWERS AND SOLUTIONS

1. a) $\dfrac{dy}{dx} = \dfrac{-x-2}{3x^3}$

$g(x) = 1+x$

$g'(x) = 1$

$h(x) = 3x^2$

$h'(x) = 6x$

$\dfrac{dy}{dx} = \dfrac{h(x)g'(x) - g(x)h'(x)}{\left(h(x)\right)^2}$

$\dfrac{dy}{dx} = \dfrac{3x^2(1) - (1+x)(6x)}{\left(3x^2\right)^2}$

$\dfrac{dy}{dx} = \dfrac{3x^2 - 6x - 6x^2}{9x^4}$

$\dfrac{dy}{dx} = \dfrac{-3x^2 - 6x}{9x^4}$

$\dfrac{dy}{dx} = \dfrac{3x(-x-2)}{9x^4}$

$\dfrac{dy}{dx} = \dfrac{-x-2}{3x^3}$

b) $f'(x) = \dfrac{5x^2 + 20x + 1}{2x^2 + 8x + 8}$

$g(x) = 5x^2 - 1$

$g'(x) = 10x$

$h(x) = 2x + 4$

$h'(x) = 2$

$f'(x) = \dfrac{h(x)g'(x) - g(x)h'(x)}{\left(h(x)\right)^2}$

$f'(x) = \dfrac{(2x+4)(10x) - \left(5x^2 - 1\right)(2)}{(2x+4)^2}$

$f'(x) = \dfrac{20x^2 + 40x - 10x^2 + 2}{(2x+4)^2}$

$f'(x) = \dfrac{10x^2 + 40x + 2}{(2x+4)^2}$

$f'(x) = \dfrac{10x^2 + 40x + 2}{4x^2 + 16x + 16}$

$f'(x) = \dfrac{2\left(5x^2 + 20x + 1\right)}{2\left(2x^2 + 8x + 8\right)}$

$f'(x) = \dfrac{5x^2 + 20x + 1}{2x^2 + 8x + 8}$

c) $\dfrac{dy}{dx} = \dfrac{\sqrt[6]{x}}{12x}$

$g(x) = x^{\frac{2}{3}}$

$g'(x) = \dfrac{2}{3}x^{-\frac{1}{3}}$

$h(x) = 2x^{\frac{1}{2}}$

$h'(x) = x^{-\frac{1}{2}}$

$\dfrac{dy}{dx} = \dfrac{h(x)g'(x) - g(x)h'(x)}{\left(h(x)\right)^2}$

$\dfrac{dy}{dx} = \dfrac{2x^{\frac{1}{2}}\left(\dfrac{2}{3}x^{-\frac{1}{3}}\right) - \left(x^{\frac{2}{3}}\right)\left(x^{-\frac{1}{2}}\right)}{4x}$

$\dfrac{dy}{dx} = \dfrac{\dfrac{4}{3}x^{\frac{1}{6}} - x^{\frac{1}{6}}}{4x}$

$\dfrac{dy}{dx} = \dfrac{\sqrt[6]{x}}{12x}$

2. a) $\dfrac{dy}{dx} = \dfrac{4x-1}{4}$

$g(x) = \left(x^4\right)(2x-1)$

$g'(x) = x^4(2) + (2x-1)\left(4x^3\right)$

$g'(x) = 2x^4 + 8x^4 - 4x^3$

$g'(x) = 10x^4 - 4x^3$

$h(x) = 4x^3$

$h'(x) = 12x^2$

$\dfrac{dy}{dx} = \dfrac{h(x)g'(x) - g(x)h'(x)}{\left(h(x)\right)^2}$

$\dfrac{dy}{dx} = \dfrac{4x^3\left(10x^4 - 4x^3\right) - \left(x^4\right)(2x-1)\left(12x^2\right)}{\left(4x^3\right)^2}$

$\dfrac{dy}{dx} = \dfrac{40x^7 - 16x^6 - 24x^7 + 12x^6}{16x^6}$

$\dfrac{dy}{dx} = \dfrac{x^6(16x-4)}{16x^6}$

$\dfrac{dy}{dx} = \dfrac{4(4x-1)}{16}$

$\dfrac{dy}{dx} = \dfrac{(4x-1)}{4}$

Or cancel first

$$y = \frac{\left(x^4\right)\left(2x-1\right)}{4x^3}$$

$$y = \frac{x\left(2x-1\right)}{4} = \frac{2x^2 - x}{4}$$

$$\frac{dy}{dx} = \frac{4x-1}{4}$$

b) $\quad f'(x) = \dfrac{6x^4 - 6x^3 - 165x^2 + 252}{\left(2x^2 - x - 21\right)^2}$

$$g(x) = 3x^3 - 12x$$
$$g'(x) = 9x^2 - 12$$
$$h(x) = (x+3)(2x-7)$$
$$h(x) = 2x^2 - x - 21$$
$$h'(x) = 4x - 1$$

$$f'(x) = \frac{h(x)g'(x) - g(x)h'(x)}{\left(h(x)\right)^2}$$

$$f'(x) = \frac{\left(2x^2 - x - 21\right)\left(9x^2 - 12\right)}{-\left(3x^3 - 12x\right)\left(4x-1\right)}{\left(2x^2 - x - 21\right)^2}$$

$$f'(x) = \frac{\begin{array}{c}18x^4 - 9x^3 - 213x^2 + 12x \\ +252 - 12x^4 + 3x^3 + 48x^2 - 12x\end{array}}{\left(2x^2 - x - 21\right)^2}$$

$$f'(x) = \frac{6x^4 - 6x^3 - 165x^2 + 252}{\left(2x^2 - x - 21\right)^2}$$

The Chain Rule

ANSWERS AND SOLUTIONS

1. a) $\quad f'(x) = 9\left(5x^3 - x\right)^8 \left(15x^2 - 1\right)$

b) $\quad \dfrac{dy}{dx} = \dfrac{(x-1)}{\sqrt{x^2 - 2x}}$

$$y = \left(x^2 - 2x\right)^{\frac{1}{2}}$$

$$\frac{dy}{dx} = \frac{1}{2}\left(x^2 - 2x\right)^{-\frac{1}{2}}(2x-2)$$

$$\frac{dy}{dx} = \frac{2(x-1)}{2\left(x^2 - 2x\right)^{\frac{1}{2}}}$$

$$\frac{dy}{dx} = \frac{x-1}{\sqrt{x^2 - 2x}}$$

c) $\quad f'(x) = 3x^2(3x-1)(5x-1) \quad g(x) = x^3$

$$g'(x) = 3x^2$$
$$h(x) = (3x-1)^2$$
$$h'(x) = 2(3x-1)(3)$$
$$h'(x) = 6(3x-1)$$
$$f'(x) = x^3\left(6(3x-1)\right) + (3x-1)^2\left(3x^2\right)$$
$$f'(x) = 3x^2(3x-1)[2x + 3x - 1]$$
$$f'(x) = 3x^2(3x-1)(5x-1)$$

d) $\dfrac{dy}{dx}=\dfrac{-15\left(2x^2+1\right)}{2\left(2x^2-3\right)^2\sqrt{5x}}$

$$y=\dfrac{(5x)^{\frac{1}{2}}}{2x^2-3}$$

$$\dfrac{dy}{dx}=\dfrac{\left(2x^2-3\right)\dfrac{1}{2}(5x)^{-\frac{1}{2}}(5)-(5x)^{\frac{1}{2}}(4x)}{\left(2x^2-3\right)^2}$$

$$\dfrac{dy}{dx}=\dfrac{\dfrac{1}{2}(5x)^{-\frac{1}{2}}\left[10x^2-15-(5x)(8x)\right]}{\left(2x^2-3\right)^2}$$

$$\dfrac{dy}{dx}=\dfrac{-30x^2-15}{2(5x)^{\frac{1}{2}}\left(2x^2-3\right)^2}$$

$$\dfrac{dy}{dx}=\dfrac{-15\left(2x^2+1\right)}{2\left(2x^2-3\right)^2\sqrt{5x}}$$

e) $f'(x)=\dfrac{3x+6}{2\sqrt{x+3}\sqrt{2x\sqrt{x+3}}}$

$$f(x)=\left(2x(x+3)^{\frac{1}{2}}\right)^{\frac{1}{2}}$$

$$f'(x)=\dfrac{1}{2}\left(2x(x+3)^{\frac{1}{2}}\right)^{-\frac{1}{2}}$$

$$\left[2x\left(\dfrac{1}{2}(x+3)^{-\frac{1}{2}}\right)(1)+(x+3)^{\frac{1}{2}}(2)\right]$$

$$f'(x)=\dfrac{(x+3)^{-\frac{1}{2}}\left[x+(x+3)(2)\right]}{2\left[2x(x+3)^{\frac{1}{2}}\right]^{\frac{1}{2}}}$$

$$f'(x)=\dfrac{3x+6}{2\sqrt{x+3}\sqrt{2x\sqrt{x+3}}}$$

ANSWERS AND SOLUTIONS

1. $f'(x)=12x-1$

$$f'(x)=\lim_{h\to0}\dfrac{f(x+h)-f(x)}{h}$$

$$=\lim_{h\to0}\dfrac{6(x+h)^2-(x+h)-\left(6x^2-x\right)}{h}$$

$$=\lim_{h\to0}\dfrac{6\left(x^2+2xh+h^2\right)-x-h-6x^2+x}{h}$$

$$=\lim_{h\to0}\dfrac{6x^2+12xh+6h^2-x-h-6x^2+x}{h}$$

$$=\lim_{h\to0}\dfrac{12xh+6h^2-h}{h}$$

$$=\lim_{h\to0}\dfrac{h\left(12x+6^2-h\right)}{h}$$

$$=\lim_{h\to0}12x+6h-1$$

$$=12x-1$$

2. a) $\dfrac{dy}{dx}=32x^3-18x^2+1$

$$y=8x^4-6x^3+x-7$$

$$\dfrac{dy}{dx}=32x^3-18x^2+1$$

b) $f'(x)=\dfrac{5x^2-6}{2\sqrt{x}}$

$$f(x)=\sqrt{x}\left(x^2-6\right)$$

$$f(x)=x^{\frac{1}{2}}\left(x^2-6\right)$$

$$f'(x)=x^{\frac{1}{2}}(2x)+\left(x^2-6\right)\left(\dfrac{1}{2}x^{\frac{-1}{2}}\right)$$

$$f'(x)=\sqrt{x}(2x)+\dfrac{\left(x^2-6\right)}{2\sqrt{x}}$$

$$f'(x)=\dfrac{2\sqrt{x}\,2x\sqrt{x}+\left(x^2-6\right)}{2\sqrt{x}}$$

$$f'(x)=\dfrac{4x^2+x^2-6}{2\sqrt{x}}$$

$$f'(x)=\dfrac{5x^2-6}{2\sqrt{x}}$$

---

c) $\dfrac{dy}{dx} = \dfrac{6x^3 - 27x^2}{(x-3)^2}$

$y = \dfrac{3x^3}{x-3}$

$\dfrac{dy}{dx} = \dfrac{(x-3)(9x^2) - 3x^3(1)}{(x-3)^2}$

$\dfrac{dy}{dx} = \dfrac{9x^3 - 27x^2 - 3x^3}{(x-3)^2}$

$\quad = \dfrac{6x^3 - 27x^2}{(x-3)^2}$

d) $f'(x) = 18x^2(x^3+4)^5$

$f'(x) = 6(x^3+4)^5 \, 3x^2$

$f'(x) = 18x^2(x^3+4)^5$

e) $f'(x) = \dfrac{x^2 + 6x - 4}{2\sqrt{x-1}(x+2)^2}$

$f'(x) = \dfrac{(x+2)\left[x\left(\frac{1}{2}\right)(x-1)^{-\frac{1}{2}}(1) + (x-1)^{\frac{1}{2}}(1)\right] - x(x-1)^{\frac{1}{2}}(1)}{(x+2)^2}$

$= \dfrac{\frac{1}{2}x(x+2)(x-1)^{-\frac{1}{2}} + (x+2)(x-1)^{\frac{1}{2}} - x(x-1)^{\frac{1}{2}}}{(x+2)^2}$

$= \dfrac{\frac{1}{2}(x-1)^{-\frac{1}{2}}\left[x(x+2) + 2(x+2)(x-1) - 2x(x-1)\right]}{(x+2)^2}$

$= \dfrac{x^2 + 2x + 2x^2 + 2x - 4 - 2x^2 + 2x}{2\sqrt{x-1}(x+2)^2}$

$= \dfrac{x^2 + 6x - 4}{2\sqrt{x-1}(x+2)^2}$

f) $f'(x) = 2x(3x^2-7)^3(15x^2-7)$

$f'(x) = x^2\left(4(3x^2-7)^3\right)(6x) + (3x^2-7)^4(2x)$

$= 24x^3(3x^2-7)^3 + 2x(3x^2-7)^4$

$= 2x(3x^2-7)^3\left(12x^2 + (3x^2-7)\right)$

$= 2x(3x^2-7)^3(15x^2-7)$

3. $3x + 16y = 14$

$y = \dfrac{1}{x^3}$

$= x^{-3}$

$y' = -3x^{-4}$

$= \dfrac{-3}{x^4}$

So, the slope at $\left(2, \dfrac{1}{2}\right)$ is

$y' = \dfrac{-3}{(2)^4}$

$= \dfrac{-3}{16}$

and the equation of the tangent is

$\dfrac{-3}{16} = \dfrac{y - \frac{1}{2}}{x - 2}$

$3x + 16y = 14$

Implicit Differentiation

ANSWERS AND SOLUTIONS

1. a) $\dfrac{dy}{dx} = -\dfrac{x}{y}$

$8x + 8y\dfrac{dy}{dx} = 0$

$8y\dfrac{dy}{dx} = -8x$

$\dfrac{dy}{dx} = \dfrac{-8x}{8y}$

$\dfrac{dy}{dx} = -\dfrac{x}{y}$

b) $\dfrac{dy}{dx} = \dfrac{3 - 4y^2}{8xy + 2y}$

$4x\left(2y\dfrac{dy}{dx}\right) + y^2(4) + 2\left(\dfrac{dy}{dx}\right) = 3$

$8xy\dfrac{dy}{dx} + 2\dfrac{dy}{dx} = 3 - 4y^2$

$\dfrac{dy}{dx}(8xy + 2) = 3 - 4y^2$

$\dfrac{dy}{dx} = \dfrac{3 - 4y^2}{8xy + 2}$

*Notice the use of the Product Rule in step 1.

c) $\dfrac{dy}{dx} = \dfrac{-2y^4}{x^3 - 4xy^3}$

$$3\dfrac{dy}{dx} - \dfrac{x^2 4y^3 \dfrac{dy}{dx} - y^4(2x)}{\left(x^2\right)^2} = 2\dfrac{dy}{dx}$$

$$3x^4 \dfrac{dy}{dx} - x^2\left(4y^3\right)\dfrac{dy}{dx} + 2xy^4 = 2x^4\dfrac{dy}{dx}$$

$$\dfrac{dy}{dx}\left(3x^4 - 4x^2y^3 - 2x^4\right) = -2xy^4$$

$$\dfrac{dy}{dx} = \dfrac{-2xy^4}{3x^4 - 4x^2y^3 - 2x^4}$$

$$\dfrac{dy}{dx} = \dfrac{-2xy^4}{x^4 - 4x^2y^3}$$

$$\dfrac{dy}{dx} = \dfrac{-2y^4}{x^3 - 4xy^3}$$

2. a) $\left.\dfrac{dy}{dx}\right|_{x=2} = \dfrac{48}{11}$

$$4x^3 - y^2 = y + 2$$

$$12x^2 - 2y\dfrac{dy}{dx} = \dfrac{dy}{dx}$$

$$\dfrac{dy}{dx}\left(-2y - 1\right) = -12x^2$$

$$\dfrac{dy}{dx} = \dfrac{12x^2}{2y + 1}$$

Find the slope at the point $(2, 5)$.

$$= \dfrac{12(2)^2}{2(5) + 1}$$

$$= \dfrac{48}{11}$$

b) $\left.\dfrac{dy}{dx}\right|_{x=6} = -\dfrac{1}{12}$

$$7xy = 21$$

$$7x\dfrac{dy}{dx} + y(7) = 0$$

$$\dfrac{dy}{dx} = \dfrac{-7y}{7x}$$

$$\dfrac{dy}{dx} = -\dfrac{y}{x}$$

Find the slope at the point $\left(6, \dfrac{1}{2}\right)$.

$$= \dfrac{-\dfrac{1}{2}}{6}$$

$$= -\dfrac{1}{12}$$

3. $3x - 2y = 13$

$$3x - y^2 + 6y = x^2 - x$$

$$3 - 2y\dfrac{dy}{dx} + 6\dfrac{dy}{dx} = 2x - 1$$

$$\dfrac{dy}{dx}\left(-2y + 6\right) = 2x - 4$$

$$\dfrac{dy}{dx} = \dfrac{x - 2}{-y + 3}$$

Find the slope at the point $(5, 1)$.

$$= \dfrac{5 - 2}{-1 + 3}$$

$$= \dfrac{3}{2}$$

Equation of a tangent at this point.

$$\dfrac{3}{2} = \dfrac{y - 1}{x - 5}$$

$$3(x - 5) = 2(y - 1)$$

$$3x - 2y = 13$$

Higher Derivatives

ANSWERS AND SOLUTIONS

1. a) $f''(x) = 18x - 18$

$$f'(x) = 9x^2 - 18x + 16$$

$$f''(x) = 18x - 18$$

b) $f''(x) = 0$

$$f'(x) = 10$$

$$f''(x) = 0$$

c) $\dfrac{d^2y}{dx^2} = \dfrac{56}{(x-7)^3}$

$\dfrac{dy}{dy} = \dfrac{(x-7)(4)-4x(1)}{(x-7)^2}$

$\dfrac{dy}{dx} = \dfrac{4x-28-4x}{(x-7)^2}$

$\dfrac{dy}{dx} = \dfrac{-28}{(x-7)^2}$

$\dfrac{d^2y}{dx^2} = \dfrac{\left(x-7^2(0)-((-28)(2(x-7)(1)))\right)}{(x-7)^4}$

$\dfrac{d^2y}{dx^2} = \dfrac{56(x-7)}{(x-7)^4}$

$\dfrac{d^2y}{dx^2} = \dfrac{56}{(x-7)^3}$

d) $\dfrac{d^2y}{dx^2} = 90(3x^2-5)(3x^2-1)$

$\dfrac{dy}{dx} = 3(3x^2-5)^2(6x)$

$\dfrac{dy}{dx} = 18x(3x^2-5)^2$

$\dfrac{d^2y}{dx^2} = 18x\left(2(3x^2-5)(6x)\right)+(3x^2-5)^2(18)$

$\dfrac{d^2y}{dx^2} = 216x^2(3x^2-5)+18(3x^2-5)^2$

$\dfrac{d^2y}{dx^2} = 18(3x^2-5)(12x^2+(3x^2-5))$

$\dfrac{d^2y}{dx^2} = 18(3x^2-5)(15x^2-5)$

$\qquad = 90(3x^2-5)(3x^2-1)$

2. a) $f''(-1) = -42$

$f'(x) = 21x^2 - 2$
$f''(x) = 42x$
$f''(-1) = 42(-1)$
$f''(-1) = -42$

b) $f''(-1) = -4$

$f'(x) = \dfrac{x^2(5)-(5x+1)(2x)}{x^4}$

$f'(x) = \dfrac{5x^2-10x^2-2x}{x^4}$

$f'(x) = \dfrac{-5x^2-2x}{x^4}$

$f'(x) = \dfrac{x(-5x-2)}{x^4}$

$f'(x) = \dfrac{(-5x-2)}{x^3}$

$f''(x) = \dfrac{x^3(-5)-(-5x-2)(3x^2)}{x^6}$

$f''(x) = \dfrac{-5x^3+15x^3+6x^2}{x^6}$

$f''(x) = \dfrac{10x^3+6x^2}{x^6}$

$f''(x) = \dfrac{x^2(10x+6)}{x^6}$

$f''(x) = \dfrac{(10x+6)}{x^4}$

$f''(-1) = \dfrac{(10(-1)+6)}{(-1)^4}$

$f''(-1) = -4$

Topic Practice Questions 2

ANSWERS AND SOLUTIONS

1. $= \dfrac{5}{2x\sqrt{x}}$

$f'(x) = \lim\limits_{h \to 0} \dfrac{f(x+h)-f(x)}{h}$

$= \lim\limits_{h \to 0} \dfrac{\dfrac{-5}{\sqrt{x+h}}+\dfrac{5}{\sqrt{x}}}{h}$

$= \lim\limits_{h \to 0} \dfrac{-5\sqrt{x}+5\sqrt{x+h}}{h\sqrt{x}\sqrt{x+h}}$

$= \lim\limits_{h \to 0} \dfrac{\left(-5\sqrt{x}+5\sqrt{x+h}\right)}{\left(h\sqrt{x}\sqrt{x+h}\right)} \times \dfrac{\left(-5\sqrt{x}-5\sqrt{x+h}\right)}{\left(-5\sqrt{x}-5\sqrt{x+h}\right)}$

$= \lim\limits_{h \to 0} \dfrac{25x-25(x+h)}{h\sqrt{x}\sqrt{x+h}\left(-5\sqrt{x}-5\sqrt{x+h}\right)}$

$= \lim\limits_{h \to 0} \dfrac{-25h}{h\sqrt{x}\sqrt{x+h}\left(-5\sqrt{x}-5\sqrt{x+h}\right)}$

$= \dfrac{-25}{x\left(-5\sqrt{x}-5\sqrt{x}\right)}$

$= \dfrac{-25}{-10x\sqrt{x}}$

$= \dfrac{5}{2x\sqrt{x}}$

2. a) Power Rule and Difference Rule

$\dfrac{dy}{dx} = 112x^6 - 1$

b) Power Rule

$f(x) = -6(x)^{-3}$
$f'(x) = 18x^{-4}$
$= \dfrac{18}{x^4}$

c) Product Rule

$\dfrac{dy}{dx} = 6x\left(\dfrac{1}{2}x^{\frac{-1}{2}}\right)+x^{\frac{1}{2}}(6)$

$= 3x^{\frac{1}{2}}+6x^{\frac{1}{2}}$

$= 9\sqrt{x}$

d) Quotient Rule

$f'(x) = \dfrac{(5-x)(2)-2x(-1)}{(5-x)^2}$

$= \dfrac{10-2x+2x}{(5-x)^2}$

$= \dfrac{10}{(5-x)^2}$

e) Power and Chain Rules

$f'(x) = \dfrac{1}{2}\left(x^2-7\right)^{\frac{-1}{2}}(2x)$

$= \dfrac{x}{\sqrt{x^2-7}}$

f) Product and Chain Rules

$\dfrac{dy}{dx} = (x-3)^2(4)+(4x+1)2(x-3)(1)$

$= 2(x-3)\left[(x-3)2+4x+1\right]$

$= 2(x-3)(6x-5)$

3. $9x-2y=3$

$\dfrac{dy}{dx} = \dfrac{(x+1)(12x)-6x^2(1)}{(x+1)^2}$

$= \dfrac{12x^2+12x-6x^2}{(x+1)^2}$

$= \dfrac{6x^2+12x}{(x+1)^2}$

The slope at (1, 3) is

$\dfrac{6(1)^2+12(1)}{(1+1)^2}$

$= \dfrac{9}{2}$

The equation of the tangent is

$\dfrac{9}{2} = \dfrac{y-3}{x-1}$
$9x-9 = 2y-6$
$9x-2y=3$

4. (2, 1)

$$f(x) = \frac{4}{x^2}$$
$$= 4x^{-2}$$
$$f'(x) = -8x^{-3}$$
$$= \frac{-8}{x^3}$$

Since the slope $= -1$

$$\frac{-8}{x^3} = -1$$
$$8 = x^3$$
$$x = 2$$

the y-coordinate is

$$f(x) = \frac{4}{2^2}$$
$$= 1$$

So, the point is (2, 1).

5. $\dfrac{dy}{dx} = \dfrac{4x - 3y}{3x + 18y^2}$

$$3x\frac{dy}{dx} + 3y = 4x - 18y^2\frac{dy}{dx}$$
$$\frac{dy}{dx}(3x + 18y^2) = 4x - 3y$$
$$\frac{dy}{dx} = \frac{4x - 3y}{3x + 18y^2}$$

6. a) $\dfrac{d^2y}{dx^2} = 24x^2 - 6$

$$\frac{dy}{dx} = 8x^3 - 6x$$
$$\frac{d^2y}{dx^2} = 24x^2 - 6$$

b) $f''(x) = \dfrac{3}{2\sqrt{x^5}}$

$$f(x) = 2x^{\frac{-1}{2}}$$
$$f'(x) = -x^{\frac{-3}{2}}$$
$$f'(x) = -\frac{1}{\sqrt{x^3}}$$
$$f''(x) = \frac{3}{2}x^{\frac{-5}{2}}$$
$$f''(x) = \frac{3}{2\sqrt{x^5}}$$

7. a) $a = 6t - 12$

$$v(t) = \frac{ds}{dt}$$
$$v(t) = 3t^2 - 12t$$
$$a(t) = \frac{dv}{dt} \quad \left(\text{also, } a(t) = \frac{d^2s}{dt^2}\right)$$
$$a(t) = 6t - 12$$

b) $a(35) = 198$

$$a(35) = 6(35) - 12$$
$$a(35) = 198$$

After 35 seconds, the acceleration is $198\,\text{m}/\text{s}^2$.

DERIVATIVES OF TRIGONOMETRIC, LOGARITHMIC, AND EXPONENTIAL FUNCTIONS

Limits of Trigonometric Functions

ANSWERS AND SOLUTIONS

1. a) $= 1$

$$\lim_{x \to 0} \frac{\sin(4x)}{4x}$$
$$= 1$$

b) $= 0$

$$\lim_{x \to 0} \frac{2 - 2\cos x}{x}$$
$$\lim_{x \to 0} \frac{-2(-1 + \cos x)}{x}$$
$$= -2\lim_{x \to 0} \frac{\cos x - 1}{x}$$
$$= -2(0)$$
$$= 0$$

c) $= \dfrac{4}{3}$

$$\lim_{\theta \to 0} \frac{\sin(4\theta)}{\sin(3\theta)}$$

$$\lim_{\theta \to 0} \frac{\dfrac{\sin(4\theta)}{4\theta}}{\dfrac{\sin(3\theta)}{4\theta}}$$

$$= \lim_{\theta \to 0} \frac{\dfrac{\sin(4\theta)}{4\theta(3)}}{\dfrac{\sin(3\theta)}{4\theta(3)}}$$

$$= \frac{1}{3}\lim_{\theta \to 0} \frac{\sin(4\theta)}{4\theta} \div \frac{1}{4}\lim_{\theta \to 0} \frac{\sin(3\theta)}{3\theta}$$

$$= \frac{1}{3}(1) \div \frac{1}{4}(1)$$

$$= \frac{4}{3}$$

d) $= 3$

$$\lim_{x \to 0} \frac{\sin(3x)}{3x^2 + x}$$
$$= \lim_{x \to 0} \frac{\sin(3x)3}{x(3x + 1)3}$$
$$= \lim_{x \to 0} \frac{\sin 3x}{3x} \lim_{x \to 0} \frac{3}{3x + 1}$$
$$= (1)\left(\frac{3}{0 + 1}\right)$$
$$= 3$$

e) $= 0$

$$\lim_{\theta \to 0} \frac{1 - \cos(2\theta)}{\theta}$$
$$\lim_{\theta \to 0} \frac{(1 - \cos 2\theta)2}{\theta(2)}$$
$$= -2\lim_{\theta \to 0} \frac{\cos 2\theta - 1}{2\theta}$$
$$= -2(0)$$
$$= 0$$

f) $= 0$

$$\lim_{x \to 0} \frac{5\tan x - 5\sin x}{x\cos x}$$
$$\lim_{x \to 0} \frac{\dfrac{5\sin x}{\cos x} - \dfrac{5\sin x}{1}}{x\cos x}$$
$$= \lim_{x \to 0} \frac{5\sin x - 5\sin x \cos x}{x\cos^2 x}$$
$$= \lim_{x \to 0} \frac{-5\sin x(\cos x - 1)}{x\cos^2 x}$$
$$= -5\lim_{x \to 0} \frac{\sin x}{x} \lim_{x \to 0} \frac{\cos x - 1}{\cos^2 x}$$
$$= -5(1)\left(\frac{1 - 1}{1^2}\right)$$
$$= 0$$

Derivatives of Trigonometric Functions Part 1: Sine and Cosine

ANSWERS AND SOLUTIONS

1. a) $\dfrac{dy}{dx} = -4\sin x$

b) $f'(x) = 30x\cos(5x^2)$

$f'(x) = 3\cos(5x^2)(10x)$

$f'(x) = 30x\cos(5x^2)$

c)

$$\dfrac{dy}{dx}$$

$$= \dfrac{\cos 2x\left(2\sin x\cos x\right) - \sin^2 x\left(-2\sin 2x\right)}{\cos^2\left(2x\right)}$$

d) $f'(x) = 42\cos^2(7x)\sin(7x)$

$f(x) = -2\left(\cos(7x)\right)^3$

$f'(x) = -6\left(\cos 7x\right)^2\left(-\sin 7x\right)(7)$

$f'(x) = 42\cos^2(7x)\sin(7x)$

e) $\dfrac{dy}{dx} = x\cos x + \sin x$

$y = x\sin x$

$\dfrac{dy}{dx} = x(\cos x) + \sin x(1)$

$\dfrac{dy}{dx} = x\cos x + \sin x$

2. $\left.\dfrac{dy}{dx}\right|_{x=\frac{\pi}{2}} = 0$

$\dfrac{dy}{dx} = 2\cos(2x)\left(-\sin(2x)(2)\right)$

$\dfrac{dy}{dx} = -2\sin(4x)$

When $x = \dfrac{\pi}{2}$

$\left.\dfrac{dy}{dx}\right|_{x=\frac{\pi}{2}} = -2\sin\left(4\left(\dfrac{\pi}{2}\right)\right)$

$\left.\dfrac{dy}{dx}\right|_{x=\frac{\pi}{2}} = -2\sin(2\pi)$

$\left.\dfrac{dy}{dx}\right|_{x=\frac{\pi}{2}} = 0$

Derivatives of Trigonometric Functions Part 2: Tangent, Cotangent, Secant, and Cosecant

ANSWERS AND SOLUTIONS

1. a) $f'(x) = -4\csc^2(2x)$

b) $\dfrac{dy}{dx} = \sec(2x)\left(\sin x\tan 2x + \cos x\right)$

$\dfrac{dy}{dx} = \sin x\sec(2x)\tan(2x)(2) + \sec(2x)\cos x$

$\dfrac{dy}{dx} = \sec(2x)\left(2\sin x\tan 2x + \cos x\right)$

c)

$$f'(x) = \dfrac{\cos x^3\sec^2(5x-4)(5)}{-\tan(5x-4)\left(-\sin(x^3)(3x^2)\right)}{\cos^2(x^3)}$$

$$f'(x) = \dfrac{5\cos x^3\sec^2(5x-4)}{+3x^2\tan(5x-4)\sin(x^3)}{\cos^2(x^3)}$$

d) $\dfrac{dy}{dx} = -18x\csc^3\left(3x^2\right)\cot\left(3x^2\right)$

$y = \left[\csc(3x^2)\right]^3$
$\dfrac{dy}{dx} = 3\left[\csc\left(3x^2\right)\right]^2\left(-\csc\left(3x^2\right)\cot\left(3x^2\right)\right)(6x)$
$\dfrac{dy}{dx} = -18x\csc^3\left(3x^2\right)\cot\left(3x^2\right)$

Topic Practice Questions 1

ANSWERS AND SOLUTIONS

1. a) $= 8$

$\lim\limits_{x\to 0}\dfrac{\sin^2(4x)}{2x^2}$
$= \lim\limits_{x\to 0}\dfrac{\sin(4x)\sin(4x)(8)}{2x^2(8)}$
$= 8\lim\limits_{x\to 0}\dfrac{\sin(4x)}{4x}\lim\limits_{x\to 0}\dfrac{\sin(4x)}{4x}$
$= 8(1)(1)$
$= 8$

b) $= 0$

$\lim\limits_{x\to 0}\dfrac{\cos x - 1}{3x}$
$= \dfrac{1}{3}\lim\limits_{x\to 0}\dfrac{\cos x - 1}{x}$
$= \dfrac{1}{3}(0)$

2. a) $\dfrac{dy}{dx} = 4\sin(2x)$

$y = 4(\sin x)^2$
$\dfrac{dy}{dx} = 8\sin x\cos x$
$\dfrac{dy}{dx} = 4\sin(2x)$

b) $f'(x) = 15\tan^2(5x)\sec^2(5x)$

$f(x) = (\tan(5x))^3$
$f'(x) = 3\tan^2(5x)\sec^2(5x)(5)$
$f'(x) = 15\tan^2(5x)\sec^2(5x)$

c) $\dfrac{dy}{dx} = -4x\sin(4x) + \cos(4x)$

$g(x) = x$
$g'(x) = 1$
$h(x) = \cos(4x)$
$h'(x) = -\sin(4x)(4)$
$h'(x) = -4\sin(4x)$
$\dfrac{dy}{dx} = x(-4\sin(4x)) + \cos(4x)$
$\dfrac{dy}{dx} = -4x\sin(4x) + \cos(4x)$

d) $f'(x) = -\dfrac{\cos x}{\sin^2 x}$

$f(x) = \dfrac{\sec x}{\tan x} = \dfrac{\dfrac{1}{\cos x}}{\dfrac{\sin x}{\cos x}} = \dfrac{1}{\sin x} = [\sin x]^{-1}$
$f'(x) = -1[\sin x]^{-2}(\cos x)$
$f'(x) = -\dfrac{\cos x}{\sin^2 x}$

e) $\dfrac{dy}{dx} = -6x\csc^3\left(x^2-1\right)\cot\left(x^2-1\right)$

$y = \left[\csc\left(x^2-1\right)\right]^3$
$\dfrac{dy}{dx} = 3\csc^2\left(x^2-1\right)\left(-\csc\left(x^2-1\right)\cot\left(x^2-1\right)\right)(2x)$
$\dfrac{dy}{dx} = -6x\csc^3\left(x^2-1\right)\cot\left(x^2-1\right)$

f) $\dfrac{dy}{dx} = \dfrac{3 - y\cos x}{\sin x - \sin y}$

$y\cos x + \sin x\left(\dfrac{dy}{dx}\right) = 3 + \sin y\dfrac{dy}{dx}$
$\sin x\dfrac{dy}{dx} - \sin y\dfrac{dy}{dx} = 3 - y\cos x$
$\dfrac{dy}{dx}(\sin x - \sin y) = 3 - y\cos x$
$\dfrac{dy}{dx} = \dfrac{3 - y\cos x}{\sin x - \sin y}$

3. $= 16$

$$\frac{dy}{dx} = 8 \tan x \sec^2 x$$

at $x = \frac{\pi}{4}$

$$\frac{dy}{dx}\Big|_{x=\frac{\pi}{4}} = 8 \tan\left(\frac{\pi}{4}\right) \sec^2\left(\frac{\pi}{4}\right)$$

$$= 8(1)\left(\sqrt{2}\right)^2$$

$$= 16$$

Derivatives of Functions with Natural Logarithms

ANSWERS AND SOLUTIONS

1. $\dfrac{dy}{dx} = \dfrac{2}{x}$

$$\frac{dy}{dx} = \frac{1}{x^2}(2x)$$

$$\frac{dy}{dx} = \frac{2x}{x^2}$$

$$\frac{dy}{dx} = \frac{2}{x}$$

2. $f'(x) = \dfrac{3x^2}{x+1} + 6x \ln(x+1)$

$g(x) = 3x^2$

$g'(x) = 6x$

$h(x) = \ln(x+1)$

$h'(x) = \dfrac{1}{x+1}(1)$

$h'(x) = \dfrac{1}{x+1}$

$f'(x) = 3x^2\left(\dfrac{1}{x+1}\right) + \ln(x+1)(6x)$

$f'(x) = \dfrac{3x^2}{x+1} + 6x \ln(x+1)$

3. $\dfrac{dy}{dx} = \dfrac{1 - 3\ln x}{x^4}$

$g(x) = \ln x$

$g'(x) = \dfrac{1}{x}$

$h(x) = x^3$

$h'(x) = 3x^2$

$$\frac{dy}{dx} = \frac{x^3\left(\dfrac{1}{x}\right) - \ln x\left(3x^2\right)}{x^6}$$

$$\frac{dy}{dx} = \frac{x^2\left(1 - 3\ln x\right)}{x^6}$$

$$\frac{dy}{dx} = \frac{1 - 3\ln x}{x^4}$$

4. $\dfrac{dy}{dx} = \dfrac{6x}{3x^2 - 1}$

$$\frac{dy}{dx} = \frac{1}{3x^2 - 1}(6x)$$

$$\frac{dy}{dx} = \frac{6x}{3x^2 - 1}$$

5. $\dfrac{dy}{dx} = \dfrac{-y^2}{xy - 1}$

$$x\frac{dy}{dx} + y(1) = \frac{1}{y}\frac{dy}{dx}$$

$$x\frac{dy}{dx} - \frac{1}{y}\frac{dy}{dx} = -y$$

$$\frac{dy}{dx}\left(x - \frac{1}{y}\right) = -y$$

$$\frac{dy}{dx} = \frac{-y}{x - \dfrac{1}{y}}$$

$$\frac{dy}{dx} = \frac{-y}{\dfrac{xy - 1}{y}}$$

$$\frac{dy}{dx} = \frac{-y^2}{xy - 1}$$

Derivatives of Exponential and Logarithmic Functions

ANSWERS AND SOLUTIONS

1. a) $\dfrac{dy}{dx} = 2^x \ln 2$

    b) $\dfrac{dy}{dx} = 8x \ln 5 \left(5^{x^2} \right)$

    $\ln y = \ln 4 + \ln 5^{x^2}$
    $\ln y = \ln 4 + x^2 \ln 5$
    $\dfrac{1}{y} \dfrac{dy}{dx} = 0 + 2 \ln 5 (x)$
    $\dfrac{dy}{dx} = 4 \left(5^{x^2} \right) 2x \ln 5$
    $\dfrac{dy}{dx} = 8x \ln 5 \left(5^{x^2} \right)$

    c) $\dfrac{dy}{dx} = 7^{x^3-x} \ln 7 \left(3x^2 - 1 \right)$

    $\ln y = \ln 7^{x^3-x}$
    $\ln y = \left(x^3 - x \right) \ln 7$
    $\ln y = x^3 \ln 7 - x \ln 7$
    $\dfrac{1}{y} \dfrac{dy}{dx} = 3x^2 \ln 7 - \ln 7$
    $\dfrac{dy}{dx} = y \ln 7 \left(3x^2 - 1 \right)$
    $\dfrac{dy}{dx} = 7^{x^3-x} \ln 7 \left(3x^2 - 1 \right)$

2. a) $\dfrac{dy}{dx} = \dfrac{1}{x \ln 7}$

    $7^y = x$
    $\ln 7^y = \ln x$
    $y \ln 7 = \ln x$
    $\ln 7 \dfrac{dy}{dx} = \dfrac{1}{x}$
    $\dfrac{dy}{dx} = \dfrac{1}{x \ln 7}$

    b) $\dfrac{dy}{dx} = \dfrac{2}{\ln 3 (x-6)}$

    $y = \log_3 (x-6)^2$
    $3^y = (x-6)^2$
    $\ln 3^y = \ln (x-6)^2$
    $y \ln 3 = 2 \ln (x-6)$
    $\ln 3 \dfrac{dy}{dx} = 2 \left(\dfrac{1}{x-6} \right)(1)$
    $\dfrac{dy}{dx} = \dfrac{2}{\ln 3 (x-6)}$

3. a) $f'(x) = 2^{\sin x} \ln 2 (\cos x)$

    Method 1:
    $y = 2^{\sin x}$
    $\ln y = \sin x \ln 2$
    $\dfrac{1}{y} \dfrac{dy}{dx} = \ln 2 (\cos x)$
    $\dfrac{dy}{dx} = y \ln 2 (\cos x)$
    $\dfrac{dy}{dx} = 2^{\sin x} \ln 2 (\cos x)$

    Method 2:
    Using $\dfrac{d}{dx} \left[b^u \right] = \left(b^u \right)(\ln b) \left(\dfrac{du}{dx} \right)$
    $\qquad f'(x) = \left(2^{\sin x} \right)(\ln 2)(\cos x)$

    $\dfrac{d}{d_x} \left[b^u \right] = \left(b^u \right)(\ln b) \left(\dfrac{d_u}{d_x} \right)$

    b) $\dfrac{dy}{dx} = 4x (1 + 2 \ln x)$

    $g(x) = 4x^2$
    $g'(x) = 8x$
    $h(x) = \ln x$
    $h'(x) = \dfrac{1}{x}$
    $\dfrac{dy}{dx} = 4x^2 \left(\dfrac{1}{x} \right) + (\ln x)(8x)$
    $\dfrac{dy}{dx} = 4x (1 + 2 \ln x)$

c) $f'(x) = 2^x x(2 + x\ln 2)$

$$g(x) = 2^x$$
$$g'(x) = 2^x \ln 2$$
$$h(x) = x^2$$
$$h'(x) = 2x$$
$$f'(x) = 2^x(2x) + x^2(2^x \ln 2)$$
$$f'(x) = 2^x x(2 + x\ln 2)$$

d) $y' = -8x^2 \tan(2x)^2 + \ln\left(\cos(2x)^2\right)$

$$y = x\ln\left(\cos(2x)^2\right)$$
$$g(x) = x$$
$$g'(x) = 1$$
$$h(x) = \ln\left(\cos(2x)^2\right)$$
$$h'(x) = \frac{1}{\cos(2x)^2}\left(-\sin(2x)^2\left(2(2x)\right)(2)\right)$$
$$h'(x) = \frac{-8x\sin(2x)^2}{\cos(2x)^2}$$
$$y' = x\frac{-8x\sin(2x)^2}{\cos(2x)^2} + \ln\left(\cos(2x)^2\right)(1)$$
$$y' = -8x^2 \tan(2x)^2 + \ln\left(\cos(2x)^2\right)$$

Topic Practice Questions 2

ANSWERS AND SOLUTIONS

1. $= \dfrac{25}{2}$

$$\lim_{x\to 0}\frac{5\sin(5x)(5)}{2x(5)}$$
$$= \lim_{x\to 0}\frac{25}{2}\frac{\sin(5x)}{5x}$$
$$= \frac{25}{2}\lim_{x\to 0}\frac{\sin(5x)}{5x}$$
$$= \frac{25}{2}(1)$$
$$= \frac{25}{2}$$

2. a) $\dfrac{dy}{dx} = -\csc x \cot x$

b) $\dfrac{dy}{dx} = -2x\sin(3x)\sin x^2 + 3\cos x^2 \cos(3x)$

$$g(x) = \sin(3x)$$
$$g'(x) = 3\cos(3x)$$
$$h(x) = \cos x^2$$
$$h'(x) = -\sin x^2(2x)$$
$$h'(x) = -2x\sin x^2$$
$$\frac{dy}{dx} = \sin 3x\left(-2x\sin x^2\right) + \cos x^2\left(3\cos(3x)\right)$$
$$\frac{dy}{dx} = -2x\sin(3x)\sin x^2 + 3\cos x^2 \cos(3x)$$

c) $\dfrac{dy}{dx} = 8\tan(2x-5)\sec^2(2x-5)$

$$\frac{dy}{dx} = 2(\tan(2x-5))^2$$
$$\frac{dy}{dx} = 4\tan(2x-5)\sec^2(2x-5)(2)$$
$$\frac{dy}{dx} = 8\tan(2x-5)\sec^2(2x-5)$$

d) $f'(x) = 4x^2 \sec(7x)\left[7x\tan(7x)+3\right]$

$$g(x) = 4x^3$$
$$g'(x) = 12x^2$$
$$h(x) = \sec(7x)$$
$$h'(x) = \sec(7x)\tan(7x)(7)$$
$$f'(x) = 4x^3 \sec(7x)\tan(7x)(7)$$
$$\qquad + \sec(7x)\left(12x^2\right)$$
$$f'(x) = 4x^2 \sec(7x)\left[7x\tan(7x)+3\right]$$

3. $= 3\sqrt{3}$

$$f(x) = 3\left(\cos(2x)\right)^2$$
$$f'(x) = 6\cos(2x)\sin(2x)(2)(-1)$$
$$f'(x) = -12\cos(2x)\sin(2x)$$
$$f'(x) = -6\sin(4x)$$

slope at $x = \dfrac{\pi}{3}$

$$f'\left(\frac{\pi}{3}\right) = -6\sin\left(\frac{4\pi}{3}\right)$$
$$= -6\left(\frac{-\sqrt{3}}{2}\right)$$
$$= 3\sqrt{3}$$

ANSWERS AND SOLUTIONS

4. **a)** $f'(x) = \dfrac{5}{x}$

$$f'(x) = 5\left(\dfrac{1}{3x}\right)(3)$$

$$f'(x) = \dfrac{5}{x}$$

b) $\dfrac{dy}{dx} = 4\left(5^{2x^2}\right)\left(1 + 4x^2 \ln 5\right)$

$$g(x) = 5^{2x^2}$$
$$g'(x) = 5^{2x^2} 4x \ln 5$$
$$h(x) = 4x$$
$$h'(x) = 4$$
$$\dfrac{dy}{dx} = 5^{2x^2}(4) + 4x\left(5^{2x^2} 4x \ln 5\right)$$
$$\dfrac{dy}{dx} = 4\left(5^{2x^2}\right)\left(1 + 4x^2 \ln 5\right)$$

c) $\dfrac{dy}{dx} = \dfrac{1}{(x-3)\ln 2}$

Method 1:
$$2^y = 3x - 9$$
$$y \ln 2 = \ln(3x - 9)$$
$$\dfrac{dy}{dx} \ln 2 = \dfrac{1}{3x-9}(3)$$
$$\dfrac{dy}{dx} = \dfrac{1}{(x-3)\ln 2}$$

Method 2:
Using $\dfrac{d}{dx}(\log_b u) = \left(\dfrac{1}{u \ln b}\right)\left(\dfrac{du}{dx}\right)$

$$\dfrac{d}{dx}\left[\log_2(3x-9)\right] = \left(\dfrac{1}{(3x-9)\ln 2}\right)(3)$$
$$= \dfrac{1}{(x-3)\ln 2}$$

d) $\dfrac{dy}{dx} = \dfrac{y \ln 2}{\dfrac{1}{y} - x \ln 2}$

$$\ln y = xy \ln 2$$
$$\dfrac{1}{y}\dfrac{dy}{dx} = x \ln 2 \dfrac{dy}{dx} + y \ln 2 (1)$$
$$\dfrac{1}{y}\dfrac{dy}{dx} - x \ln 2 \dfrac{dy}{dx} = y \ln 2$$
$$\dfrac{dy}{dx}\left(\dfrac{1}{y} - x \ln 2\right) = y \ln 2$$
$$\dfrac{dy}{dx} = \dfrac{y \ln 2}{\dfrac{1}{y} - x \ln 2}$$
$$\dfrac{dy}{dx} = \dfrac{y \ln 2}{\dfrac{1 - x \ln 2}{y}}$$
$$\dfrac{dy}{dx} = \dfrac{y^2 \ln 2}{1 - xy \ln 2}$$

5. **a)** $f'(x) = \dfrac{1}{x}\sin(2\ln(2x))$

$$f(x) = \left(\sin(\ln(2x))\right)^2$$
$$f'(x) = 2\sin(\ln 2x)\cos(\ln 2x)\left(\dfrac{1}{2x}(2)\right)$$
$$f'(x) = \dfrac{1}{x}\sin(2\ln(2x))$$

b) $\dfrac{dy}{dx} = 5^{x\sin x} \ln 5 (x\cos x + \sin x)$

Method 1:
$$\ln y = x \sin x \ln 5$$
$$\dfrac{1}{y}\dfrac{dy}{dx} = x \ln 5 \cos x + \ln 5 \sin x (1)$$
$$\dfrac{dy}{dx} = y\left(\ln 5 (x\cos x + \sin x)\right)$$
$$\dfrac{dy}{dx} = 5^{x\sin x} \ln 5 (x\cos x + \sin x)$$

Method 2:
Using $\dfrac{d}{dx}(b^u) = (b^u)(\ln b)\left(\dfrac{du}{dx}\right)$

$$\dfrac{d}{dx}\left(5^{x\sin x}\right) = \left(5^{x\sin x}\right)(\ln 5)\left[x\cos x + \sin x(1)\right]$$

EXTREME VALUES AND CURVE SKETCHING

Intercepts and Zeros

ANSWERS AND SOLUTIONS

1. a) $x = 3, y = -6$

$$y = 2(0) - 6$$
$$y = -6$$
$$0 = 2x - 6$$
$$3 = x$$

b) $x = 0,\ x = 1,\ y = 0$

$$y = x(x-1)$$
$$= 0(0-1)$$
$$= 0$$
$$0 = x(x-1)$$
$$x = 0,\ x = 1$$

c) $x = \dfrac{2}{3},\ x = -4,\ y = -8$

$$y = 3(0)^2 + 10(0) - 8$$
$$= -8$$
$$0 = 3x^2 + 10x - 8$$
$$= (3x-2)(x+4)$$
$$x = \frac{2}{3},\ x = -4$$

d) $x = 0,\ x = \pi,\ y = 0$

$$y = 3\sin(0)$$
$$= 0$$
$$0 = 3\sin x$$
$$0 = \sin x$$
$$x = 0,\ x = \pi$$

e) $x = 0,\ x = \dfrac{1}{4}, y = 0$

$$y = \frac{4(0)^2 - (0)}{3(0) - 7}$$
$$= 0$$
$$0 = \frac{4x^2 - x}{3x - 7}$$
$$0 = 4x^2 - x$$
$$= x(4x-1)$$
$$x = 0,\ x = \frac{1}{4}$$

f) $y = \dfrac{3 \pm \sqrt{65}}{4}, y = -7$

$$y = 2(0)^2 - 3(0) - 7$$
$$= -7$$
$$x = \frac{3 \pm \sqrt{(-3)^2 - 4(2)(-7)}}{2(2)}$$
$$= \frac{3 \pm \sqrt{65}}{4}$$

Symmetry of Functions

ANSWERS AND SOLUTIONS

1. a) even

$$f(-x) = 4(-x)^2 - 3$$
$$= 4x^2 - 3$$
$$f(x) = f(-x)$$

The function is even.

b) not even

$$f(-x) = 2(-x)^3 + 3(-x) - 1$$
$$= -2x^3 - 3x - 1$$
$$f(x) \neq f(-x)$$

The function is not even.

c) even

$$f(-x) = 4(-x)^4 + 2(-x)^2 - 1$$
$$= 4x^4 + 2x^2 - 1$$
$$f(x) = f(-x)$$

The function is even.

d) even

$$f(-x) = 2\cos(-x) + 3$$
$$= 2\cos(x) + 3$$
$$f(x) = f(-x)$$

The function is even.

2. a) odd

$$-f(x) = -3x^3$$
$$f(-x) = 3(-x)^3$$
$$= -3x^3$$
$$-f(x) = f(-x)$$

The function is odd.

b) not odd

$$-f(x) = -(4x^2 - x)$$
$$= -4x^2 + x$$
$$f(-x) = 4(-x)^2 - (-x)$$
$$= 4x^2 + x$$
$$-f(x) \neq f(-x)$$

The function is not odd.

c) odd

$$-f(x) = -2(2x^3 - 5x)$$
$$= -2x^3 + 5x$$
$$f(-x) = 2(-x)^3 - 5(-x)$$
$$= -2x^3 + 5x$$
$$-f(x) = f(-x)$$

The function is odd.

d) odd

$$-f(x) = -\left(\frac{1}{2}\sin(2x)\right)$$
$$= -\frac{1}{2}\sin(2x)$$
$$f(-x) = \frac{1}{2}\sin(2(-x))$$
$$= -\frac{1}{2}\sin(2x)$$
$$-f(x) = f(-x)$$

The function is odd.

3. a) symmetric about the y-axis

$$f(-x) = 3(-x)^2 - 5$$
$$= 3x^2 - 5$$
$$-f(x) = -(3x^2 - 5)$$
$$= -3x^2 + 5$$
$$f(x) = f(-x)$$

The function is even, therefore, is symmetric about the y–axis.

b) symmetric about the origin

$$f(-x) = 2(-x)^3 - 7(-x)$$
$$= -2x^3 + 7x$$
$$-f(x) = -(2x^3 - 7x)$$
$$= -2x^3 + 7x$$
$$-f(x) = f(-x)$$

The function is odd, therefore, is symmetric about the origin.

c) no symmetry

$$f(-x) = (-x)^3 - (-x)^2$$
$$= -x^3 - x^2$$
$$-f(x) = -(x^3 - x^2)$$
$$= -x^3 + x^2$$
$$-f(x) \neq f(-x)$$
$$f(x) \neq f(-x)$$

The function is not even nor odd, therefore, it has no symmetry

d) symmetric about the origin

$$y = 4\sin x \cos x$$
$$y = 2\sin(2x)$$

$$f(-x) = 2\sin(2(-x))$$
$$= -2\sin(2x)$$
$$-f(x) = -2\sin(2x)$$
$$-f(x) = f(-x)$$

The function is odd, therefore, is symmetric about the origin.

Intervals of Increase and Decrease and Maximum and Minimum Values

ANSWERS AND SOLUTIONS

1. a) Decreasing: $(-\infty, 4)$

Increasing: $(4, \infty)$

Local minimum at $(4, f(4))$

Minimum value = $f(4) = 7$

$y = 2x^2 - 16x + 39$

$y' = 4x - 16$

$0 = 4x - 16$

$x = 4$

Critical value is $x = 4$

Test values:

$f'(0) = 4(0) - 16$
$\quad = $ negative

$f'(5) = 4(5) - 16$
$\quad = $ positive

Decreasing: $(-\infty, 4)$

Increasing: $(4, \infty)$

Local minimum at $(4, f(4))$

Minimum value = $f(4) = 7$

b) Decreasing: $(-\infty, 3) \cup (3, \infty)$

There are no maximum or minimum values.

$f(x) = \dfrac{2}{x-3}$

$f'(x) = \dfrac{-2}{(x-3)^2}$

$f'(x)$ cannot equal zero

$f(x)$ is undefined when $x = 3$

So, 3 is a critical value.

Test values:

$f'(0) = \dfrac{-2}{(0-3)^2}$
$\quad = $ negative

$f'(4) = \dfrac{-2}{(4-3)^2}$
$\quad = $ negative

Decreasing: $(-\infty, 3) \cup (3, \infty)$

There are no maximum or minimum values.

c) Increasing: $\left(0, \dfrac{\pi}{2}\right) \cup \left(\dfrac{3\pi}{2}, 2\pi\right)$

Decreasing: $\left(\dfrac{\pi}{2}, \dfrac{3\pi}{2}\right)$

Maximum value:

$f\left(\dfrac{\pi}{2}\right) = 3\sin\left(\dfrac{\pi}{2}\right) + 2$
$\quad = 5$

Minimum value:

$f\left(\dfrac{3\pi}{2}\right) = 3\sin\left(\dfrac{3\pi}{2}\right) + 2$
$\quad = -1$

$f(x) = 3\sin(x) + 2, 0 < x \le 2\pi$

$f'(x) = 3\cos(x)$

$0 = 3\cos(x)$

$0 = \cos(x)$

$x = \dfrac{\pi}{2} \quad x = \dfrac{3\pi}{2}$

Test values:

$f'\left(\dfrac{\pi}{3}\right) = 3\cos\left(\dfrac{\pi}{3}\right)$
$\quad = $ positive

$f'(\pi) = 3\cos(\pi)$
$\quad = $ negative

$f'\left(\dfrac{5\pi}{3}\right) = 3\cos\left(\dfrac{5\pi}{3}\right)$
$\quad = $ positive

Increasing: $\left(0, \dfrac{\pi}{2}\right) \cup \left(\dfrac{3\pi}{2}, 2\pi\right)$

Decreasing: $\left(\dfrac{\pi}{2}, \dfrac{3\pi}{2}\right)$

Maximum value:

$f\left(\dfrac{\pi}{2}\right) = 3\sin\left(\dfrac{\pi}{2}\right) + 2$
$\quad = 5$

Minimum value:

$f\left(\dfrac{3\pi}{2}\right) = 3\sin\left(\dfrac{3\pi}{2}\right) + 2$
$\quad = -1$

Since the function
$f(x) = 3\sin x + 2, 0 \le x \le 2\pi$ has a restricted domain, local maximum or minimum values will also occur at the endpoints.

$f(0) = 3\sin(0) + 2 = 2$

Since the function is increasing in the interval $\left(0,\dfrac{\pi}{2}\right)$, 2 is a local minimum

$f(2\pi) = 3\sin(2\pi) + 2 = 2$

Since the function is decreasing in the interval $\left(\dfrac{3\pi}{2}, 2\pi\right)$, 2 is a local maximum.

$f(x) = 3\sin x + 2, 0 \le x \le 2\pi$, at its endpoints, $(0,2)$ and $(2\pi,2)$ to see this:

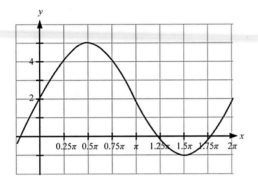

d) Decreasing: $\left(0,\dfrac{\pi}{4}\right)\cup\left(\dfrac{\pi}{2},\dfrac{3\pi}{4}\right)$

Increasing: $\left(\dfrac{\pi}{4},\dfrac{\pi}{2}\right)$

Minimum value:

$y = 2\cos^2\left(2\left(\dfrac{\pi}{4}\right)\right)$

$= 0$

Maximum value:

$y = 2\cos^2\left(2\left(\dfrac{\pi}{2}\right)\right)$

$= 2$

$y = 2\cos^2(2x), 0 < x < \dfrac{3\pi}{4}$

$f'(x) = 4\cos(2x)(-\sin(2x)(2))$

$\quad\quad = -8\cos(2x)\sin(2x)$

$\quad\quad = -4(2\sin(2x)\cos(2x))$

$\quad\quad = -4\sin(4x)$

$0 = -4\sin(4x)$

$0 = \sin 4x$

$x = \dfrac{\pi}{4} \quad x = \dfrac{\pi}{2}$

Test values:

$f'\left(\dfrac{\pi}{6}\right) = -4\sin\left(4\left(\dfrac{\pi}{6}\right)\right)$

$\quad\quad = \text{negative}$

$f'\left(\dfrac{\pi}{3}\right) = -4\sin\left(4\left(\dfrac{\pi}{3}\right)\right)$

$\quad\quad = \text{positive}$

$f'\left(\dfrac{2\pi}{3}\right) = -4\sin\left(4\left(\dfrac{2\pi}{3}\right)\right)$

$\quad\quad = \text{negative}$

Decreasing: $\left(0,\dfrac{\pi}{4}\right)\cup\left(\dfrac{\pi}{2},\dfrac{3\pi}{4}\right)$

Increasing: $\left(\dfrac{\pi}{4},\dfrac{\pi}{2}\right)$

Minimum value:

$y = 2\cos^2\left(2\left(\dfrac{\pi}{4}\right)\right)$

$= 0$

Maximum value:

$y = 2\cos^2\left(2\left(\dfrac{\pi}{2}\right)\right)$

$= 2$

Concavity and Points of Inflection

ANSWERS AND SOLUTIONS

1. **a)** concave down, negative

   b) concave up, positive

   c) increasing, positive

   d) decreasing, negative

   e) inflection point, zero

   f) local maximum, zero

   g) local minimum, zero

2. **a)** Concave up: $(-\infty, \infty)$ and, therefore, it has no inflection points.

$$f(x) = x^2 - 8x$$
$$f'(x) = 2x - 8$$
$$f''(x) = 2$$

Since the second derivative is always positive, the function is always concave up.

Concave up: $(-\infty, \infty)$ and, therefore, it has no inflection points.

b) Concave down: $\left(-\infty, \dfrac{1}{3}\right)$

Concave upward: $\left(\dfrac{1}{3}, \infty\right)$

$\therefore$ There is an inflection point at
$$\left(\frac{1}{3}, f\left(\frac{1}{3}\right)\right) = \left(\frac{1}{3}, \frac{206}{27}\right)$$

$$f(x) = 5x^3 - 5x^2 + 8$$
$$f'(x) = 15x^2 - 10x$$
$$f''(x) = 30x - 10$$
$$0 = 30x - 10$$
$$\frac{1}{3} = x$$

Test values: 0 and 1
$$f''(0) = 30(0) - 10$$
$$= \text{negative}$$
$$f''(1) = 30(1) - 10$$
$$= \text{positive}$$

Concave downward: $\left(-\infty, \dfrac{1}{3}\right)$

Concave upward: $\left(\dfrac{1}{3}, \infty\right)$

$\therefore$ There is an inflection point at
$$\left(\frac{1}{3}, f\left(\frac{1}{3}\right)\right) = \left(\frac{1}{3}, \frac{206}{27}\right)$$

c) Concave up: $(-\infty, 0)$

Concave down: $(0, \infty)$

Since the function is not defined when $x = 0$, there is no inflection point.

$$f(x) = \frac{x^2 - 1}{x}$$
$$f'(x) = \frac{x^2 + 1}{x^2}$$
$$f''(x) = -\frac{2}{x^3}$$

Since $f''(x)$ is undefined when $x = 0$, it is the potential inflection point.

Test values: -1 and 1
$$f''(-1) = -\frac{2}{(-1)^3}$$
$$= \text{positive}$$
$$f''(1) = -\frac{2}{(1)^3}$$
$$= \text{negative}$$

Concave up: $(-\infty, 0)$

Concave down: $(0, \infty)$

Since the function is not defined when $x = 0$, there is no inflection point.

d) Concave down: $\left(0, \dfrac{\pi}{4}\right) \cup \left(\dfrac{3\pi}{4}, \pi\right)$

Concave up: $\left(\dfrac{\pi}{4}, \dfrac{3\pi}{4}\right)$

Inflection points:
$$\left(\frac{\pi}{4}, f\left(\frac{\pi}{4}\right)\right) \text{ and } \left(\frac{3\pi}{4}, f\left(\frac{3\pi}{4}\right)\right)$$
$$\left(\frac{\pi}{4}, -\frac{\pi}{4}\right) \text{ and } \left(\frac{3\pi}{4}, -\frac{3\pi}{4}\right)$$
$$(0, \pi)$$

$$f(x) = 5\cos(2x) - x$$
$$f'(x) = -10\sin(2x) - 1$$
$$f''(x) = -20\cos(2x)$$
$$0 = -20\cos(2x)$$
$$0 = \cos(2x)$$
$$x = \frac{\pi}{4} \quad x = \frac{3\pi}{4}$$

Test values: $\dfrac{\pi}{6}$ and $\dfrac{\pi}{2}$ and $\dfrac{5\pi}{6}$

$$f''\left(\dfrac{\pi}{6}\right) = -20\cos\left(2\left(\dfrac{\pi}{6}\right)\right)$$
$$= \text{negative}$$

$$f''\left(\dfrac{\pi}{2}\right) = -20\cos\left(2\left(\dfrac{\pi}{2}\right)\right)$$
$$= \text{positive}$$

$$f''\left(\dfrac{5\pi}{6}\right) = -20\cos\left(2\left(\dfrac{5\pi}{6}\right)\right)$$
$$= \text{negative}$$

Concave down: $\left(0,\dfrac{\pi}{4}\right)\cup\left(\dfrac{3\pi}{4},\pi\right)$

Concave up: $\left(\dfrac{\pi}{4},\dfrac{3\pi}{4}\right)$

Inflection points:
$$\left(\dfrac{\pi}{4}, f\left(\dfrac{\pi}{4}\right)\right) \text{ and } \left(\dfrac{3\pi}{4}, f\left(\dfrac{3\pi}{4}\right)\right)$$
$$\left(\dfrac{\pi}{4}, -\dfrac{\pi}{4}\right) \text{ and } \left(\dfrac{3\pi}{4}, -\dfrac{3\pi}{4}\right)$$

3. a) (b, c)

b) $(0, d)$

c) $(a, 0)$

d) $(a, b)\cup(c, d)$

4.

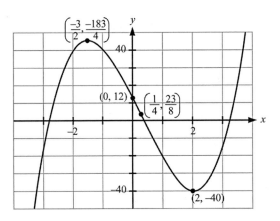

$$f'(x) = 12x^2 - 6x - 36$$
$$f'(x) = 6(2x+3)(x-2)$$
$$0 = 6(2x+3)(x-2)$$
$$x = -\dfrac{3}{2} \quad x = 2$$

Test values: -2, 0, and 3
$$f'(-2) = \text{positive}$$
$$f'(0) = \text{negative}$$
$$f'(3) = \text{positive}$$

The function is increasing on $\left(-\infty, -\dfrac{3}{2}\right)\cup(2, \infty)$

and decreasing on $\left(-\dfrac{3}{2}, 2\right)$.

There is a local maximum at $\left(-\dfrac{3}{2}, f\left(\dfrac{3}{2}\right)\right)$, which

is $\left(-\dfrac{3}{2}, \dfrac{183}{4}\right)$, and a local minimum at $(2, f(2))$,

which is $(2, -40)$.
$$f''(x) = 24x - 6$$
$$0 = 24x - 6$$
$$x = \dfrac{1}{4}$$

Test values: 0 and 1
$$f''(0) = \text{negative}$$
$$f''(1) = \text{positive}$$

The function is concave down on the interval
$\left(-\infty, \dfrac{1}{4}\right)$ and concave up on $\left(\dfrac{1}{4}, \infty\right)$.

There is an inflection point at $\left(\dfrac{1}{4}, f\left(\dfrac{1}{4}\right)\right)$, which

is $\left(\dfrac{1}{4}, \dfrac{23}{8}\right)$.

y-intercept:
$$f(0) = 12$$

5. a)

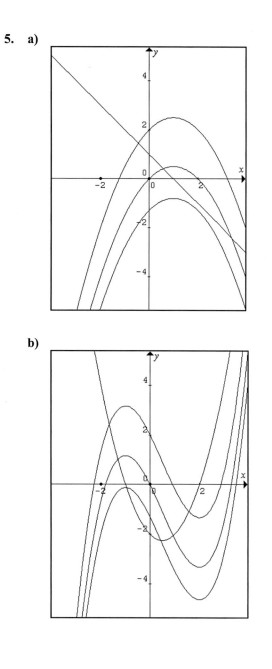

b)

ANSWERS AND SOLUTIONS

1. Let a be one number and b be the other number. Let S be the sum and P the product.

$$S = a + b$$

and $P = ab$

$$100 = ab$$

$$\frac{100}{a} = b$$

So,

$$S = a + \frac{100}{a}$$

$$\frac{dS}{da} = 1 - \frac{100}{a^2}$$

$$0 = 1 - \frac{100}{a^2}$$

$$\frac{100}{a^2} = 1$$

$$\sqrt{100} = a$$

$$10 = a$$

We ignore the negative square root value. Check where the function is increasing or decreasing around the critical number:

when $a = 1$,

$$\frac{dS}{da} = 1 - \frac{100}{1^2}$$

$$= \text{negative}$$

when $a = 20$,

$$\frac{dS}{da} = 1 - \frac{100}{20^2}$$

$$= \text{positive}$$

decreasing −		increasing +
1	10	20
test value	critical number	test value

Since $\dfrac{dS}{da}$ changes from negative to positive at

$a = 10$, the original function, $S = a + \dfrac{100}{a}$, reaches

a local minimum.

When $a = 10$,

$$b = \frac{100}{10}$$

$$= 10$$

The 2 positive numbers whose product is 100 and whose sum is a minimum are 10 and 10.

2. Let l be the length of the rectangle and w be the width. P is the perimeter of the rectangle and A is its area.

$$P = 2l + 2w$$

$$A = lw$$
$$8\ 000 = lw$$
$$l = \frac{8\ 000}{w}$$

$$P = 2\left(\frac{8\ 000}{w}\right) + 2w$$

$$P = \frac{16\ 000}{w} + 2w$$
$$P = 16\ 000w^{-1} + 2w$$

$$\frac{dP}{dw} = \frac{-16\ 000}{w^2} + 2$$

$$0 = \frac{-16\ 000}{w^2} + 2$$

$$\frac{16\ 000}{w^2} = 2$$

$$8\ 000 = w^2$$
$$\sqrt{8\ 000} = w$$
$$40\sqrt{5} = w$$

Check where the function is increasing or decreasing around the critical number: when $w = 1$, when $w = 1\ 000$,

$$\frac{dP}{dw} = \frac{-16\ 000}{1^2} + 2 \qquad \frac{dP}{dw} = \frac{-16\ 000}{1\ 000^2} + 2$$
$$= \text{negative} \qquad\qquad = \text{positive}$$

decreasing   increasing
−   +

0        $40\sqrt{5}$ 1 000
test value   critical   test value
             number

Therefore, the minimum perimeter occurs when $w = 40\sqrt{5}$ cm and

$$l = \frac{8\ 000}{40\sqrt{5}}$$
$$= \frac{200}{\sqrt{5}} \text{ cm}$$
$$= \frac{200}{\sqrt{5}} \times \frac{\sqrt{5}}{\sqrt{5}}$$
$$= \frac{200\sqrt{5}}{5}$$
$$= 40\sqrt{5} \text{ cm}$$

The dimensions of the rectangle: the width is $40\sqrt{5}$ cm and the length is $40\sqrt{5}$ cm.

3. Let θ be the angle at A.

Area of the triangle $= \frac{1}{2}$ base $\times$ height

$$\text{Area} = \frac{1}{2}(AB)(BC)$$

Express AB and BC in terms of θ:

$$\sin(\theta) = \frac{BC}{40} \qquad\qquad \cos(\theta) = \frac{AB}{40}$$

$$BC = 40\sin(\theta) \qquad\qquad AB = 40\cos(\theta)$$

$$\text{Area} = \frac{1}{2}(40\cos(\theta))(40\sin(\theta))$$
$$= 800\cos(\theta)\sin(\theta)$$
$$= 400(2\cos(\theta)\sin(\theta))$$
$$= 400\sin(2\theta)$$

Use the identity: $2(\sin A)(\cos A) = \sin(2A)$

$$\frac{dA}{d\theta} = 400(\cos(2\theta))2$$

$$\frac{dA}{d\theta} = 800\cos(2\theta)$$

$$0 = 800\cos(2\theta)$$

$$0 = \cos(2\theta)$$

$$\theta = \frac{\pi}{4}$$

Since θ is one of the acute angles in the right triangle, it must be less than $\frac{\pi}{2}$.

Check where the function is increasing or decreasing around the critical number:

when $\theta = 0$,   when $\theta = \frac{\pi}{2}$,

$$\frac{dA}{d\theta} = 800\cos(2(0)) \qquad \frac{dA}{d\theta} = 800\cos(2(90))$$
$$= 800\cos(0) \qquad\qquad = 800\cos(180)$$
$$= \text{positive} \qquad\qquad = \text{negative}$$

decreasing   increasing
−   +

0        $\frac{\pi}{4}$ $\frac{\pi}{2}$

So, there is a local maximum when $\theta = \frac{\pi}{4}$.

The maximum area is:

$$A = 400\sin\left[2\left(\frac{\pi}{4}\right)\right]$$
$$= 400\sin\left(\frac{\pi}{2}\right)$$
$$= 400(1)$$
$$= 400\ \text{cm}^2$$

4. $= 15\ 000\ \text{m}^2$

Let l be the length and let w be the width.

Let A be area: $A = lw$
Let F be the length of fence:

$$F = 2l + 3w$$
$$600 = 2l + 3w$$
$$\frac{600 - 3w}{2} = l$$
$$300 - \frac{3}{2}w = l$$

Substitute l into the expression for area:

$$A = \left(300 - \frac{3}{2}w\right)w$$
$$A = 300w - \frac{3}{2}w^2$$

Find the derivative of this function and set it equal to zero:

$$\frac{dA}{dw} = 300 - 3w$$
$$0 = 300 - 3w$$
$$3w = 300$$
$$w = 100$$

Check where the function is increasing or decreasing around the critical number:

when $w = 0$,   when $w = 200$,

$$\frac{dA}{dw} = 300 - 3w \qquad \frac{dA}{dw} = 300 - 3(200)$$
$$= 300 - 3(0) \qquad\qquad = -300$$
$$= \text{positive} \qquad\qquad = \text{negative}$$

```
decreasing              increasing
    −                       +
────┼───────┼───────┼────
    0      100      200
test value  critical  test value
            number
```

Therefore, a maximum area occurs when

$w = 100$ m.

$$A = 300(100) - \frac{3}{2}(100)^2$$
$$= 30\ 000 - 15\ 000$$
$$= 15\ 000\ \text{m}^2$$

5.

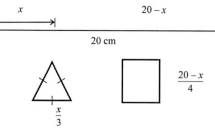

Let x be the length of one portion of wire and $(20 - x)$ will be the other.

Let $\dfrac{x}{3}$ be the side length of the triangle.

Let $\dfrac{20 - x}{4}$ be the side length of the square.

The area of an equilateral triangle is given by:

$$A = \frac{\sqrt{3}a^2}{4}\text{, where } a \text{ is the length of a side.}$$

The combined area, A, of the equilateral triangle and square is:

$$A = \frac{\sqrt{3}\left(\frac{x}{3}\right)^2}{4} + \left(\frac{20 - x}{4}\right)^2$$
$$= \frac{\sqrt{3}x^2}{36} + \frac{400 - 40x + x^2}{16}$$
$$= \frac{4\sqrt{3}x^2 + 3\ 600 - 360x + 9x^2}{144}$$
$$= \frac{4\sqrt{3}x^2}{144} + \frac{3\ 600}{144} - \frac{360x}{144} + \frac{9x^2}{144}$$

Find $\dfrac{dA}{dx}$ and set it to zero.

$$\frac{dA}{dx} = \frac{8\sqrt{3}x}{144} + 0 - \frac{360}{144} + \frac{18x}{144}$$
$$0 = \frac{8\sqrt{3}x - 360 + 18x}{144}$$
$$0 = 8\sqrt{3}x - 360 + 18x$$
$$360 = x\left(8\sqrt{3} + 18\right)$$
$$x = \frac{360}{8\sqrt{3} + 18}$$
$$x \doteq 11.3$$

Test the sign of $\dfrac{dA}{dx}$ at $x = 11$ and $x = 12$.

(Before and after the critical value of 11.3)
At $x = 11$,
$$\frac{dA}{dx} = \frac{8\sqrt{3}(11) - 360 + 18(11)}{144} \doteq -0.067$$

At $x = 12$,
$$\frac{dA}{dx} = \frac{8\sqrt{3}(12) - 360 + 18(12)}{144} \doteq +0.155$$

Since the first derivative changed from *negative to positive* across the critical value of 11.3, the original function was decreasing before, and increasing after the critical value of 11.3 and reached a local minimum at $x = 11.3$.

A minimum total area of the equilateral triangle and square occurs when $x = 11.3$cm.

The wire should be cut so that $\dfrac{360}{8\sqrt{3}+18}$ cm is used for the equilateral triangle and

$\left(20 - \dfrac{360}{8\sqrt{3}+18}\right)$ cm is used for the square.

Topic Practice Questions 1

ANSWERS AND SOLUTIONS

1. The function is even and has symmetry about the *y*-axis.

$$f(x) = \frac{4x^4 - 1}{x^2}$$

$$f(-x) = \frac{4(-x)^4 - 1}{(-x)^2}$$

$$= \frac{4x^4 - 1}{x^2}$$

$$-f(x) = -\left(\frac{4x^4 - 1}{x^2}\right)$$

$$= -\frac{4x^4 - 1}{x^2}$$

Since $f(x) = f(-x)$ and $-f(x) \neq f(-x)$, the function is even and has symmetry about the *y*-axis.

2. **a)** $f(x) = x^2 - 4x + 1$

$$f(x) = x^2 - 4x + 1$$
$$f'(x) = 2x - 4$$
$$0 = 2x - 4$$
$$x = 2$$

Test values: 0 and 3
$$f'(0) = 2(0) - 4$$
$$= \text{negative}$$
$$f'(0) = 2(3) - 4$$
$$= \text{positive}$$

Interval of decrease: $(-\infty, 2)$

Interval of increase: $(2, \infty)$

Minimum value:
$$f(2) = (2)^2 - 4(2) + 1$$
$$= -3$$

b) Intervals of increase: $(-\infty, -1) \cup (1, \infty)$

Intervals of decrease: $(-1, 0) \cup (0, 1)$

Maximum value: $f(-1) = -2$

Minimum value: $f(1) = 2$

$$f'(x) = \frac{x(2x) - (x^2 + 1)(1)}{x}$$

$$= \frac{x^2 - 1}{x}$$

$$0 = \frac{x^2 - 1}{x}$$

$$0 = x^2 - 1$$

$$x = \pm 1$$

Also, the function is not defined when $x = 0$, so the critical values are 0 and ± 1.
Test values: $-2, -0.5, 0.5, 2$
$$f'(-2) = \text{positve}$$
$$f'(-0.5) = \text{negative}$$
$$f(0.5) = \text{negative}$$
$$f(2) = \text{positive}$$

Intervals of increase: $(-\infty, -1) \cup (1, \infty)$

Intervals of decrease: $(-1, 0) \cup (0, 1)$

Maximum value: $f(-1) = -2$

Minimum value: $f(1) = 2$

3. **a)** $f'(x) = 3x^2 + 4x - 1$

$f''(x) = 6x + 4$
$0 = 6x + 4$
$x = \dfrac{-2}{3}$

Test values: -1 and 0
$f''(-1) = \text{negative}$
$f''(0) = \text{positive}$

Concave down: $\left(-\infty, -\dfrac{2}{3}\right)$

Concave up: $\left(-\dfrac{2}{3}, \infty\right)$

Inflection point: $\left(\dfrac{-2}{3}, f\left(\dfrac{-2}{3}\right)\right)$
$= \left(\dfrac{-2}{3}, \dfrac{142}{27}\right)$

b) $f(x) = 2\sin x;\ 0 < x < 2\pi$

$f'(x) = 2\cos x$
$f''(x) = -2\sin x$
$0 = -2\sin x$
$0 = \sin x$
$x = \pi$

Test values: $\dfrac{\pi}{2}$ and $\dfrac{3\pi}{2}$

$f''\left(\dfrac{\pi}{2}\right) = \text{negative}$

$f''\left(\dfrac{3\pi}{2}\right) = \text{positive}$

Concave up: $(\pi, 2\pi)$
Concave down: $(0, \pi)$
Inflection point: $(\pi, f(\pi)) = (\pi, 0)$

4. $SA = 2\pi r^2 + 2\pi rh$

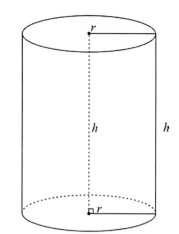

Using $V = \pi r^2 h$:
$355 = \pi r^2 h$
$\dfrac{355}{\pi r^2} = h$

Substitute:
$SA = 2\pi r^2 + 2\pi r\left(\dfrac{355}{\pi r^2}\right)$
$= 2\pi r^2 + \dfrac{710}{r}$
$= 2\pi r^2 + 710r^{-1}$

$\dfrac{d(SA)}{dr} = 4\pi r - \dfrac{710}{r^2}$

$0 = 4\pi r - \dfrac{710}{r^2}$

$r = \sqrt[3]{\dfrac{710}{4\pi}}$
$\doteq 3.84$

Test values: 3 and 4

$\left.\dfrac{d(SA)}{dr}\right|r = 3 = 4\pi(3) - \dfrac{710}{r^2}$
$= \text{negative}$

$\left.\dfrac{d(SA)}{dr}\right|r = 4 = 4\pi(4) - \dfrac{710}{r^2}$
$= \text{positive}$

$\therefore$ a minimum occurs when $r = \sqrt[3]{\dfrac{710}{4\pi}}$

Calculate the other dimension, h:

$h = \dfrac{355}{\pi r^2} = \dfrac{355}{\pi\left(\sqrt[3]{\dfrac{710}{4\pi}}\right)^2} \doteq 7.67$

This can should have a radius of approximately 3.8 cm and a height of approximately 7.67 cm.

Vertical Asymptotes

ANSWERS AND SOLUTIONS

1. a) $f(x) = \dfrac{1}{x+1}$

The function is undefined when
$$x + 1 = 0$$
$$x = -1$$
(potential asymptote)

$$\lim_{x \to -1^+} \left(\frac{1}{x+1} \right) = +\infty$$

$$\lim_{x \to -1^-} \left(\frac{1}{x+1} \right) = -\infty$$

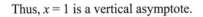

Thus, $x = 1$ is a vertical asymptote.

b) $f(x) = \dfrac{2}{x^2 + 2x - 3}$

The function is undefined when
$$x^2 + 2x - 3 = 0.$$
$$(x+3)(x-1) = 0$$
$$x = -3 \text{ and } x = 1 \quad \text{(potential asymptote)}$$

$$\lim_{x \to 1^+} \left[\frac{2}{(x+3)(x-1)} \right] = +\infty$$

$$\lim_{x \to 1^-} \left[\frac{2}{(x+3)(x-1)} \right] = -\infty$$

$$\lim_{x \to -3^+} \left[\frac{2}{(x+3)(x-1)} \right] = -\infty$$

$$\lim_{x \to -3^-} \left[\frac{2}{(x+3)(x-1)} \right] = +\infty$$

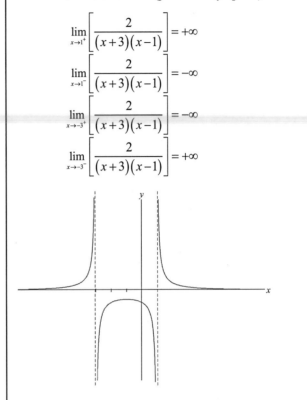
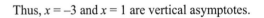

Thus, $x = -3$ and $x = 1$ are vertical asymptotes.

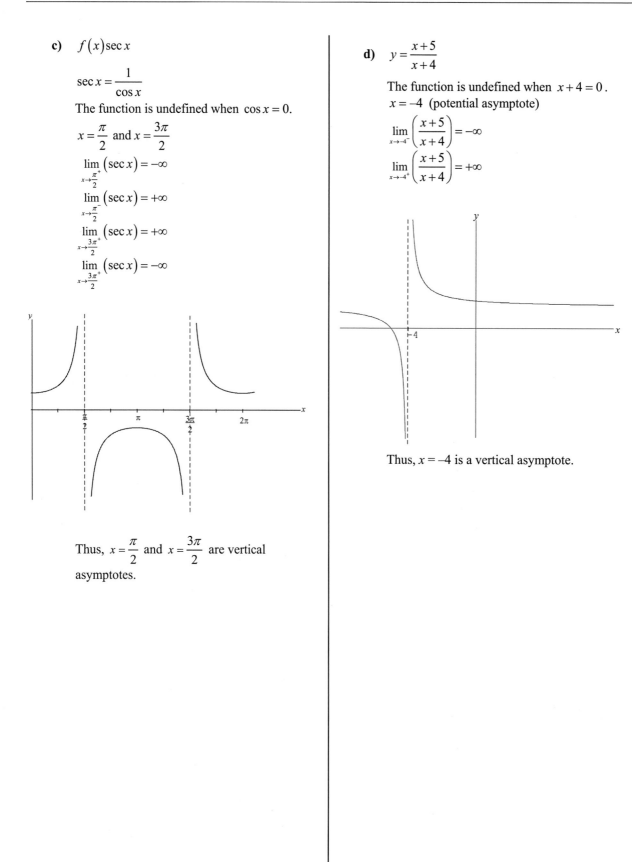

c) $f(x)\sec x$

$$\sec x = \frac{1}{\cos x}$$

The function is undefined when $\cos x = 0$.

$$x = \frac{\pi}{2} \text{ and } x = \frac{3\pi}{2}$$

$$\lim_{x \to \frac{\pi}{2}^+}\left(\sec x\right) = -\infty$$

$$\lim_{x \to \frac{\pi}{2}^-}\left(\sec x\right) = +\infty$$

$$\lim_{x \to \frac{3\pi}{2}^+}\left(\sec x\right) = +\infty$$

$$\lim_{x \to \frac{3\pi}{2}^+}\left(\sec x\right) = -\infty$$

Thus, $x = \frac{\pi}{2}$ and $x = \frac{3\pi}{2}$ are vertical asymptotes.

d) $y = \frac{x+5}{x+4}$

The function is undefined when $x + 4 = 0$.
$x = -4$ (potential asymptote)

$$\lim_{x \to -4^-}\left(\frac{x+5}{x+4}\right) = -\infty$$

$$\lim_{x \to -4^+}\left(\frac{x+5}{x+4}\right) = +\infty$$

Thus, $x = -4$ is a vertical asymptote.

Horizontal Asymptotes

ANSWERS AND SOLUTIONS

1. **a)** $y = 0$

$$\lim_{x \to \infty} \frac{x^2}{x^3 - 4} = \lim_{x \to \infty} \frac{\dfrac{x^2}{x^3}}{\dfrac{x^3}{x^3} - \dfrac{4}{x^3}}$$

$$= \lim_{x \to \infty} \frac{\dfrac{1}{x}}{1 - \dfrac{4}{x^3}}$$

$$= \frac{\lim\limits_{x \to \infty} \dfrac{1}{x}}{\lim\limits_{x \to \infty} 1 - \lim\limits_{x \to \infty} \dfrac{4}{x^3}}$$

$$= \frac{0}{1 - 0}$$

$$= 0$$

There is a horizontal asymptote at $y = 0$.

b) $y = \dfrac{1}{2}$

$$\lim_{x \to \infty} \frac{2x^2 - x}{4x^2 - 3} = \lim_{x \to \infty} \frac{\dfrac{2x^2}{x^2} - \dfrac{x}{x^2}}{\dfrac{4x^2}{x^2} - \dfrac{3}{x^2}}$$

$$= \lim_{x \to \infty} \frac{2 - \dfrac{1}{x}}{4 - \dfrac{3}{x^2}}$$

$$= \frac{\lim\limits_{x \to \infty} 2 - \lim\limits_{x \to \infty} \dfrac{1}{x}}{\lim\limits_{x \to \infty} 4 - \lim\limits_{x \to \infty} \dfrac{3}{x^2}}$$

$$= \frac{2 - 0}{4 - 0} = \frac{2 - 0}{4 - 0} = \frac{1}{2}$$

There is a horizontal asymptote at $y = \dfrac{1}{2}$.

c) There are no horizontal asymptotes.

$$\lim_{x \to \infty} \frac{-5x^3 - 4x^2}{3x^2 + x} = \lim_{x \to \infty} \frac{\dfrac{-5x^3}{x^2} - \dfrac{4x^2}{x^2}}{\dfrac{3x^2}{x^2} + \dfrac{x}{x^2}}$$

$$= \lim_{x \to \infty} \frac{-5x - 4}{3 + \dfrac{1}{x}}$$

$$= \frac{\lim\limits_{x \to \infty}(-5x) - \lim\limits_{x \to \infty} 4}{\lim\limits_{x \to \infty} 3 + \lim\limits_{x \to \infty} \dfrac{1}{x}}$$

$$= \frac{-\infty - 4}{3 + 0}$$

$$= -\infty$$

Therefore, there are no horizontal asymptotes.

d) $y = -\dfrac{2}{3}$

$$\lim_{x \to \infty} \frac{-4x^3 + 2x^2 - 1}{6x^3 - x + 5}$$

$$= \lim_{x \to \infty} \frac{\dfrac{-4x^3}{x^3} + \dfrac{2x^2}{x^3} - \dfrac{1}{x^3}}{\dfrac{6x^3}{x^3} - \dfrac{x}{x^3} + \dfrac{5}{x^3}}$$

$$= \lim_{x \to \infty} \frac{-4 + \dfrac{2}{x} - \dfrac{1}{x^3}}{6 - \dfrac{1}{x^2} + \dfrac{5}{x^3}}$$

$$= \frac{\lim\limits_{x \to \infty}(-4) + \lim\limits_{x \to \infty} \dfrac{2}{x} - \lim\limits_{x \to \infty} \dfrac{1}{x^3}}{\lim\limits_{x \to \infty} 6 - \lim\limits_{x \to \infty} \dfrac{1}{x^2} + \lim\limits_{x \to \infty} \dfrac{5}{x^3}}$$

$$= \frac{-4 + 0 - 0}{6 - 0 + 0}$$

$$= \frac{-4}{6} = \frac{-2}{3}$$

Therefore, the horizontal asymptote
is $y = -\dfrac{2}{3}$.

2. a) The vertical asymptotes:
$$x - 3 = 0$$
$$x = 3$$

$$\lim_{x \to 3^+} \frac{2x+1}{x-3} = \frac{2(3)+1}{(\text{very small positive number})}$$
$$= \infty$$

$$\lim_{x \to 3^-} \frac{2x+1}{x-3} = \frac{2(3)+1}{(\text{very small negative number})}$$
$$= -\infty$$

Vertical asymptote at $x = 3$

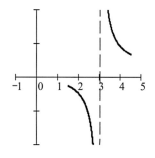

The horizontal asymptotes:
$$\lim_{x \to \infty} \frac{2x+1}{x-3}$$

$$= \lim_{x \to \infty} \frac{\dfrac{2x}{x} + \dfrac{1}{x}}{\dfrac{x}{x} - \dfrac{3}{x}}$$

$$= \lim_{x \to \infty} \frac{2 + \dfrac{1}{x}}{1 - \dfrac{3}{x}}$$

$$= \frac{\lim\limits_{x \to \infty} 2 + \lim\limits_{x \to \infty} \dfrac{1}{x}}{\lim\limits_{x \to \infty} 1 - \lim\limits_{x \to \infty} \dfrac{3}{x}}$$

$$= \frac{2+0}{1-0}$$
$$= 2$$

Therefore, the horizontal asymptote is at $y = 2$.

b) $f(x) = \dfrac{-4x^2 - x}{x^2 - 2x - 15}$

Find the vertical asymptotes:
$$x^2 - 2x - 15 = 0$$
$$(x-5)(x+3) = 0$$
$$x = 5 \text{ and } x = -3$$

$$\lim_{x \to 5^+} \frac{-4x^2 - x}{(x-5)(x+3)} = -\infty$$

$$\lim_{x \to 5^-} \frac{-4x^2 - x}{(x-5)(x+3)} = +\infty$$

$$\lim_{x \to -3^+} \frac{-4x^2 - x}{(x-5)(x+3)} = +\infty$$

$$\lim_{x \to -3^-} \frac{-4x^2 - x}{(x-5)(x+3)} = -\infty$$

Therefore, there are vertical asymptotes at $x = -3$ and $x = 5$.
Find the horizontal asymptotes:
$$\lim_{x \to \infty} \frac{-4x^2 - x}{x^2 - 2x - 15}$$

$$= \lim_{x \to \infty} \frac{\dfrac{-4x^2}{x^2} - \dfrac{x}{x^2}}{\dfrac{x^2}{x^2} - \dfrac{2x}{x^2} - \dfrac{15}{x^2}}$$

$$= \lim_{x \to \infty} \frac{-4 - \dfrac{1}{x}}{1 - \dfrac{2}{x} - \dfrac{15}{x^2}}$$

$$= \frac{\lim\limits_{x \to \infty}(-4) - \lim\limits_{x \to \infty} \dfrac{1}{x}}{\lim\limits_{x \to \infty} 1 - \lim\limits_{x \to \infty} \dfrac{2}{x} - \lim\limits_{x \to \infty} \dfrac{15}{x^2}}$$

$$= \frac{-4 - 0}{1 - 0 - 0} = -4$$

Therefore, there is a horizontal asymptote at $y = -4$.

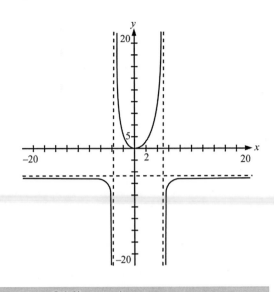

Oblique Asymptotes

ANSWERS AND SOLUTIONS

1. Because the degree of the numerator exceeds that of the denominator by 1, the functions that will have an oblique asymptote are those given in a, c, and d.

   Because the degree of the numerator does not exceed that of the denominator by 1, the functions that will **not** have an oblique asymptote are those given in b, e, and f.

2. **a)** $y = 2x$

$$x \overline{)2x^2 + 3} \quad 2x \; R3$$

$$\frac{2x^2 + 3}{x} = 2x + \frac{3}{x}$$

$$f(x) - 2x = \frac{3}{x}$$

$$\lim_{x \to \infty}\left[f(x) - 2x\right] = \lim_{x \to \infty}\frac{3}{x}$$
$$= 0$$

$\therefore$ The equation of the asymptote is $y = 2x$.

b) $y = 3x - 1$

$$x - 2 \overline{)3x^2 - 7x} \quad 3x - 1 \; R - 2$$

$$\frac{3x^2 - 7x}{x - 2} = 3x - 1 + \frac{-2}{x - 2}$$

$$f(x) - (3x - 1) = -\frac{2}{x - 2}$$

$$\lim_{x \to \infty}\left[f(x) - (3x - 1)\right] = \lim_{x \to \infty}-\frac{2}{x - 2}$$

$$= \lim_{x \to \infty}-\frac{\dfrac{2}{x}}{\dfrac{x}{x} - \dfrac{2}{x}}$$

$$= -\frac{\lim\limits_{x \to \infty}\dfrac{2}{x}}{\lim\limits_{x \to \infty}1 - \lim\limits_{x \to \infty}\dfrac{2}{x}}$$

$$= -\frac{0}{1 - 0}$$
$$= 0$$

$\therefore$ The equation of the asymptote is $y = 3x - 1$.

c) $y = 6x$

$$x^2 + 1 \overline{)6x^3 - 5x} \quad 6x \; R - 11x$$

$$\frac{6x^3 - 5x}{x^2 + 1} = 6x - \frac{11x}{x^2 + 1}$$

$$f(x) - 6x = -\frac{11x}{x^2 + 1}$$

$$\lim_{x \to \infty}\left[f(x) - 6x\right] = \lim_{x \to \infty}-\frac{11x}{x^2 + 1}$$

$$= \lim_{x \to \infty}-\frac{\dfrac{11x}{x^2}}{\dfrac{x^2}{x^2} + \dfrac{1}{x^2}}$$

$$= -\frac{\lim\limits_{x \to \infty}\dfrac{11}{x}}{\lim\limits_{x \to \infty}1 + \lim\limits_{x \to \infty}\dfrac{1}{x^2}}$$

$$= -\frac{0}{1 + 0}$$
$$= 0$$

$\therefore$ The equation of the asymptote is $y = 6x$.

d) $y = -4x - 6$

$$x^2 - 2x \overline{) -4x^3 + 2x^2 + x - 4 } \quad \begin{array}{c} -4x - 6 \text{ R } -11x - 4 \end{array}$$

$$\frac{-4x^3 + 2x^2 + x - 4}{x^2 - 2x} = -4x - 6 + \frac{-11x - 4}{x^2 - 2x}$$

$$f(x) - (-4x - 6) = \frac{-11x - 4}{x^2 - 2x}$$

$$\lim_{x \to \infty} \left[f(x) - (-4x - 6) \right] = \lim_{x \to \infty} \frac{-11x - 4}{x^2 - 2x}$$

$$= \lim_{x \to \infty} \frac{\dfrac{-11x}{x^2} - \dfrac{4}{x^2}}{\dfrac{x^2}{x^2} - \dfrac{2x}{x^2}}$$

$$= \frac{\displaystyle\lim_{x \to \infty} \frac{-11}{x} - \lim_{x \to \infty} \frac{4}{x^2}}{\displaystyle\lim_{x \to \infty} 1 - \lim_{x \to \infty} \frac{2}{x}}$$

$$= \frac{0 - 0}{1 - 0}$$

$$= 0$$

$\therefore$ The equation of the asymptote is $y = -4x - 6$.

Topic Practice Questions 2

ANSWERS AND SOLUTIONS

1. a) $(-\infty, a) \cup (0, d)$

b) $(a, 0) \cup (d, \infty)$

c) (b, c)

d) a, 0, and d

2. i) a)

$$f'(x) = 15x^2 - 10x$$
$$0 = 5x(3x - 2)$$
$$x = 0, \frac{2}{3}$$

Test values: -1, $\dfrac{1}{2}$, and 1

$$f'(-1) = 15(-1)^2 - 10(-1)$$
$$= \text{positive}$$

$$f'\left(\frac{1}{2}\right) = 15\left(\frac{1}{2}\right)^2 - 10\left(\frac{1}{2}\right)$$
$$= \text{negative}$$

$$f'(1) = 15(1)^2 - 10(1)$$
$$= \text{positive}$$

Intervals of increase: $(-\infty, 0) \cup \left(\dfrac{2}{3}, \infty\right)$

Interval of decrease: $\left(0, \dfrac{2}{3}\right)$

b) Maximum value: $f(0) = -15$

Minimum value: $f\left(\dfrac{2}{3}\right) = \dfrac{-425}{27}$

c) $f''(x) = 30x - 10$

$$0 = 30x - 10$$
$$x = \frac{1}{3}$$

Test values: 0 and 1
$$f''(0) = \text{negative}$$
$$f''(1) = \text{positive}$$

$\therefore$ Concave up $\left(\dfrac{1}{3}, \infty\right)$

Concave down $\left(-\infty, \dfrac{1}{3}\right)$

d) Inflection point: $\left(\dfrac{1}{3}, f\left(\dfrac{1}{3}\right)\right) = \left(\dfrac{1}{3}, \dfrac{-415}{27}\right)$

ii) a)

$$f'(x) = 6x^2 + 6x - 120$$
$$0 = 6(x+5)(x-4)$$
$$x = -5, 4$$

Test values: -6, 0, and 5

$f''(-6) = $ positive
$f''(0) = $ negative
$f''(5) = $ positive

Increasing: $(-\infty, -5) \cup (4, \infty)$

Decreasing: $(-5, 4)$

b) Maximum: $f(-5) = 473$

Minimum: $f(4) = -256$

c) $f''(x) = 12x + 6$
$$0 = 12x + 6$$
$$x = -\frac{1}{2}$$

Test values: -1 and 0

$f''(-1) = $ negative
$f''(0) = $ positive

Concave down: $\left(-\infty, -\frac{1}{2}\right)$

Concave up $\left(-\frac{1}{2}, \infty\right)$

d) Inflection point:

$$\left(-\frac{1}{2}, f\left(-\frac{1}{2}\right)\right) = \left(-\frac{1}{2}, \frac{217}{2}\right)$$

3. a) $x = -2$, $y = -\dfrac{2}{9}$

x-intercept:
$$0 = \frac{x+2}{x^2 - 9}$$
$$0 = x + 2$$
$$x = -2$$

y-intercept
$$y = \frac{0+2}{0^2 - 9}$$
$$y = -\frac{2}{9}$$

b) The vertical asymptotes are at $x = 3$ and $x = -3$.

Vertical asymptote:
$$x^2 - 9 = 0$$
$$x = \pm 3$$

$$\lim_{x \to 3^-} \left[\frac{x+2}{(x+3)(x-3)}\right] = -\infty$$

$$\lim_{x \to 3^+} \left[\frac{x+2}{(x+3)(x-3)}\right] = +\infty$$

$$\lim_{x \to -3^-} \left[\frac{x+2}{(x+3)(x-3)}\right] = -\infty$$

$$\lim_{x \to -3^+} \left[\frac{x+2}{(x+3)(x-3)}\right] = \infty$$

The vertical asymptotes are at $x = 3$ and $x = -3$.

c) $y = 0$

$$f(x) = \frac{x+2}{x^2 - 9}$$

$$\lim_{x \to \infty} f(x) = \lim_{x \to \infty} \frac{x+2}{x^2 - 9}$$

$$= \lim_{x \to \infty} \frac{\dfrac{x}{x^2} + \dfrac{2}{x^2}}{\dfrac{x^2}{x^2} - \dfrac{9}{x^2}}$$

$$= \frac{\displaystyle\lim_{x \to \infty} \frac{1}{x} + \lim_{x \to \infty} \frac{2}{x^2}}{\displaystyle\lim_{x \to \infty} 1 - \lim_{x \to \infty} \frac{9}{x^2}}$$

$$= \frac{0+0}{1-0}$$

$$= 0$$

and $\displaystyle\lim_{x \to -\infty} f(x) = 0$

The equation of the horizontal asymptote is $y = 0$.

d) $f'(x) = \dfrac{(x^2 - 9) - (x + 2)(2x)}{(x^2 - 9)^2}$

$f'(x) = \dfrac{-x^2 - 4x - 9}{(x^2 - 9)^2}$

Critical values:
The numerator will never be zero.
$-x^2 - 4x - 9 = 0$

$x = \dfrac{4 \pm \sqrt{(-4)^2 - 4(-1)(-9)}}{2(-1)}$

$= \dfrac{4 \pm \sqrt{-20}}{-2}$

The denominator is zero when $x = \pm 3$

Test values: $x = -4, 0,$ and 4

$f'(-4) = \dfrac{-(-4)^2 - 4(-4) - 9}{\left[(-4)^2 - 9\right]^2} = -\dfrac{9}{49}$

$f'(0) = \dfrac{-(0)^2 - 4(0) - 9}{\left[(0)^2 - 9\right]^2} = -\dfrac{1}{9}$

$f'(4) = \dfrac{-(4)^2 - 4(4) - 9}{\left[(4)^2 - 9\right]^2} = -\dfrac{41}{49}$

There are no intervals of increase.
Intervals of decrease:
$(-\infty, -3) \cup (-3, 3) \cup (3, \infty)$
There are no maximum or minimum values.

e)

$f'(x) = \dfrac{-x^2 - 4x - 9}{(x^2 - 9)^2}$

$f''(x) = \dfrac{(x^2 - 9)^2(-2x - 4) - (-x^2 - 4x - 9)(2)(x^2 - 9)(2x)}{(x^2 - 9)^4}$

$f''(x) = \dfrac{\left[(x^2 - 9)(x + 2) + (-x^2 - 4x - 9)2x\right](-2(x^2 - 9))}{(x^2 - 9)^4}$

$f''(x) = \dfrac{-2\left[x^3 + 2x^2 - 9x - 18 - 2x^3 - 8x^2 - 18x\right]}{(x^2 - 9)^3}$

$f''(x) = \dfrac{2(x^3 + 6x^2 + 27x + 18)}{(x^2 - 9)^3}$

Critical values:
The numerator is zero when
$x^3 + 6x^2 + 27x + 18 = 0$
This occurs when $x \doteq -0.796$

The denominator is zero when $x = \pm 3$
Test values: $x = -4, -2, -1, 0, 2,$ and 4

$f''(-4) = \dfrac{2\left[(-4)^3 + 6(-4)^2 + 27(-4) + 18\right]}{\left[(-4)^2 - 9\right]^3}$

$= \dfrac{-116}{343}$

$f''(-2) = \dfrac{2\left[(-2)^3 + 6(-2)^2 + 27(-2) + 18\right]}{\left[(-2)^2 - 9\right]^3}$

$= \dfrac{-40}{-125}$

$f''(-1) = \dfrac{2\left[(-1)^3 + 6(-1)^2 + 27(-1) + 18\right]}{\left[(-1)^2 - 9\right]^3}$

$= \dfrac{-8}{-512}$

$f''(0) = \dfrac{2\left[(0)^3 + 6(0)^2 + 27(0) + 18\right]}{\left[(0)^2 - 9\right]^3}$

$= \dfrac{36}{-729}$

$f''(2) = \dfrac{2\left[(2)^3 + 6(2)^2 + 27(2) + 18\right]}{\left[(2)^2 - 9\right]^3}$

$= \dfrac{208}{-125}$

$f''(4) = \dfrac{2\left[(4)^3 + 6(4)^2 + 27(4) + 18\right]}{\left[(4)^2 - 9\right]^3}$

$= \dfrac{572}{343}$

The original function is concave up in the intervals: $(-3, -0.786) \cup (3, \infty)$

The original function is concave down in the intervals: $(-\infty, -3) \cup (-0.786, 3)$

Since the sign of the second derivative changes at $x = -0.786$, a point of inflection exists at $\left(-0.786, f(0.786)\right) \doteq (-0.786, -0.145)$

f)

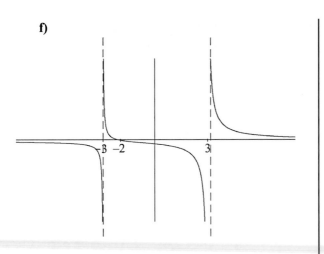

4. **a)** $y = 4$

x-intercept
$$0 = \frac{x^2 + 4x + 4}{x+1}$$
$$0 = (x+2)(x+2)$$
$$x = -2$$

y-intercept
$$y = \frac{0^2 + 4(0) + 4}{0+1}$$
$$y = 4$$

b) $x = -1$

$$x + 1 = 0$$
$$x = -1$$

$$\lim_{x \to -1^-} \frac{(x+2)^2}{x+1}$$
$$= \frac{1}{\text{very small negative}}$$
$$= -\infty$$

$$\lim_{x \to -1^+} \frac{(x+2)^2}{x+1}$$
$$= \frac{1}{\text{very small positive}}$$
$$= \infty$$

There is a vertical asymptote at $x = -1$.

c) $y = x + 3$

$$\begin{array}{r} x + 3 \ \text{R1} \\ x+1{\overline{\smash{\big)}\,x^2 + 4x + 4}} \end{array}$$

$$\frac{x^2 + 4x + 4}{x+1} = x + 3 + \frac{1}{x+1}$$
$$f(x) - (x+3) = \frac{1}{x+1}$$
$$\lim_{x \to \infty} \left[f(x) - (x+3) \right] = \lim_{x \to \infty} \frac{1}{x+1}$$
$$= \lim_{x \to \infty} \frac{\frac{1}{x}}{\frac{x}{x} + \frac{1}{x}}$$
$$= \frac{\lim_{x \to \infty} \frac{1}{x}}{\lim_{x \to \infty} 1 + \lim_{x \to \infty} \frac{1}{x}}$$
$$= \frac{0}{1+0}$$
$$= 0$$

$\therefore$ There is an oblique asymptote at $y = x + 3$.

d) $f'(x) = \frac{(x+1)(2x+4) - (x^2 + 4x + 4)(x)}{(x+1)^2}$

$$f'(x) = \frac{2x^2 + 6x + 4 - x^2 - 4x - 4}{(x+1)^1}$$
$$f'(x) = \frac{x^2 + 2x}{(x+1)^2} = \frac{x(x+2)}{(x+1)^2}$$

Critical values:
The numerator is zero when $x = -2$ or 0
The denominator is undefined when $x = -1$
Test values: $x = -3, -1.5, -0.5,$ and 1

$$f'(-3) = \frac{-3(-3+2)}{(-3+1)^2} = \frac{3}{4}$$
$$f'(-1.5) = \frac{-1.5(-1.5+2)}{(-1.5+1)^2} = \frac{-0.75}{0.25}$$
$$f'(-0.5) = \frac{-0.5(-0.5+2)}{(-0.5+1)^2} = \frac{-0.75}{0.25}$$
$$f'(-1) = \frac{1(1+2)}{(1+1)^2} = \frac{3}{4}$$

The original function is increasing in the intervals: $(-\infty, -2) \cup (0, \infty)$
The original function is decreaseing in the intervals: $(-2, -1) \cup (-1, 0)$

The original function has a maximum value of

$$f(-2) = \frac{(-2)^2 + 4(-2) + 4}{-2 + 1} = 0$$

The original function has a minimum value of

$$f(0) = \frac{(0)^2 + 4(0) + 4}{0 + 1} = 4$$

e)

$$f'(x) = \frac{x^2 + 2x}{(x+1)^2}$$

$$f''(x) = \frac{(x+1)^2(2x+2)}{-(x^2+2x)(2)(x+1)(1)}{(x+1)^4}$$

$$f''(x) = \frac{2(x+1)\left[\left[(x+1)^2 - (x^2+2x)\right]\right]}{(x+1)^4}$$

$$f''(x) = \frac{2}{(x+1)^3}$$

Critical values:
The numerator cannot equal zero.
The denominator is zero when $x = -1$
Test values: $x = -2, 0$

$$f''(-2) = \frac{2}{(-2+1)^3} = \frac{2}{-1}$$

$$f''(0) = \frac{2}{(0+1)^3} = \frac{2}{1}$$

The original function is concave down in the interval $(-\infty, -1)$.

The original function is concave up in the interval $(-1, \infty)$.

The sign of the second derivative does change at $x = -1$. However, the original function is undefined at $x = -1$. There are no points of inflection.

f)

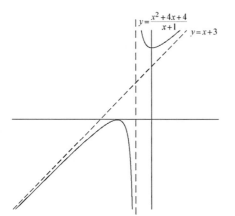

5. Let s be the length of the base and let h be the height of the box.
$$SA = 2s^2 + 4sh$$

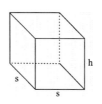

Using the volume formula, we can isolate h.
$$V = s^2 h$$
$$h = \frac{1\ 000}{s^2}$$

Substitute:

$$SA = 2s^2 + 4s\left(\frac{1\ 000}{s^2}\right)$$
$$= 2s^2 + 4\ 000s^{-1}$$
$$\frac{d(SA)}{ds} = 4s - \frac{4\ 000}{s^2}$$
$$0 = 4s - \frac{4\ 000}{s^2}$$
$$\frac{4\ 000}{s^2} = 4s$$
$$4\ 000 = 4s^3$$
$$s = 10$$

Test values: 9 and 11
$$\frac{d(SA)}{ds} = 4(9) - \frac{4\ 000}{(9)^2}$$
$$= 36 - \frac{4\ 000}{36}$$
$$= \text{negative}$$

$$\frac{d(SA)}{ds} = 4(11) - \frac{4\ 000}{(11)^2}$$
$$= 44 - \frac{4\ 000}{121}$$
$$= \text{positive}$$

Since the first derivative changes from negative to positive at $s = 10$, the surface area function,

$$SA = 2s^2 + 4s\left(\frac{1\ 000}{s^2}\right), \text{ reached a minimum value.}$$

Substituting, we find
$$h = \frac{1\ 000}{(10)^2}$$
$$h = 10$$

The dimensions of the box of minimum surface area: a base length of 10 cm and a height of 10 cm.

6.

Area $= \dfrac{1}{2}$ (base)(height)

$b = 2(10)\cos\theta \quad h = 10\sin\theta$

$$A = \frac{1}{2}bh$$
$$= \frac{1}{2}\big(2(10\cos\theta)\big)(10\sin\theta)$$
$$= 100\sin\theta\cos\theta$$
$$= 50\sin(2\theta)$$

$$\frac{dA}{d\theta} = 50\cos(2\theta)(2)$$
$$= 100\cos(2\theta)$$

We know that θ is acute.

$$0 = 100\cos(2\theta)$$
$$0 = \cos(2\theta)$$
$$\theta = \frac{\pi}{4}$$

Test values: $\dfrac{\pi}{6}$ and $\dfrac{\pi}{3}$

$$\frac{dA}{d\theta} = 100\cos\left(2\left(\frac{\pi}{6}\right)\right)$$
$$= \text{positive}$$

$$\frac{dA}{d\theta} = 100\cos\left(2\left(\frac{\pi}{3}\right)\right)$$
$$= \text{negative}$$

$\therefore$ A maximum area occurs when $\theta = \dfrac{\pi}{4}$

$$A = 50\sin\left(2\left(\frac{\pi}{4}\right)\right)$$
$$= 50$$

50 cm^2 is the maximum possible area of an isosceles triangle whose equal sides each measure 10 cm.

7. $f'(x) = -3x^2 + 8x + 3$

$$f'(x) = -(3x+1)(x-3)$$
$$0 = -(3x+1)(x-3)$$
$$x = -\frac{1}{3} \quad x = 3$$

Test values: -1, 0 and 4

$$f'(-1) = \text{negative}$$
$$f'(0) = \text{positive}$$
$$f'(4) = \text{negative}$$

The function is decreasing on $\left(-\infty, -\dfrac{1}{3}\right] \cup (3, \infty)$

and increasing on $\left(-\dfrac{1}{3}, 3\right)$.

There is a local minimum at $\left(-\dfrac{1}{3}, \dfrac{121}{27}\right)$ and a local

maximum at $(3, 23)$.

$$f''(x) = -6x + 8$$
$$0 = -6x + 8$$
$$x = \frac{4}{3}$$

Test values: 0 and 2

$$f''(0) = \text{positive}$$
$$f''(2) = \text{negative}$$

The function is concave up on $\left(-\infty, \dfrac{4}{3}\right)$ and

concave down on $\left(\dfrac{4}{3}, \infty\right)$, and there is an

inflection point at $\left(\dfrac{4}{3}, \dfrac{371}{27}\right)$.

y-intercept: 5

APPLICATIONS OF DERIVATIVES

Distance, Velocity, and Acceleration

ANSWERS AND SOLUTIONS

1. a) $t = 183.676$ s

$$h = -4.9t^2 + 900t + 2.4$$

$$t = \frac{-(900) \pm \sqrt{(900)^2 - 4(-4.9)(2.4)}}{2(-4.9)}$$

$$t = 183.676 \text{ s}$$

b) Maximum velocity = 900 m/s
Minimum velocity = –900 m/s

$$h = -4.9t^2 + 900t + 2.4$$

$$v = \frac{dh}{dt} = -9.8t + 900$$

Since this problem involves a restricted domain of $0 \le t \le 183.676$, the endpoints of the velocity-time function must be considered. The velocity-time function is linear.

$$v(0) = -9.8(0) + 900$$
$$= 900 \text{ m/s}$$
$$v(183.676) = -9.8(183.676) + 900$$
$$= -900 \text{ m/s}$$

Since a linear function cannot have any points where its first derivative would be zero, these endpoint values are the maximum and minimum values of the velocity.

c) $v = 312$ m/s upward

$$v = -9.8(60) + 900$$

$$v = 312 \text{ m/s upward}$$

2. a) Maximum velocity = 0 m/s
Minimum velocity = –21.909 m/s

$$h = -0.8t^2 + 150$$
$$0 = -0.8t^2 + 150$$
$$t = \sqrt{\frac{150}{0.8}}$$
$$t = 13.693 \text{ s}$$

$$h = -0.8t^2 + 150$$
$$v = \frac{dh}{dt} = -1.6t$$

Since this problem involves a restricted domain of $0 \le t \le 13.693$, the endpoints of the velocity-time function must be considered. The velocity-time function is linear.

$$v(0) = -1.6(0) = 0$$
$$v(13.693) = -1.6(13.693) = -21.909$$

Since a linear function cannot have any points where its first derivative would be zero, these endpoint values are the maximum and minimum values of the velocity.

b) $a = -1.6$ m/s²

$$v = -1.6t$$
$$a = \frac{dv}{dt} = -1.6$$
$$a = -1.6 \text{ m/s}^2$$

3. a) Neptune:
$$h = -5.88t^2 - 8t + 200$$
$$v = \frac{dh}{dt} = -11.68t - 8$$
$$a = \frac{dv}{dt} = -11.68 \text{ m/s}^2$$

Mars:
$$h = -1.85t^2 - 8t + 200$$
$$v = \frac{dh}{dt} = -3.7t - 8$$
$$a = \frac{dv}{dt} = -3.7 \text{ m/s}^2$$

Venus:
$$h = -4.45t^2 - 8t + 200$$
$$v = \frac{dh}{dt} = -8.9t - 8$$
$$a = \frac{dv}{dt} = -8.9 \text{ m/s}^2$$

b) Maximum speed is –60.199 m/s.

$$0 = -4.45t^2 - 8t + 200$$

$$t = \frac{-(-8) \pm \sqrt{(-8)^2 - 4(-4.45)(200)}}{2(-4.45)}$$

$$t = 5.865 \text{ s}$$

Since this problem involves a restricted domain of $0 \le t \le 5.865$, the endpoint values of the velocity-time function must be considered.

$$v(t) = -8.9t - 8$$
$$v(0) = -8.9(0) - 8 = -8$$
$$v(5.865) = -8.9(5.865) - 8 = -60.199$$

Since a linear function cannot have any points where its first derivative would be zero, these endpoint values are the maximum and minimum values of the velocity. The object has a maximum velocity of –8 m/s and a minimum velocity of –60.199 m/s. The absolute value of –60.199 is the value of the object's maximum speed.

c) Difference maximum speeds is speed 29.3 m/s

Neptune:

$$t = \frac{-(-8) \pm \sqrt{(-8)^2 - 4(-5.8)(200)}}{2(-5.8)}$$

$$t = 5.22... \text{ s}$$
$$v = -11.6t - 8$$
$$= -11.6(5.22... \text{ s}) - 8$$
$$\doteq -68.59 \text{ m/s}$$

The maximum speed of the object on Neptune is 68.59 m/s.

Mars:

$$t = \frac{-(-8) \pm \sqrt{(-8)^2 - 4(-1.85)(200)}}{2(-1.85)}$$

$$t = 8.458... \text{ s}$$
$$v = -3.7t - 8$$
$$= -3.7(8.458... \text{ s}) - 8$$
$$\doteq -39.29 \text{ m/s}$$

The maximum speed of the object on Mars is 39.29 m/s.

Difference: $68.59 - 39.29 = 29.3$ m/s

Rate of Change Involving Area and Volume

ANSWERS AND SOLUTIONS

1. a) $= 900 \text{ m}^3/\text{s}$

$$V = s^3$$
$$\frac{dV}{dt} = 3s^2 \frac{ds}{dt}$$
When $s = 10$ m
$$= 3(10 \text{ m})^2 (3 \text{ m/s})$$
$$= 900 \text{ m}^3/\text{s}$$

b) $A = \pi r^2 \quad 15 = \pi r^2, \quad r = \sqrt{\frac{15}{\pi}}$ m

$$\frac{dA}{dt} = \pi 2r \frac{dr}{dt}$$
When $A = 15$ m^2
$$-1.2 \text{ m}^2/\text{s} = 2\pi\left(\sqrt{\frac{15}{\pi}} \text{ m}\right)\frac{dr}{dt}$$
$$\frac{dr}{dt} = \frac{-1.2 \text{ m}^2/\text{s}}{2\pi\left(\sqrt{\frac{15}{\pi}} \text{ m}\right)}$$
$$\frac{dr}{dt} = \frac{-3}{5\sqrt{15\pi}} \text{ m/s}$$

2. $\frac{ds}{dt} = \frac{1}{20}$ cm/s

$$A = s^2$$
$$\frac{dA}{dt} = 2s \frac{ds}{dt}$$
When $s = 200$ cm
$$20 \text{ cm}^2/\text{s} = 2s \frac{ds}{dt}$$
$$20 \text{ cm}^2/\text{s} = 2(200 \text{ cm})\frac{ds}{dt}$$
$$\frac{20 \text{ cm}^2/\text{s}}{400 \text{ cm}} = \frac{ds}{dt}$$
$$\frac{ds}{dt} = \frac{1}{20} \text{ cm/s}$$

3. $\dfrac{40}{49\pi}$ cm/s

$$V = \dfrac{4}{3}\pi r^3$$

$$\dfrac{dV}{dt} = 4\pi r^2 \dfrac{dr}{dt}$$

When $r = 3.5$ cm

$$-40 \text{ cm}^3/\text{s} = 4\pi(3.5 \text{ cm})^2 \dfrac{dr}{dt}$$

$$\dfrac{-40 \text{ cm}^3/\text{s}}{4\pi(3.5 \text{ cm})^2} = \dfrac{dr}{dt}$$

$$\dfrac{dr}{dt} = \dfrac{-40 \text{ cm}^3/\text{s}}{4(12.25 \text{ cm}^2)\pi}$$

$$= \dfrac{-40}{49\pi} \text{ cm/s}$$

Since this rate of change is negative, the radius is decreasing at a rate of $\dfrac{40}{49\pi}$ cm/s .

4. $\dfrac{dh}{dt} = \dfrac{1}{5\pi}$ m/min

$$V = \dfrac{1}{3}\pi r^2 h$$

$$\dfrac{r}{h} = \dfrac{2}{5}, \ r = \dfrac{2}{5}h$$

When $r = 3$, $h = \dfrac{15}{2}$

$$V = \dfrac{1}{3}\pi\left(\dfrac{2}{5}h\right)^2 h$$

$$= \dfrac{4}{75}\pi h^3$$

$$\dfrac{dV}{dt} = \dfrac{4}{25}\pi h^2 \dfrac{dh}{dt}$$

$$1.8 = \dfrac{900}{100}\pi \dfrac{dh}{dt}$$

$$180 = 900\pi \dfrac{dh}{dt}$$

$$\dfrac{180}{900\pi} = \dfrac{dh}{dt}$$

$$\dfrac{1}{5\pi} = \dfrac{dh}{dt}$$

5. $\dfrac{ds}{dt} = \dfrac{3}{10}$ m/s

$$V = s^3$$

$$SA = 6s^2$$

$$40 \text{ m}^2 = 6s^2$$

$$s = \sqrt{\dfrac{20}{3}}$$

$$\dfrac{dV}{dt} = 3s^2 \dfrac{ds}{dt}$$

When $SA = 40$ m^2

$$6 \text{ m}^3/\text{s} = 3\left(\sqrt{\dfrac{20}{3}} \text{ m}\right)^2 \dfrac{ds}{dt}$$

$$\dfrac{ds}{dt} = \dfrac{3}{10} \text{ m/s}$$

Rates of Change Involving Triangles

ANSWERS AND SOLUTIONS

1. $\dfrac{dz}{dt} \doteq 2.69$ m/s

$$\dfrac{dx}{dt} = 2 \text{ m/s}$$

$$\dfrac{dy}{dt} = 1.8 \text{ m/s}$$

After 5 minutes:
$x = 600$ m , $y = 540$ m,

$$z = \sqrt{600^2 + 540^2}$$

$$= 60\sqrt{181} \text{ m}$$

$$z^2 = x^2 + y^2$$

Differentiating implicitly:

$$2z\frac{dz}{dt} = 2x\frac{dx}{dt} + 2y\frac{dy}{dt}$$

$$\frac{dz}{dt} = \frac{x\dfrac{dx}{dt} + y\dfrac{dy}{dt}}{z}$$

$$\frac{dz}{dt}\Big|_{t=5\text{ min}} = \frac{600(2) + 540(1.8)}{60\sqrt{181}}$$

$$= \frac{36.2}{\sqrt{181}}$$

$$= \frac{181}{5\sqrt{181}}$$

$$= \frac{181}{5\sqrt{181}} \times \frac{\sqrt{181}}{\sqrt{181}}$$

$$= \frac{181\sqrt{181}}{5(181)}$$

$$= \frac{\sqrt{181}}{5}$$

$$\doteq 2.69 \text{ m/s}$$

2. $= \dfrac{17}{70}$ m/s

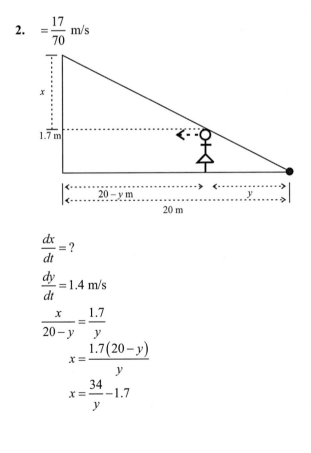

$$\frac{dx}{dt} = ?$$

$$\frac{dy}{dt} = 1.4 \text{ m/s}$$

$$\frac{x}{20-y} = \frac{1.7}{y}$$

$$x = \frac{1.7(20-y)}{y}$$

$$x = \frac{34}{y} - 1.7$$

Differentiating implicitly:

$$\frac{dx}{dt} = \left(\frac{-34}{y^2}\right)\left(\frac{dy}{dt}\right)$$

$$\frac{dx}{dt}\Big|_{y=14\text{ m}} = \frac{-34}{(14\text{ m})^2}(1.4 \text{ m/s})$$

$$= \frac{-47.6}{196}$$

$$= \frac{-17}{70} \text{ m/s}$$

The length of the shadow is decreasing at a rate of $\dfrac{17}{70}$ m/s .

3. $\dfrac{dz}{dt}\Big|_{z=30} = 2\sqrt{3}$ m/s

$$\frac{dx}{dt} = 4$$

$$\frac{dz}{dt} = ?$$

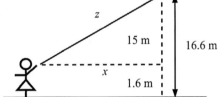
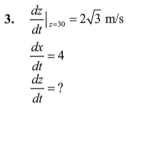

When $z = 30$ m,

$$x = \sqrt{30^2 - 15^2}$$

$$= \sqrt{675}$$

$$= 15\sqrt{3} \text{ m}$$

$$z^2 = x^2 + 15^2$$

Differentiating implicitly:

$$2z\frac{dz}{dt} = 2x\frac{dx}{dt}$$

$$\frac{dz}{dt} = \frac{x\dfrac{dx}{dt}}{z}$$

When $z = 30$ m

$$\frac{dz}{dt}\Big|_{z=30} = \frac{(15\sqrt{3})(4)}{30}$$

$$= 2\sqrt{3} \text{ m/s}$$

4. The angle is decreasing at a rate of $\frac{1}{8}$ rad/sec.

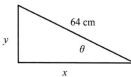

$$\frac{dy}{dt} = -5 \text{ cm/s}$$
$$\frac{d\theta}{dt} = ?$$

When $x = 40$ cm, then $\cos\theta = \frac{40}{64}$,

$$\sin\theta = \frac{y}{64 \text{ cm}}$$

Differentiating implicitly:

$$\cos\theta \frac{d\theta}{dt} = \left(\frac{1}{64 \text{ cm}}\right)\left(\frac{dy}{dt}\right)$$

$$\frac{d\theta}{dt} = \frac{\left(\frac{1}{64}\right)\left(\frac{dy}{dt}\right)}{\cos\theta}$$

When $x = 40$

$$\frac{d\theta}{dt}\bigg|_{x=40} = \frac{\left(\frac{1}{64}\right)(-5)}{\frac{40}{64}}$$

$$\frac{d\theta}{dt} = \frac{-1}{8} \text{ rad/s}$$

The angle is decreasing at a rate of $\frac{1}{8}$ rad/sec.

5. The base is changing at a rate of -3.6 cm/min

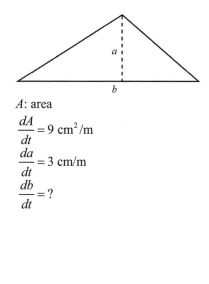

A: area

$$\frac{dA}{dt} = 9 \text{ cm}^2/\text{m}$$
$$\frac{da}{dt} = 3 \text{ cm/m}$$
$$\frac{db}{dt} = ?$$

when $A = 300$ cm^2 and $a = 20$ cm,

$$b = \frac{2(300 \text{ cm}^2)}{20 \text{ cm}}$$
$$= 30 \text{ cm}$$

$$A = \frac{1}{2}ab$$

Differentiating implicitly:

$$\frac{dA}{dt} = \frac{1}{2}a\frac{db}{dt} + \frac{1}{2}b\frac{da}{dt}$$

When $a = 20$ cm

$$9 = \frac{1}{2}(20 \text{ cm})\frac{db}{dt} + \frac{1}{2}(30 \text{ cm})(3 \text{ cm/m})$$

$$\frac{9-45}{10} = \frac{db}{dt}$$

$$\frac{db}{dt} = -3.6 \text{ cm/min}$$

The base is decreasing at a rate of 3.6 cm/min when the altitude is 20 cm and the area is 300 cm^2.

6. The angle is increasing at a rate of 0.176 rad/s.

$$\frac{da}{dt} = 3.5 \text{ cm/s}$$
$$\frac{dA}{dt} = ?$$

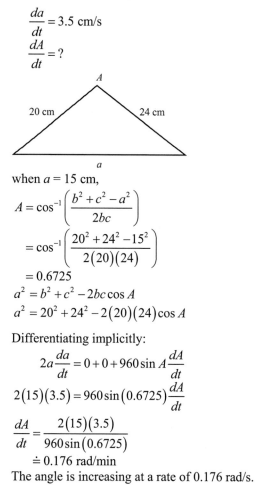

when $a = 15$ cm,

$$A = \cos^{-1}\left(\frac{b^2 + c^2 - a^2}{2bc}\right)$$

$$= \cos^{-1}\left(\frac{20^2 + 24^2 - 15^2}{2(20)(24)}\right)$$

$$= 0.6725$$

$$a^2 = b^2 + c^2 - 2bc\cos A$$

$$a^2 = 20^2 + 24^2 - 2(20)(24)\cos A$$

Differentiating implicitly:

$$2a\frac{da}{dt} = 0 + 0 + 960\sin A\frac{dA}{dt}$$

$$2(15)(3.5) = 960\sin(0.6725)\frac{dA}{dt}$$

$$\frac{dA}{dt} = \frac{2(15)(3.5)}{960\sin(0.6725)}$$

$$\doteq 0.176 \text{ rad/min}$$

The angle is increasing at a rate of 0.176 rad/s.

Topic Practice Questions 1

ANSWERS AND SOLUTIONS

1. **a)** $t \doteq 4.71$

$$t = \frac{-5 \pm \sqrt{(5)^2 - 4(-4.9)(85)}}{2(-4.9)}$$

$$t \doteq 4.71$$

b) Maximum speed: $\doteq 19.5$ m/s

$$v = \frac{dh}{dt} = -9.8t + 5$$

Since this problem involves a restricted domain of $0 \le t \le 4.71$, the endpoint values of the velocity-time function must be considered.

$$v(0) = -9.8(0) + 5 = 5 \text{ m/s}$$
$$v(4.71) = -9.8(4.71) + 5 = -41.16 \text{ m/s}$$

Since a linear function cannot have any points where its first derivative would be zero, these endpoint values are the maximum and minimum values of the velocity.

The maximum speed reached by the object is 41.16 m/s.

c) $= -19.5$ m/s

$$v(t) = -9.8t + 5$$
$$v(2.5) = -9.8(2.5 \text{ s}) + 5$$
$$= -19.5 \text{ m/s}$$

d) $v = -9.8t + 5$

$$a = \frac{dv}{dt} = -9.8$$

The acceleration is a constant value of -9.8 m/s^2.

2. $\dfrac{dr}{dt} = -\dfrac{3}{50\pi}$ m/s

$$V = \frac{4}{3}\pi r^3$$

Differentiation implicitly:

$$\frac{dV}{dt} = \frac{4}{3}\pi\left(3r^2\right)\left(\frac{dr}{dt}\right)$$

$$\frac{dr}{dt} = \frac{\left(\dfrac{dV}{dt}\right)}{4\pi r^2}$$

At the given values:

$$\frac{dr}{dt} = \frac{-6 \text{ m/s}^3}{4\pi(5 \text{ m})^2}$$

$$= -\frac{3}{50\pi} \text{ m/s}$$

3. **C:** circumference

$$\frac{dr}{dt} = 20 \text{ cm/s}$$
$$\frac{dC}{dt} = ?$$

$$C = 2\pi r$$
$$\frac{dC}{dt} = 2\pi \frac{dr}{dt}$$
$$\frac{dC}{dt}\bigg|_{A=10\ 000} = 2\pi(20 \text{ cm/s})$$
$$= 40\pi \text{ cm/s}$$

4.

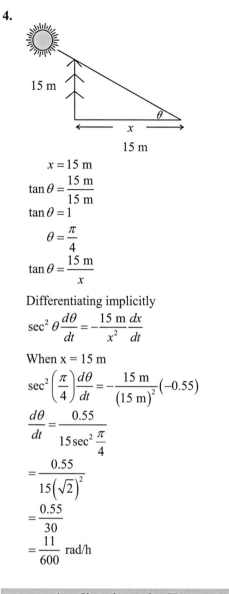

$x = 15$ m

$\tan \theta = \dfrac{15 \text{ m}}{15 \text{ m}}$

$\tan \theta = 1$

$\theta = \dfrac{\pi}{4}$

$\tan \theta = \dfrac{15 \text{ m}}{x}$

Differentiating implicitly

$\sec^2 \theta \dfrac{d\theta}{dt} = -\dfrac{15 \text{ m}}{x^2} \dfrac{dx}{dt}$

When x = 15 m

$\sec^2 \left(\dfrac{\pi}{4}\right) \dfrac{d\theta}{dt} = -\dfrac{15 \text{ m}}{\left(15 \text{ m}\right)^2}(-0.55)$

$\dfrac{d\theta}{dt} = \dfrac{0.55}{15 \sec^2 \dfrac{\pi}{4}}$

$= \dfrac{0.55}{15\left(\sqrt{2}\right)^2}$

$= \dfrac{0.55}{30}$

$= \dfrac{11}{600}$ rad/h

Applications in Economics

ANSWERS AND SOLUTIONS

1. a) $C'(x) = 4.2 + 0.02x$

b) $= \$24.20$

$C'(1\ 000) = 4.2 + 0.02(1\ 000)$
$= 4.2 + 20$
$= \$24.20$

c) 1 790 units need to be produced.

$40 = 4.2 + 0.02x$

$x = \dfrac{35.8}{0.02}$

$x = 1\ 790$

1 790 units need to be produced to give a marginal cost of $40.

2. a) $R(x) = 6x - 0.008x^2$

$R(x) = xp(x)$
$= x(6 - 0.008x)$
$R(x) = 6x - 0.008x^2$

b) $R'(x) = 6 - 0.016x$

c) $= \$-4.40$

$R'(650) = 6 - 0.016(650)$
$= \$-4.400$

3. a) $P(x) = R(x) - C(x)$

$P(x) = \left(6x - 0.008x^2\right)$
$\quad - \left(55 + 1.9x - 0.009x^2 + 0.000\ 08x^3\right)$
$P(x) = -0.000\ 08x^3 + 0.001x^2 + 4.1x - 55$

b) $P'(x) = -0.000\ 24x^2 + 0.002x + 4.1$

Set $P'(x) = 0$ and solve for x:

$0 = -0.000\ 24x^2 + 0.002x + 4.1$

$x = \dfrac{-(0.002) \pm \sqrt{(0.002)^2 - 4(-0.000\ 24)(4.1)}}{2(-0.000\ 24)}$

$\doteq 134.936$

Test values: $x = 130, 140$

$P'(130) = -0.000\ 24(130)^2 + 0.002(130) + 4.1$
$= +0.304$

$P'(140) = -0.000\ 24(140)^2 + 0.002(140) + 4.1$
$= -0.324$

Since the value of the derivative function changed from positive to negative, the profit function reached a maximum value. To maximize profit, 135 items should be produced.

Applications in Biological Sciences

ANSWERS AND SOLUTIONS

1. **a)** Decay function because $k = \dfrac{-\ln 3}{7}$, which is negative.

   b) Growth function because $k = \dfrac{1}{4}\ln 2$, which is positive.

2. **a)** $f'(t) = 35e^{\frac{-\ln 3}{40}t}\left(\dfrac{-\ln 3}{40}\right)$

   $f'(t) = \dfrac{-7\ln 3}{8}e^{\frac{-\ln 3}{40}t}$

   b) $f'(20) = \dfrac{-7\ln 3}{8}e^{\frac{-\ln 3}{40}(20)}$
   $\doteq 0.55$ grams/day

3. **a)** $f'(t) = \dfrac{1\,500\ln 3}{7}e^{\frac{\ln 3}{7}t}$

   $f'(5) = \dfrac{1\,500\ln 3}{7}e^{\frac{\ln 3}{7}(5)}$
   $\doteq 515.99$
   After 5 hours, the growth rate is 516 bacteria/hour.

b) $f'(t) = 2\,000$

$2\,000 = \dfrac{1\,500\ln 3}{7}e^{\frac{\ln 3}{7}t}$

$\dfrac{14\,000}{1\,500\ln 3} = e^{\frac{\ln 3}{7}t}$

$\dfrac{28}{3\ln 3} = e^{\frac{\ln 3}{7}t}$

$\ln\left(\dfrac{28}{3\ln 3}\right) = \ln\left(e^{\frac{\ln 3}{7}t}\right)$

$\ln\left(\dfrac{28}{3\ln 3}\right) = \dfrac{\ln 3}{7}t$

$t = \dfrac{\ln\left(\dfrac{28}{3\ln 3}\right)}{\dfrac{\ln 3}{7}}$

$\doteq 13.632$ h

4. **a)** $f(t) = Ae^{kt}$

   $25 = 100e^{k(30)}$

   $\dfrac{25}{100} = e^{k(30)}$

   $\ln\left(\dfrac{1}{4}\right) = 30k$

   $k = \dfrac{\ln\left(\dfrac{1}{4}\right)}{30}$

   $k = \dfrac{\ln\left(4^{-1}\right)}{30}$

   $k = \dfrac{-\ln(4)}{30}$

   The mass after t days is given by
   $f(t) = 100e^{\frac{-\ln 4}{30}t}$.

   b) $f'(t) = 100e^{\frac{-\ln 4}{30}t}\left(\dfrac{-\ln 4}{30}\right)$

   The decay rate after t days is given by
   $f'(t) = \dfrac{-10\ln 4}{3}e^{\frac{-\ln 4}{30}t}$.

c) $f'(t) = -3$

$$-3 = \frac{-10\ln 4}{3}e^{\frac{-\ln 4}{30}t}$$

$$\frac{9}{10\ln 4} = e^{\frac{-\ln 4}{30}t}$$

$$\ln\left(\frac{9}{10\ln 4}\right) = \frac{-\ln 4}{30}t$$

$$t = \frac{-30}{\ln 4}\ln\left(\frac{9}{10\ln 4}\right)$$

$$\doteq 9.35 \text{ days}$$

Newton's Method

ANSWERS AND SOLUTIONS

1. $\doteq 3.46$

$$f(x) = x^2 - 12$$
$$f'(x) = 2x$$

$$x_2 = x_1 - \frac{f(x_1)}{f'(x_1)}$$

$$= 2 - \frac{(2)^2 - 12}{2(2)}$$

$$= 2 + 2$$

$$x_2 = 4$$

$$x_3 = 4 - \frac{(4)^2 - 12}{2(4)}$$

$$= 4 - \frac{1}{2}$$

$$= 3.5$$

$$x_4 = 3.5 - \frac{(3.5)^2 - 12}{2(3.5)}$$

$$\doteq 3.46$$

2. $\doteq 2.68$

$$f(x) = x^3 - 5x - 5$$
$$f'(x) = 3x^2 - 5$$

$$x_2 = x_1 - \frac{f(x_1)}{f'(x_1)}$$

$$= 2 - \frac{(2)^3 - 5(2) - 5}{3(2)^2 - 5}$$

$$= 2 - \frac{8 - 10 - 5}{12 - 5}$$

$$= 2 - \frac{-7}{7}$$

$$x_2 = 3$$

$$x_3 = x_2 - \frac{f(x_2)}{f'(x_2)}$$

$$= 3 - \frac{(3)^3 - 5(3) - 5}{3(3)^2 - 5}$$

$$x_3 = 3 - \frac{27 - 15 - 5}{27 - 5}$$

$$= 3 - \frac{7}{22}$$

$$\doteq 2.68$$

3. $x_3 \doteq 3.1416$

$$f(x) = \sin x$$
$$f'(x) = \cos x$$

$$x_2 = x_1 - \frac{f(x_1)}{f'(x_1)}$$

$$x_2 = 3 - \frac{\sin(3)}{\cos(3)}$$

$$x_2 \doteq 3.1425$$

$$x_3 = x_2 - \frac{f(x_2)}{f'(x_2)}$$

$$x_3 = 3.1425 - \frac{\sin(3.1425)}{\cos(3.1425)}$$

$$x_3 \doteq 3.1416$$

4. $x_3 \doteq 2.196$

$$f(x) = x^2 - 2 - \frac{x+4}{x} = x^2 - 3 - \frac{4}{x}$$

$$f'(x) = 2x + \frac{4}{x^2}$$

$$x_2 = x_1 - \frac{f(x_1)}{f'(x_1)}$$

$$x_2 = 2 - \frac{(2)^2 - 3 - \frac{4}{2}}{2(2) + \frac{4}{(2)^2}}$$

$$x_2 = 2.2$$

$$x_3 = 2.2 - \frac{(2.2)^2 - 3 - \frac{4}{2.2}}{2(2.2) + \frac{4}{(2.2)^2}}$$

$$x_3 = 2.196$$

5. $x_3 = 1.0472$

$$f(x) = 4\sin^2 x - 3$$
$$f'(x) = 8\sin x \cos x$$
$$= 4\sin 2x$$

$$x_2 = 1 - \frac{4\sin^2(1) - 3}{4\sin(2(1))}$$

$$x_2 \doteq 1.0461$$

$$x_3 = 1.0461 - \frac{4\sin^2(1.0461) - 3}{4\sin(2(1.0461))}$$

$$x_3 \doteq 1.0472$$

ANSWERS AND SOLUTIONS

1. a) Maximum velocity $= -6$ m/s
Minimum velocity $= -14.52$ m/s
Maximum speed $= 14.52$ m/s

When $h = 0$:
$$0 = -4.9t^2 - 6t + 9$$
$$t = \frac{-(-6) \pm \sqrt{(-6)^2 - 4(-4.9)(9)}}{2(-4.9)}$$
$$t \doteq 0.87$$

$$V = \frac{dh}{dt} = -9.8t - 6$$

at $t \doteq 0.87$:
The restricted domain for this problem is $0 \le t \le 0.87$. The endpoints of the linear velocity-time function must be considered.
$$v(0) = -9.8(0) - 6$$
$$= -6 \text{ m/s}$$
$$v(0.87) = -9.8(0.87) - 6$$
$$= -14.52 \text{ m/s}$$

The maximum velocity is -6 m/s.
The minimum velocity is -14.52 m/s.
The maximum speed is 14.52 m/s.

b) $t = 0.41$ s
$$-10 = -9.8t - 6$$
$$t = 0.41 \text{ s}$$

2. a) $= -144\pi$ m^2/s
$$A = 4\pi r^2$$
$$\frac{dA}{dt} = 8\pi r \frac{dr}{dt}$$
$$\frac{dA}{dt}\Big|_{r=12} = 8\pi(12)(-1.5)$$
$$= -144\pi \text{ m}^2\text{/s}$$

b) $\dfrac{dr}{dt} = \dfrac{25}{18\pi}$ cm/s

$$A = 2\pi r^2 + 2\pi r (2r)$$
$$= 6\pi r^2$$
$$\dfrac{dA}{dt} = 12\pi r \dfrac{dr}{dt}$$
$$\dfrac{dr}{dt} = \dfrac{\dfrac{dA}{dt}}{12\pi r}$$
$$\dfrac{dr}{dt}\bigg|_{r=3} = \dfrac{50}{12\pi(3)}$$
$$\dfrac{dr}{dt}\bigg|_{r=3} = \dfrac{25}{18\pi} \text{ cm/s}$$

3. a) $\dfrac{dh}{dt}\bigg|_{h=4} = -\dfrac{49}{72\pi}$ m/s

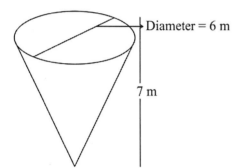

Diameter = 6 m

7 m

$r = 3$ m

$\dfrac{h}{r} = \dfrac{7 \text{ m}}{3 \text{ m}}$

$\therefore r = \dfrac{3}{7}h$

$V = \dfrac{1}{3}\pi r^2 h$

$= \dfrac{1}{3}\pi \left(\dfrac{3}{7}h\right)^2 h$

$= \dfrac{3}{49}\pi h^3$

$\dfrac{dV}{dt} = -2$

$\dfrac{dh}{dt} = ?$

$r = \dfrac{3}{7}h$

$\dfrac{dV}{dt} = \dfrac{9}{49}\pi h^2 \dfrac{dh}{dt}$

$\dfrac{dh}{dt} = \dfrac{49\dfrac{dV}{dt}}{9\pi h^2}$

$\dfrac{dh}{dt}\bigg|_{h=4} = \dfrac{49(-2)}{9\pi(4)^2}$

$\dfrac{dh}{dt}\bigg|_{h=4} = -\dfrac{49}{72\pi}$ m/s

b) when $r = 1$ m, $h = \dfrac{7}{3}$

$\dfrac{dh}{dt} = \dfrac{49\dfrac{dV}{dt}}{9\pi h^2}$

$\dfrac{dh}{dt}\bigg|_{h=\frac{7}{3}} = \dfrac{49(-2)}{9\pi\left(\dfrac{7}{3}\right)^2}$

$\dfrac{dh}{dt}\bigg|_{h=\frac{7}{3}} = \dfrac{\cancel{4}9(-2)}{\cancel{9}\pi\left(\dfrac{\cancel{4}9}{\cancel{9}}\right)}$

$\dfrac{dh}{dt}\bigg|_{h=\frac{7}{3}} = -\dfrac{2}{\pi}$ m/s

4. Let x be the horizontal distance between them.
Let y be the vertical distance between them.
Let z be the shortest distance between them.

a)

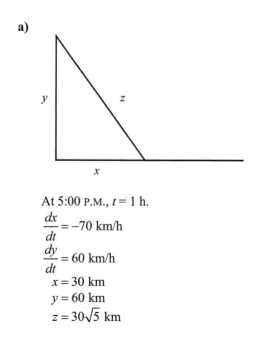

At 5:00 P.M., $t = 1$ h.

$\dfrac{dx}{dt} = -70$ km/h

$\dfrac{dy}{dt} = 60$ km/h

$x = 30$ km

$y = 60$ km

$z = 30\sqrt{5}$ km

$$z^2 = x^2 + y^2$$
$$2z\frac{dz}{dt} = 2x\frac{dx}{dt} + 2y\frac{dy}{dt}$$
$$\frac{dz}{dt} = \frac{x\frac{dx}{dt} + y\frac{dy}{dt}}{z}$$
$$\frac{dz}{dt}\Big|_{t=1} = \frac{30(-70) + (60)(60)}{30\sqrt{5}}$$
$$= \frac{1\,500}{30\sqrt{5}} \text{ km/h}$$
$$= \frac{50}{\sqrt{5}} \text{ km/h}$$
$$= \frac{50}{\sqrt{5}} \times \frac{\sqrt{5}}{\sqrt{5}} \text{ km/h}$$
$$= \frac{50\sqrt{5}}{5} \text{ km/h}$$
$$= 10\sqrt{5} \text{ km/h}$$

b) At 6:30 P.M., $t = 2.5$ h.

After $2\frac{1}{2}$ hrs, we are 75 m west.

$$\frac{dx}{dt} = 70 \text{ km/h}$$
$$\frac{dy}{dt} = 60 \text{ km/h}$$
$$x = 75 \text{ km}$$
$$y = 150 \text{ km}$$
$$z = 75\sqrt{5}$$
$$\frac{dz}{dt}\Big|_{t=2.5} = \frac{75(70) + 150(60)}{75\sqrt{5}}$$
$$\frac{dz}{dt}\Big|_{t=2.5} = \frac{14\,250}{75\sqrt{5}}$$
$$\frac{dz}{dt}\Big|_{t=2.5} = \frac{190}{\sqrt{5}} \text{ km/h}$$
$$\frac{dz}{dt}\Big|_{t=2.5} = \frac{190}{\sqrt{5}} \times \frac{\sqrt{5}}{\sqrt{5}} \text{ km/h}$$
$$\frac{dz}{dt}\Big|_{t=2.5} = \frac{190\sqrt{5}}{5} \text{ km/h}$$
$$\frac{dz}{dt}\Big|_{t=2.5} = 38\sqrt{5} \text{ km/h}$$

5. a) = \$5.60/item

$$C'(x) = 3 + 0.026x$$
$$C'(100) = 3 + (0.026)(100)$$
$$= \$5.60$$

b) $R'(800) = \$34$/item

$$R(x) = xp(x)$$
$$= x(2 + 0.02x)$$
$$= 2x + 0.02x^2$$
$$R'(x) = 2 + 0.04x$$
$$R'(800) = 34$$

c) $x = 71$

$$C'(x) = R'(x)$$
$$3 + 0.026x = 2 + 0.04x$$
$$1 = 0.014x$$
$$x = 71.4$$

Approximately 71 items should be produced for maximum profit to be reached.

6. a) $f(t) = 325\ln(3)e^{\frac{\ln 3}{2}t}$

$$f(t) = Ae^{kt}$$
$$1\,950 = 650e^{k(2)}$$
$$\frac{1\,950}{650} = e^{2k}$$
$$3 = e^{2k}$$
$$\ln 3 = 2k$$
$$k = \frac{\ln 3}{2}$$

The function is $f(t) = 650e^{\frac{\ln 3}{2}t}$

b) $f'(10) \doteq 86\,762.9$ bacteria/h

$$f'(t) = 650e^{\frac{\ln 3}{2}t}\left(\frac{\ln 3}{2}\right)$$
$$= 325\ln(3)e^{\frac{\ln 3}{2}t}$$
$$f'(10) = 325\ln(3)e^{\frac{\ln 3}{2}(10)}$$
$$\doteq 86\,762.9$$

7. a) $= \dfrac{179}{385}$

$\doteq 0.465$

$f(x) = x^3 + 2x - 1$

$f'(x) = 3x^2 + 2$

$x_1 = 1$

$x_2 = 1 - \dfrac{x^3 + 2x - 1}{3x^2 + 2}$

$\quad = 1 - \dfrac{(1)^3 + 2(1) - 1}{3(1)^2 + 2}$

$\quad = \dfrac{3}{5}$

$x_3 = \dfrac{3}{5} - \dfrac{\left(\dfrac{3}{5}\right)^3 + 2\left(\dfrac{3}{5}\right) - 1}{3\left(\dfrac{3}{5}\right)^2 + 2}$

$\quad = \dfrac{179}{385}$

$\quad \doteq 0.465$

b) $= \dfrac{27}{5}$

$f(x) = x^2 - 4x - 5$

$f'(x) = 2x - 4$

$x_1 = 3$

$x_2 = 3 - \dfrac{x^2 - 4x - 5}{2x - 4}$

$\quad = 3 - \dfrac{(3)^2 - 4(3) - 5}{2(3) - 4}$

$\quad = 7$

$x_3 = 7 - \dfrac{(7)^2 - 4(7) - 5}{2(7) - 4}$

$\quad = \dfrac{27}{5}$

ANTIDERIVATIVES AND AREA

The Antiderivative

ANSWERS AND SOLUTIONS

1. a) $y = -x^3 - x^2 + x + C$

$\dfrac{dy}{dx} = -3x^2 - 2x + 1$

$dy = \left(-3x^2 - 2x + 1\right)dx$

$\int 1\,dy = \int \left(-3x^2 - 2x + 1\right)dx$

$y + C_1 = -3\left[\dfrac{x^{2+1}}{(2+)}\right] - 2\left[\dfrac{x^{1+1}}{(1+1)}\right] + 1x + C_2$

$y = -x^3 - x^2 + x + C$

b) $p = 3\ln|z| + \dfrac{3}{z} - \dfrac{1}{z^2} + C$

$\dfrac{dp}{dz} = \dfrac{3}{z} - \dfrac{3}{z^2} + \dfrac{2}{z^3}$

$dp = \left(\dfrac{3}{z} - \dfrac{3}{z^2} + \dfrac{2}{z^3}\right)dz$

$\int 1\,dp = \int \left(\dfrac{3}{z} - \dfrac{3}{z^2} + \dfrac{2}{z^3}\right)dz$

$\int 1\,dp = 3\int \left(\dfrac{1}{z}\right)dz - 3\int \left(z^{-2}\right)dz + 2\int \left(z^{-3}\right)dz$

$p + C_1 = 3\ln|z| - 3\left[\dfrac{z^{-2+1}}{(-2+1)}\right] + 2\left[\dfrac{z^{-3+1}}{(-3+1)}\right] + C_2$

$p = 3\ln|z| + 3z^{-1} - z^{-2} + C$

$p = 3\ln|z| + \dfrac{3}{z} - \dfrac{1}{z^2} + C$

c) $y = \tan x + C$

$\dfrac{dy}{dx} = \sec^2 x$

$dy = \left(\sec^2 x\right)dx$

$\int 1\,dy = \int \left(\sec^2 x\right)dx$

$y + C_1 = \tan x + C_2$

$y = \tan x + C$

d) $u = \dfrac{1}{2}y^2 - \sin y$

$$\dfrac{du}{dy} = y - \cos y$$

$$du = (y - \cos y)\,dy$$

$$\int 1\,du = \int (y - \cos y)\,dy$$

$$u + C_1 = \dfrac{1}{2}y^2 - \sin y + C_2$$

$$u = \dfrac{1}{2}y^2 - \sin y + C$$

2. a) $\displaystyle\int (x^5)\,dx = \dfrac{1}{6}x^6 + C$

b) $\displaystyle\int (5^x)(\ln 5)\,dx = 5^x + C$

c) $\displaystyle\int (\sin^2 x + \cos^2 x)\,dx = x + C$

Since $\sin^2 x + \cos^2 x = 1$,

$$\int (\sin^2 x + \cos^2 x)\,dx$$
$$= \int (1)\,dx$$
$$= x + C$$

d) $\displaystyle\int (27e^x)\,dx = 27e^x + C$

3. a) $\displaystyle\int (5x - 3)^{12}\,dx = \dfrac{1}{65}(5x - 3)^{13} + C$

Let $u = 5x - 3$

$$\dfrac{du}{dx} = 5 \text{ or } dx = \dfrac{du}{5}$$

$$\int (5x - 3)^{12}\,dx$$
$$= \int (u)^{12}\left(\dfrac{du}{5}\right)$$
$$= \dfrac{1}{5}\int (u)^{12}\,du$$
$$= \dfrac{1}{5}\left[\dfrac{u^{12+1}}{(12+1)} + C_1\right]$$
$$= \dfrac{1}{65}(u)^{13} + C$$
$$= \dfrac{1}{65}(5x - 3)^{13} + C$$

b) $\displaystyle\int \left(\sqrt{4x^2 - 10x}\right)(4x - 5)\,dx$

$$= \dfrac{1}{3}(4x^2 - 10x)^{\frac{3}{2}} + C$$

Let $u = 4x^2 - 10x$

$$\dfrac{du}{dx} = 8x - 10 \text{ or } du = (8x - 10)\,dx \text{ or}$$

$$dx = \dfrac{du}{(8x - 10)}$$

$$\int \left(\sqrt{4x^2 - 10x}\right)(4x - 5)\,dx$$

$$= \int (u)^{\frac{1}{2}}(4x - 5)\left(\dfrac{du}{8x - 10}\right)$$

$$= \int (u)^{\frac{1}{2}}(4x - 5)\left(\dfrac{du}{2(4x - 5)}\right)$$

$$= \dfrac{1}{2}\int (u)^{\frac{1}{2}}\,du$$

$$= \dfrac{1}{2}\left[\dfrac{u^{\frac{1}{2}+1}}{\left(\dfrac{1}{2}+1\right)} + C_1\right]$$

$$= \dfrac{1}{2}\left[\dfrac{u^{\frac{3}{2}}}{\left(\dfrac{3}{2}\right)} + C_1\right]$$

$$= \dfrac{1}{2}\left[\dfrac{2}{3}u^{\frac{3}{2}} + C_1\right]$$

$$= \dfrac{1}{3}(4x^2 - 10x)^{\frac{3}{2}} + C$$

c) $\int \left[\cos^4\left(8x\right)\right]\left[\sin\left(8x\right)\right]dx =$

$-\dfrac{1}{40}\cos^5\left(8x\right)+C$

Let $u = \cos\left(8x\right)$

$\dfrac{du}{dx} = -8\sin\left(8x\right)$

$dx = \dfrac{du}{-8\sin\left(8x\right)}$

$\int \left[\cos^4\left(8x\right)\right]\left[\sin\left(8x\right)\right]dx$

$\int \left(u\right)^4 \left(\sin\left(8x\right)\right)\dfrac{du}{-8\sin\left(8x\right)}$

$= -\dfrac{1}{8}\int\left(u\right)^4 du$

$= -\dfrac{1}{8}\left[\dfrac{u^{4+1}}{\left(4+1\right)}+C_1\right]$

$= -\dfrac{1}{40}\cos^5\left(8x\right)+C$

d) $\int\left(e^{\ln(4x)}\right)\left(\dfrac{1}{x}\right)dx = e^{\ln(4x)}+C$

Let $u = \ln(4x)$

$\dfrac{du}{dx} = \left(\dfrac{1}{4x}\right)(4) = \dfrac{1}{x}$

$dx = \dfrac{du}{\dfrac{1}{x}}$

$\int\left(e^{\ln(4x)}\right)\left(\dfrac{1}{x}\right)dx$

$= \int\left(e^u\right)\left(\dfrac{1}{x}\right)\left(\dfrac{du}{\dfrac{1}{x}}\right)$

$= \int\left(e^u\right)du$

$= e^{\ln(4x)}+C$

Differential Equations with Initial Conditions

ANSWERS AND SOLUTIONS

1. a) $a(t) = t+1$

$\dfrac{dv}{dt} = t+1$

$v = \dfrac{t^2}{2}+t+C$ $\qquad v(0) = 0$

$v = \dfrac{t^2}{2}+t$

$0 = \dfrac{0^2}{2}+0+C$

Therefore, $C = 0$.

$\dfrac{ds}{dt} = v$

$\dfrac{ds}{dt} = \dfrac{t^2}{2}+t$

$s = \dfrac{t^3}{6}+\dfrac{t^2}{2}+C$ $\qquad s(0) = 0$

$s = \dfrac{t^3}{6}+\dfrac{t^2}{2}$

$0 = \dfrac{0^3}{6}+\dfrac{0^2}{2}+C$

Therefore, $C = 0$.

To be complete, $s(t) = \dfrac{t^3}{6}+\dfrac{t^2}{2}$ for all $t \geq 0$.

Note that we use the $s(t)$ (displacement as a function of time) notation instead of our usual s notation because the question gives acceleration as a function of time.

b) $a = 3\sin t$

$v = \int (3\sin t)\,dt$

$v = -3\cos t + C_1$

Assigning inital velocity information gives the velocity function.

$1 = -3\cos(0) + C_1$

$1 = -3(1) + C_1$

$C_1 = 4$

$v = 4 - 3\cos t$

$s = \int (4 - 3\cos t)\,dt$

$s = 4t - 3\sin t + C_2$

Use initial conditions for displacement:

$1 = 4(0) - 3\sin(0) + C_2$

$C_2 = 1$

$s = 1 + 4t - 3\sin t$

c) $\dfrac{d^2 y}{dx^2} = x - 1$

$\dfrac{dy}{dx} = \int (x-1)\,dx$

$\dfrac{dy}{dx} = \dfrac{1}{2}x^2 - x + C_1$

Using (0, 1)

$1 = \dfrac{1}{2}(0) - (0) + C_1$

$C_1 = 1$

$\dfrac{dy}{dx} = \dfrac{1}{2}x^2 - x + 1$

$y = \int \left(\dfrac{1}{2}x^2 - x + 1 \right) dx$

$y = \dfrac{1}{6}x^3 - \dfrac{1}{2}x^2 + x + C_2$

Using (1, 2)

$2 = \dfrac{1}{6} - \dfrac{1}{2} + 1 + C_2$

$C_2 = \dfrac{4}{3}$

$y = \dfrac{x^3}{6} - \dfrac{x^2}{2} + x + \dfrac{4}{3}$

d) $v = 2t - 1$

$s = \int (2t - 1)\,dt$

$s = t^2 - t + C$

It is important to note that this result relates displacement and time.

At $t = 3$, we find that $s(3) = 6 + C$, and at $t = 5$, we find that $s(5) = 20 + C$.

Since the object did not change direction in the time interval (3, 5), the distance traveled in that interval is $s(5) - s(3) = 14$ m.

e) $y = A\sin 4x + B\cos 4x$

$1 = A\sin 2\pi + B\cos 2\pi$

$B = 1$

$y' = 4A\cos 4x - 4(1)\sin 4x$

$1 = 4A\cos 2\pi - 4\sin 2\pi$

$A = \dfrac{1}{4}$

$y = \dfrac{1}{4}\sin 4x + 1\cos 4x$

f) First, we find k from Hooke's Law $(F = ks)$. The spring is stretched from 0.1 m to 0.2 m by applying 10 N. So, $10 = k(0.1)$ or $k = 100$.

Set up the equation for the second differential:

$s'' + \dfrac{k}{m}s = 0$

Since we know mass is 0.5 kg,

$s'' + 200s = 0$

$s = A\sin\left(\sqrt{200}t\right) + B\cos\left(\sqrt{200}t\right)$

$(0.3 - 0.1) = A\sin(0) + B\cos(0)$

$B = 0.2$

$s' = \sqrt{200}A\cos\left(\sqrt{200}t\right) - \sqrt{200}B\sin\left(\sqrt{200}t\right)$

From this equation, we note that at time zero, the displaced spring is held at rest. So, this derivative equals zero (at time zero). This gives:

$0 = \sqrt{200}A\cos(0)$

$A = 0$

$s = 0.2\cos\left(\sqrt{200}t\right)$

(from the original equation)

g) Let $y =$ the number of rabbits present at any time, t, in years.

For continuous exponential growth:

$y = Ae^{kt}$

Using $(0, 100)$:

$y = 100e^{kt}$

Using $(2, 900)$

$900 = 100e^{2k}$

$9 = e^{2k}$

$\ln 9 = \ln e^{2k}$

$\ln 9 = 2k$

$k = \dfrac{\ln 9}{2} = 1.099$

$y = 100e^{\left(\frac{\ln 9}{2}\right)t}$

At $t = 3$:

$y(3) = 100e^{\left(\frac{\ln 9}{2}\right)(3)}$

$y(3) = 2\,700$

Topic Practice Questions 1

ANSWERS AND SOLUTIONS

1. $\displaystyle \int \left(2x^2 - 3\right) dx = \frac{2x^3}{3} - 3x + C$

2. $\displaystyle \int \left(2e^{2x} - \sin x\right) dx = e^{2x} + \cos x + C$

$\displaystyle \int \left(2e^{2x} - \sin x\right) dx = 2\int \left(e^{2x}\right) dx - \int (\sin x) dx$

Let $u = 2x$

$\dfrac{du}{dx} = 2$

$dx = \dfrac{du}{2}$

$2\int \left(e^{2x}\right) dx - \int (\sin x) dx$

$= \left[2\int \left(e^u\right)\left(\dfrac{du}{2}\right)\right] - \left[-\cos(x) + C_2\right]$

$= \int \left(e^u\right) du - \left[-\cos(x) + C_2\right]$

$= \left[e^{2x} + C_1\right] - \left[-\cos(x) + C_2\right]$

$= e^{2x} + \cos x + C$

3. $f(x) = 3x - 3\ln|x| + C$, where $x \neq 0$

4. $s = \dfrac{t^3}{3} - t + 1$

$s = \int \left(t^2 - 1\right) dt$

$s = \dfrac{t^3}{3} - t + C$

Using $(0, 1)$

$1 = (0) - (0) + C$

$C = 1$

$s = \dfrac{t^3}{3} - t + 1$

5. $F(x) = \dfrac{x^2}{2} - 1$

$F(x) = \int (x) dx$

$F(x) = \dfrac{x^2}{2} + C$

Given that point $\left(1, \dfrac{-1}{2}\right)$ lies on $F(x)$:

$\dfrac{-1}{2} = \dfrac{1^2}{2} + C$

$C = -1$

$F(x) = \dfrac{x^2}{2} - 1$

6. $y = \dfrac{1}{5}\sin 10x$

$y'' + 100y = 0$

$y = A\sin 10x + B\cos 10x$

$0 = A\sin 0 + B\cos 0$

$B = 0$

$y = A\sin 10x$

$y' = 10A\cos 10x$

$2 = 10A\cos 0$

$A = \dfrac{1}{5}$

$y = \dfrac{1}{5}\sin 10x$

7. $\int\left(\cos^3 x\right)dx = \sin x - \dfrac{1}{3}\sin^3 x + C$

$\int\left(\cos^3 x\right)dx$

$= \int\left(\cos^2 x\right)\left(\cos x\right)dx$

$= \int\left(1 - \sin^2 x\right)\left(\cos x\right)dx$

$= \int\left(\cos x - \cos x \sin^2 x\right)dx$

$= \int\left(\cos x\right)dx - \int\left[\sin x\right]^2\left(\cos x\right)dx$

Let $u = \sin x. \dfrac{du}{dx} = \cos x$ or $dx = \dfrac{du}{\cos x}$

$\int\left(\cos x\right)dx - \int\left[\sin x\right]^2\left(\cos x\right)dx$

$= \int\left(\cos x\right)dx - \int\left[u\right]^2\left(\cos x\right)\left(\dfrac{du}{\cos x}\right)$

$= \int\left(\cos x\right)dx - \int\left(u^2\right)du$

$= \left[\sin x + C_1\right] - \left[\dfrac{1}{3}u^3 + C_2\right]$

$= \sin x - \dfrac{1}{3}\sin^3 x + C$

Signed Area

ANSWERS AND SOLUTIONS

1. a) Signed area $\doteq 1.1$

$f(x) = \dfrac{1}{x}$

The general antiderivative function is

$A(x) = \ln|x| + C$

The signed area in the interval [1, 3] is:

$A(3) - A(1)$

$= \left[\ln 3 + C\right] - \left[\ln 1 + C\right]$

$= \ln 3 - \ln 1$

$\doteq 1.1$

b) Signed area $= 2$

$f(x) = \sin x$

The general antiderivative function is:

$A(x) = -\cos x + C$

The signed area in the interval $\left[0, \pi\right]$ is:

$A(\pi) - A(0)$

$= \left[-\cos \pi + C\right] - \left[-\cos 0 + C\right]$

$= \left[1\right] - \left[-1\right]$

$= 2$

c) Signed area $= \dfrac{32}{3}$

$f(x) = 2x^2 - 2$

The general antiderivative function is:

$A(x) = \dfrac{2}{3}x^3 - 2x + C$

The signed area in the interval [2, 3] is:

$A(3) - A(2)$

$= \left[\dfrac{2}{3}(3)^3 - 2(3) + C\right] - \left[\dfrac{2}{3}(2)^3 - 2(2) + C\right]$

$= \left[12\right] - \left[\dfrac{4}{3}\right]$

$= \dfrac{32}{3}$

d) Signed area $= \dfrac{28}{9}$

$f(x) = \dfrac{2}{3}x^{\frac{1}{2}}$

The general antiderivative function is:

$A(x) = \dfrac{2}{3}\left(\dfrac{x^{\frac{1}{2}+1}}{\left(\dfrac{1}{2}+1\right)}\right) = \dfrac{2}{3}\left(\dfrac{2}{3}x^{\frac{3}{2}}\right) = \dfrac{4}{9}x^{\frac{3}{2}}$

The signed area in the interval [1, 4] is:

$A(4) - A(1)$

$= \left[\dfrac{4}{9}(4)^{\frac{3}{2}} + C\right] - \left[\dfrac{4}{9}(1)^{\frac{3}{2}} + C\right]$

$= \left[\dfrac{32}{9}\right] - \left[\dfrac{4}{9}\right]$

$= \dfrac{28}{9}$

e) Signed area $= -9$

$f(x) = x^2 - 4x$

The general antiderivative function is:

$A(x) = \dfrac{1}{3}x^3 - 2x^2 + C$

The signed area in the interval [0, 3] is:

$A(3) - A(0)$

$= \left[\dfrac{1}{3}(3)^3 - 2(3)^2 + C\right] - \left[\dfrac{1}{3}(0)^3 - 2(0)^2 + C\right]$

$= \left[-9\right] - \left[0\right]$

$= -9$

f) Signed area = e − 1

$$f(x) = e^x$$

The general antiderivative function is:

$$A(x) = e^x + C$$

The signed area in the interval [0, 1] is:

$$A(1) - A(0)$$
$$= \left[e^1 + C \right] - \left[e^0 + C \right]$$
$$= e - 1$$

The Definite Integral

ANSWERS AND SOLUTIONS

1. Approximate signed area = 2

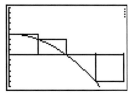

Each rectangle has its left edge contacting the function $f(x) = 4 - x^2$

The width of each rectangle is $\dfrac{4-0}{4} = 1$

The height of the first rectangle is $f(0) = 4$

The height of the second rectangle is $f(1) = 3$.

The height of the third rectangle is $f(2) = 0$.

The height of the fourth rectangle is $f(3) = -5$.

The total signed area of the 4 rectangles is:

$$(1)(4) + (1)(3) + (1)(0) + (1)(-5) = 2$$

2. a) $\displaystyle \int_{-4}^{3} \left(4 - x^2 \right) dx = -\frac{7}{3}$

$$\int_{-4}^{3} \left(4 - x^2 \right) dx = \left(4x - \frac{1}{3}x^3 + C \right)\Big|_{-4}^{3}$$
$$= \left[4(3) - \frac{1}{3}(3)^3 + C \right] - \left[4(-4) - \frac{1}{3}(-4)^3 + C \right]$$
$$= [3] - \left[\frac{16}{3} \right]$$
$$= -\frac{7}{3}$$

Using a graphing calculator:

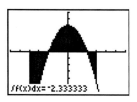

b) $\displaystyle \int_{\frac{\pi}{2}}^{\frac{5\pi}{3}} \left(\sin t + \cos t \right) dt = \frac{-3 - \sqrt{3}}{2}$

$$\int_{\frac{\pi}{2}}^{\frac{5\pi}{3}} \left(\sin t + \cos t \right) dt = \left(-\cos t + \sin t + C \right)\Big|_{\frac{\pi}{2}}^{\frac{5\pi}{3}}$$

$$= \left[-\cos\left(\frac{5\pi}{3} \right) + \sin\left(\frac{5\pi}{3} \right) + C \right]$$
$$- \left[-\cos\left(\frac{\pi}{2} \right) + \sin\left(\frac{\pi}{2} \right) + C \right]$$
$$= \left[-\frac{1}{2} - \frac{\sqrt{3}}{2} \right] - [-0 + 1]$$
$$= -\frac{1}{2} - \frac{\sqrt{3}}{2} - \frac{2}{2}$$
$$= \frac{-3 - \sqrt{3}}{2}$$

Using a graphing calculator:

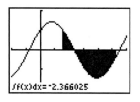

c) $\displaystyle \int_{2}^{3} \left(\frac{1}{x} \right) dx = \ln 3 - \ln 2$

$$\int_{2}^{3} \left(\frac{1}{x} \right) dx = \left(\ln|x| + C \right)\Big|_{2}^{3}$$
$$= \left[\ln|3| \right] - \left[\ln|2| \right]$$
$$= \ln 3 - \ln 2$$

Using a graphing calculator:

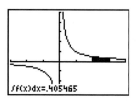

d) $\int_{-1}^{3}\left(e^{2p}\right)dp=\frac{1}{2}\left[e^{6}-e^{-2}\right]$

$\int_{-1}^{3}\left(e^{2p}\right)dp=\left(\frac{1}{2}e^{2p}+C\right)\Big|_{-1}^{3}$

$=\left[\frac{1}{2}e^{2(3)}+C\right]-\left[\frac{1}{2}e^{2(-1)}+C\right]$

$=\frac{1}{2}\left(e^{6}-e^{-2}\right)$

Using a graphing calculator:

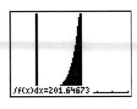

3. a) $p(x)=\frac{1}{2}x^2+x$

$p(x)=\int_{-2}^{x}(t+1)dt=\left(\frac{1}{2}t^2+t+C\right)\Big|_{-2}^{x}$

$p(x)=\left[\frac{1}{2}x^2+x+C\right]-\left[\frac{1}{2}(-2)^2+(-2)+C\right]$

$p(x)=\frac{1}{2}x^2+x$

b) $p(-2)=\frac{1}{2}(-2)^2+(-2)=0$

$p(3)=\frac{1}{2}(3)^2+(3)=\frac{15}{2}$

$p(-3)=\frac{1}{2}(-3)^2+(-3)=\frac{3}{2}$

4. Area $=\dfrac{1+\sqrt{3}}{2}$

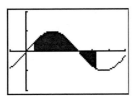

The function $f(x)=\sin x$ has a zero of $\dfrac{\pi}{2}$.

The total area is:

$\left|\int_{\frac{\pi}{6}}^{\frac{\pi}{2}}(\sin x)dx\right|+\left|\int_{\frac{\pi}{2}}^{\frac{4\pi}{3}}(\sin x)dx\right|$

$=\left|(-\cos x+C)\Big|_{\frac{\pi}{6}}^{\frac{\pi}{2}}\right|+\left|(-\cos x+C)\Big|_{\frac{\pi}{2}}^{\frac{4\pi}{3}}\right|$

$=\left|\left[-\cos\left(\frac{\pi}{2}\right)\right]-\left[-\cos\left(\frac{\pi}{6}\right)\right]\right|$

$+\left|\left[-\cos\left(\frac{4\pi}{3}\right)\right]-\left[-\cos\left(\frac{\pi}{2}\right)\right]\right|$

$=\left|[-(0)]-\left[-\frac{\sqrt{3}}{2}\right]\right|+\left|\left[-\left(-\frac{1}{2}\right)\right]-[-(0)]\right|$

$=\frac{\sqrt{3}}{2}+\frac{1}{2}$

$=\frac{1+\sqrt{3}}{2}$

5. $x=5$ or -2

$\int_{2}^{x}(2t-3)dt=12$

$(t^2-3t+C)\Big|_{2}^{x}=12$

$\left[x^2-3x+C\right]-\left[2^2-3(2)+C\right]=12$

$x^2-3x+2=12$

$x^2-3x-10=0$

$(x-5)(x+2)=0$

6. -7

Using the property

$\int_{a}^{c}\left[f(x)\right]dx=\int_{a}^{b}\left[f(x)\right]dx+\int_{b}^{c}\left[f(x)\right]dx$

Substitute: $a=2$, $b=4$, $c=5$

$\int_{2}^{5}\left[f(x)\right]dx=\int_{2}^{4}\left[f(x)\right]dx+\int_{4}^{5}\left[f(x)\right]dx$

$\int_{2}^{5}\left[f(x)\right]dx=10+(-17)$

$\int_{2}^{5}\left[f(x)\right]dx=-7$

7. 7

Using the property
$$\int_a^b \left[f(x)\right]dx = -\int_b^a \left[f(x)\right]dx$$
$$\int_2^4 \left[f(x)\right]dx = -\int_4^2 \left[f(x)\right]dx = -10$$
and
$$\int_4^5 \left[f(x)\right]dx = -\int_5^4 \left[f(x)\right]dx = -(-17) = 17$$

Substitute: $a = 2$, $b = 4$, $c = 5$
$$\int_2^5 \left[f(x)\right]dx = \int_2^4 \left[f(x)\right]dx + \int_2^5 \left[f(x)\right]dx$$
$$\int_2^5 \left[f(x)\right]dx = (-10) + (17)$$
$$\int_2^5 \left[f(x)\right]dx = 7$$

8. Determine the average value of the function $f(x) = 4 - x^2$ in the interval [0, 3]. The function has a value of 1 at the point $\left(\sqrt{3}, 1\right)$.

Using: Average value $= \dfrac{\int_a^b f(x)\,dx}{b-a}$

$$\dfrac{\int_0^3 \left(4 - x^2\right) dx}{3 - 0}$$
$$= \dfrac{\left(4x - \frac{1}{3}x^3 + C\right)\Big|_0^3}{3}$$
$$= \dfrac{\left(4(3) - \frac{1}{3}(3)^3\right) - (0)}{3}$$
$$= \dfrac{12 - 9}{3}$$
$$= 1$$

The average value of the function $f(x) = 4 - x^2$ in the interval [0, 3] is 1.

To determine where this function assumes its average value, solve the equation.
$$4 - x^2 = 1$$
$$-x^2 = -3$$
$$x^2 = 3$$
$$x = \pm\sqrt{3}$$

Only $\sqrt{3}$ needs to be considered because $-\sqrt{3}$ is not in the interval [0, 3].
$$f\left(\sqrt{3}\right) = 4 - \left(\sqrt{3}\right)^2$$
$$f\left(\sqrt{3}\right) = 1$$

The function has a value of 1 at the point $\left(\sqrt{3}, 1\right)$.

ANSWERS AND SOLUTIONS

1. a) Area $= \dfrac{2}{3}$

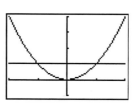

Area =
$$\int_0^1 \left(1 - x^2\right) dx = \left(x - \frac{1}{3}x^3 + C\right)\Big|_0^1$$
$$= \left[1 - \frac{1}{3}\right] - [0] = \frac{2}{3}$$

b) Area $= \dfrac{4}{3}$

$$\int_{-1}^1 \left(1 - x^2\right) dx = \left(x - \frac{1}{3}x^3 + C\right)\Big|_{-1}^1$$
$$= \left[1 - \frac{1}{3}\right] - \left[-1 + \frac{1}{3}\right] = \frac{4}{3}$$

c) Area $= 2.79$

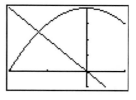

We need to find the intersection points for $y = -x^2 + 4$ and $y = -2x$. Solving $-x^2 + 4 = -2x$ using the quadratic formula yields the roots $1 \pm \sqrt{5}$.

Enclosed area $= \int_{1-\sqrt{5}}^0 \left(-x^2 + 4 + 2x\right) dx$
$$= \left(-\frac{1}{3}x^3 + 4x + x^2 + C\right)\Big|_{1-\sqrt{5}}^0$$
$$= [0] - \left[-\frac{1}{3}\left(1 - \sqrt{5}\right)^3 + 4\left(1 - \sqrt{5}\right) + \left(1 - \sqrt{5}\right)^2\right]$$
$$\doteq 2.787$$

d) Area $= \dfrac{32}{3}$

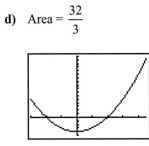

The quadratic function $y = x^2 - 4$ will intersect the x-axis at ± 2. This function will also intersect the line $x = 4$ at the point $(4, 12)$.

Enclosed area $= \displaystyle\int_2^4 (x^2 - 4)\, dx$

$$= \left[\frac{1}{3}x^3 - 4x + C \right]\Big|_2^4$$

$$= \left[\frac{1}{3}(4)^3 - 4(4) \right] - \left[\frac{1}{3}(2)^3 - 4(2) \right]$$

$$= \left[\frac{16}{3} \right] - \left[-\frac{16}{3} \right]$$

$$= \frac{32}{3}$$

e) Area $= \sqrt{2} - 1$

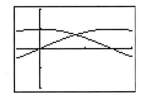

The functions intersect when $\sin x = \cos x$.

The root we use is $\dfrac{\pi}{4}$.

Enclosed area $= \displaystyle\int_0^{\frac{\pi}{4}} (\cos x - \sin x)\, dx$

$$= (\sin x + \cos x + C)\Big|_0^{\frac{\pi}{4}}$$

$$= \left[\sin \frac{\pi}{4} + \cos \frac{\pi}{4} \right] - \left[\sin 0 + \cos 0 \right]$$

$$= \left[\frac{\sqrt{2}}{2} + \frac{\sqrt{2}}{2} \right] - [0 + 1]$$

$$= \sqrt{2} - 1$$

f) Area $= \dfrac{45}{4}$

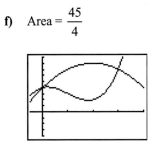

The functions intersect when

$$x^3 - 3x^2 + x + 4 = -x^2 + 4x + 4$$
$$x^3 - 2x^2 - 3x = 0$$
$$x(x^2 - 2x - 3) = 0$$
$$x(x - 3)(x + 1) = 0$$
$$x = 0, 3, -1$$

Enclosed area $=$

$$\int_0^3 \left(\left[-x^2 + 4x + 4 \right] - \left[x^3 - 3x^2 + x + 4 \right] \right) dx$$

$$\int_0^3 \left(-x^3 + 2x^2 + 3x \right) dx$$

$$= \left(-\frac{1}{4}x^4 + \frac{2}{3}x^3 + \frac{3}{2}x^2 + C \right)\Big|_0^3$$

$$= \left[-\frac{1}{4}(3)^4 + \frac{2}{3}(3)^3 + \frac{3}{2}(3)^2 \right] - [0]$$

$$= \frac{45}{4}$$

Area Using Numerical Methods

ANSWERS AND SOLUTIONS

1. a) Area approximation $= 0.863\ 4$

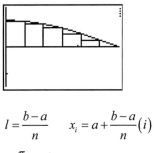

$$l = \frac{b-a}{n} \qquad x_i = a + \frac{b-a}{n}(i)$$

$$= \frac{\dfrac{\pi}{2}}{6} \qquad x_i = 0 + \frac{\pi}{12}(i)$$

$$= \frac{\pi}{12} \qquad A = \frac{\pi}{12}\sum_{i=1}^{6} \cos\left(0 + \frac{\pi}{12}i\right)$$

$$A \doteq 0.8634$$

b) Signed area = 1

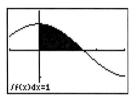

Signed area =

$$\int_0^{\frac{\pi}{2}} (\cos x)\, dx = (\sin x + C)\Big|_0^{\frac{\pi}{2}}$$

$$= \left[\sin\frac{\pi}{2}\right] - [\sin 0] = 1$$

The actual area under the curve is 1 unit squared. So, our approximation is not too far off, considering that we use only 6 rectangles.

2. a)
$$l = \frac{b-a}{n}$$
$$= \frac{3-1}{4}$$
$$= \frac{1}{2}$$

The width of each rectangle is $\frac{1}{2}$.

b) The rectangles would have the following sub-interval boundaries:

1 to $\frac{3}{2}$

$\frac{3}{2}$ to 2

2 to $\frac{5}{2}$

$\frac{5}{2}$ to 3

These are the values for x.

c) For Reimann Sums, we wish to use the lower of the two heights of each rectangle for the lower sum (m) and the greater height for the upper sum (M). But, be careful not to just use the values of x determined in (b). We need to first apply the function, since the height of each rectangle is not x, but rather $f(x)$.

For the lower sum (m) the heights of the rectangles would be $m = \frac{2}{3}, \frac{1}{2}, \frac{2}{5}, \frac{1}{3}$.

For the upper sum (M), the heights of the rectangles would be $M = 1, \frac{2}{3}, \frac{1}{2}, \frac{2}{5}$.

Mentally check to insure each $M > m$.

3. a)
$$\frac{b-a}{n} = \frac{1}{2}$$

$$0 \to \frac{1}{2} \to 1 \to \frac{3}{2} \to 2$$
$$A = \frac{1}{2}\left(\frac{1}{2}\right)\left[1 + 2(1.5) + 2(3) + 2\left(\frac{11}{2}\right) + 9\right]$$
$$A = \frac{30}{4}$$
$$A \approx 7.5$$

Using the formula and $f(x_i)$, our approximation is 7.5 units squared.

b) $f(x) = 2x^2 + 1$

$$\int_0^2 (2x^2 + 1)\, dx = \left(\frac{2}{3}x^3 + x + C\right)\Big|_0^2$$
$$= \left[\frac{16}{3} + 2\right] - [0]$$
$$= \frac{22}{3}$$

Our approximation in **a)** above is not too far off for only 4 trapezoids.

Topic Practice Questions 2

ANSWERS AND SOLUTIONS

1. a)
$$\int\left(\frac{e^{-x}}{2} + 2\cos x\right) dx = -\frac{e^{-x}}{2} + 2\sin x + C$$
$$= 2\sin x - \frac{e^{-x}}{2} + C$$

b) $\int (\sin x - \pi)\, dx = -\cos x - \pi x + C$

2. $t \doteq 3.19\text{s}$

Let the ground be the reference point and the downward direction be the negative direction. The initial velocity is 0 m/s and velocities are decreasing throughout this problem.

Thus, $a = -9.8 \text{ m/s}^2$

Integrate to find the velocity-time function:

$v(t) = \int (-9.8)\,dt$

$v(t) = -9.8t + C_1$

Using the initial condition that the velocity is 0 at $t = 0$

$0 = -9.8(0) + C_1$

$C_1 = 0$

$v(t) = -9.8$

Integrate to find the displacement-time function:

$s(t) = \int (-9.8t)\,dt$

$s(t) = -4.9t^2 + C_2$

Using the initial condition that the displacement is 50 m at $t = 0$, $C_2 = 50$.

$s(t) = -4.9t^2 + 50$

The stone hits the ground when displacement is zero, so this will allow us to find time.

$0 = -4.9t^2 + 50$

$t^2 = \dfrac{50}{4.9}$

$t \doteq 3.19$

We need only use the positive time of 3.19 seconds.

3. Using Hooke's Law, we start with $F = ks$ and apply the given information to find the constant (k).

$F = ks$

$1 = k(0.02)$

$k = 50$

Now (again using Hooke's Law), we set up the second-degree differential equation.

$\dfrac{d^2s}{dt^2} + \dfrac{50}{0.1}s = 0$ and the solution

$\dfrac{d^2s}{dt^2} + 500s = 0$

$s = A\sin\sqrt{\dfrac{k}{m}}\,t + B\cos\sqrt{\dfrac{k}{m}}\,t$

$s = A\sin\sqrt{500}t + B\cos\sqrt{500}t$

We use the initial conditions that at time zero,

$s = 0.02$

$0.02 = 0 + B\cos 0$

$B = 0.02$

Differentiate s to obtain $\dfrac{ds}{dt}$ and apply the conditions that at time zero, $\dfrac{ds}{dt} = 0$.

$\dfrac{ds}{dt} = \sqrt{500}A\cos\left(\sqrt{500}t\right) - \sqrt{500}B\sin\left(\sqrt{500}t\right)$

$0 = \sqrt{500}A\cos(0) - (0)$

$A = 0$

$s = 0.02\cos\left(\sqrt{500}t\right)$

4. **a)** The function touches the x-axis when $y = 0$ or at $\left(-\dfrac{1}{3}, 0\right)$.

b) The area of this triangle is equal to one-half the base times the height, or

$A = \dfrac{\left(\dfrac{7}{3}\right)(7)}{2}$

$A = \dfrac{49}{6}$

The base is from $\left[-\dfrac{1}{3}, 2\right]$, and at $x = 2$, the height is 7.

c) $\int_{-\frac{1}{3}}^{2}(3x+1)\,dx$

$= \left(\dfrac{3}{2}x^2 + x + C\right)\Big|_{-\frac{1}{3}}^{2}$

$= \left[\dfrac{3}{2}(2)^2 + 2\right] - \left[\dfrac{3}{2}\left(-\dfrac{1}{3}\right)^2 + \left(-\dfrac{1}{3}\right)\right]$

$= [8] - \left[-\dfrac{1}{6}\right] = \dfrac{49}{6}$

5. a) The signed area under function f in the interval [0, 3] is:

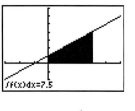

$$\int_0^3 (x+1)\,dx = \left(\frac{1}{2}x^2 + x + C_1\right)\Big|_0^3$$
$$= \left[\frac{1}{2}(3)^2 + 3\right] - [0]$$
$$= \frac{15}{2}$$

The signed area under function g in the Interval [0, 3] is:

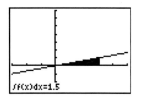

$$\int_0^3 \left(\frac{1}{3}x\right)dx = \left(\frac{1}{6}x^2 + C_2\right)\Big|_0^3$$
$$= \left[\frac{1}{6}(3)^2\right] - [0]$$
$$= \frac{3}{2}$$

The area between the 2 functions in the interval [0 , 3] is the difference of these 2 calculated areas.

$$\frac{15}{2} - \frac{3}{2} = 6$$

b) The difference function, d, (upper–lower) in the interval [0, 3] is:

$$d(x) = f(x) - g(x)$$
$$d(x) = (x+1) - \left(\frac{1}{3}x\right)$$
$$d(x) = \frac{2}{3}x + 1$$

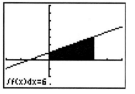

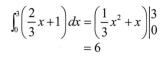

$$\int_0^3 \left(\frac{2}{3}x + 1\right)dx = \left(\frac{1}{3}x^2 + x\right)\Big|_0^3$$
$$= 6$$

6. Approximation of area $= 34$ units squared.

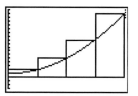

The width of each rectangle is $\dfrac{4-0}{4} = 1$

The area of the 4 rectangles is:

$$A = \frac{b-a}{n}\left[f(1) + f(2) + f(3) + f(4)\right]$$
$$A = 1(2 + 5 + 10 + 17)$$
$$A = 34$$

This is an approximation for the area under the function f in the interval [0, 4]. To find the actual area, evaluate the following definite integral:

$$\int_0^4 (x^2 + 1)\,dx$$
$$= \left(\frac{1}{3}x^3 + x + C\right)\Big|_0^4$$
$$= \left[\frac{1}{3}(4)^3 + 4\right] - [0]$$
$$= \frac{64}{3} + \frac{12}{3}$$
$$= \frac{76}{3}$$

There is a considerable difference between the approximate value and the actual value due to the fact that only 4 rectangles were used in the approximation, creating an over-approximation.

7. Approximate area = 25.5 units squared

The width of each trapezoid is $\dfrac{b-a}{n}=\dfrac{1}{2}$.

Over 8 trapezoids, we get the following intervals:

$$\left[0,\frac{1}{2}\right],\ \left[\frac{1}{2},1\right],\ \left[1,\frac{3}{2}\right],\ \left[\frac{3}{2},2\right],$$

$$\left[2,\frac{5}{2}\right],\ \left[\frac{5}{2},3\right],\ \left[3,\frac{7}{2}\right],\ \left[\frac{7}{2},4\right]$$

$$A \doteq \frac{1}{2}\left(\frac{b-a}{n}\right)$$
$$\left[f(a)+2f(x)_1+2f(x)_2+\ldots+f(b)\right]$$

$$A \doteq \frac{1}{4}\begin{bmatrix}1+2\left(\dfrac{5}{4}\right)+2(2)+2\left(\dfrac{13}{4}\right)+2(5)\\[2mm]+2\left(\dfrac{29}{4}\right)+2(10)+2\left(\dfrac{53}{4}\right)+17\end{bmatrix}$$

$$A \doteq \frac{1}{4}(102)$$
$$A \doteq 25.5$$

This approximation is very close to the exact value of the area under the curve over the given interval. There are two reasons that this approximation is more accurate than the approximation found using a rectangular approximation with four rectangles. First, we are using more trapezoids, which makes the width of each one less and the difference in $f(x)$ over the sub-interval less. Second, we are using trapezoids, which approximate the curve more closely than do rectangles.

8. Area under $f(x)=\dfrac{1}{2+\sin^2 x}$ over the interval

$[0,\pi]$. Using four trapezoids, $\dfrac{b-a}{n}=\dfrac{\pi}{4}$

Intervals are $\left[0,\dfrac{\pi}{4}\right],\ \left[\dfrac{\pi}{4},\dfrac{\pi}{2}\right],\ \left[\dfrac{\pi}{2},\dfrac{3\pi}{4}\right],\ \left[\dfrac{3\pi}{4},\pi\right]$

$$A \doteq \frac{1}{2}\left(\frac{\pi-0}{4}\right)\left[f(0)+2f\left(\frac{\pi}{4}\right)+2f\left(\frac{\pi}{2}\right)+2f\left(\frac{3\pi}{4}\right)+f(\pi)\right]$$

$$A \doteq \frac{1}{2}\left(\frac{\pi}{4}\right)\left[\left(\frac{1}{2}\right)+2\left(\frac{2}{5}\right)+2\frac{1}{3}+2\left(\frac{2}{5}\right)+\left(\frac{1}{2}\right)\right]$$

$$A \doteq \frac{1}{2}\left(\frac{\pi}{4}\right)\left(\frac{49}{15}\right)$$

$$A \doteq 1.283$$

9. a) $\displaystyle\int_{-2}^{4}\left(3x^2+2x-1\right)dx = 78$

$$\int_{-2}^{4}\left(3x^2+2x-1\right)dx$$
$$=\left(x^3+x^2-x+c\right)\Big|_{-2}^{4}$$
$$=\left[4^3+4^2-4\right]-\left[(-2)^3+(-2)^2-(-2)\right]$$
$$=[76]-[-2]$$
$$=78$$

b) $\displaystyle\int_{0}^{\pi}\left(\cos 10x\right)dx = 0$

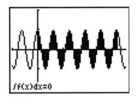

$$\int_{0}^{\pi}\left(\cos 10x\right)dx$$
$$=\left(\frac{1}{10}\sin 10x+C\right)\Big|_{0}^{\pi}$$
$$=\left[\frac{1}{10}\sin 10\pi\right]-\left[\frac{1}{10}\sin 0\right]$$
$$=[0]-[0]$$
$$=0$$

10. a) $p(-1)=0$

$$p(-1)=\int_{-1}^{-1}\left[3t^2-4\right]dt$$

Since the lower and upper limits of integration are equal, no signed area has been accumulated.

b) $p'(-1)=-1$

Since $3t^2-4$ is the integrand of the definite integral, it is the **derivative** of function p, expressed in a variable, t.
$$p'(t)=3t^2-4$$

Thus, $p'(-1)=3(-1)^2-4=-1$

c) $p(x) = x^3 - 4x - 3$

$$p(x) = \int_{-1}^{x} (3t^2 - 4)\,dt$$
$$= (t^3 - 4t + C)\Big|_{-1}^{x}$$
$$= [x^3 - 4x] - [(-1)^3 - 4(-1)]$$
$$= x^3 - 4x - 3$$

d) $p(5) = 22$

$$p(5) = (5)^3 - 4(5)^2 - 3$$
$$= 125 - 100 - 3$$
$$= 22$$

11. 0.70

Using: Average value $= \dfrac{\int_a^b f(x)\,dx}{b-a}$

$$\dfrac{\int_{\frac{\pi}{6}}^{\frac{\pi}{3}} (\cos x)\,dx}{\dfrac{\pi}{3} - \dfrac{\pi}{6}}$$

$$= \dfrac{(\sin x + C)\Big|_{\frac{\pi}{6}}^{\frac{\pi}{3}}}{\dfrac{\pi}{6}}$$

$$= \dfrac{\left(\sin \dfrac{\pi}{3}\right) - \left(\sin \dfrac{\pi}{6}\right)}{\dfrac{\pi}{6}}$$

$$= \dfrac{\dfrac{\sqrt{3}}{2} - \dfrac{1}{2}}{\dfrac{\pi}{6}}$$

$$\doteq 0.70$$

12. a) $g(2) = 9$

$$g(2) = \int_{-4}^{x} [f(t)]\,dt$$

The value of $g(2)$ is the accumulated signed area under function f in the interval $[-4, 2]$. We can evaluate this signed area simply by determining the area of the triangle formed.

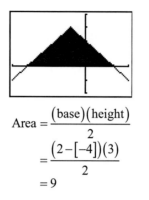

$$\text{Area} = \dfrac{(\text{base})(\text{height})}{2}$$
$$= \dfrac{(2 - [-4])(3)}{2}$$
$$= 9$$

b) $g'(2) = 0$

$$g(x) = \int_{-4}^{x} [f(t)]\,dt$$

The integrand, which is function f, is the **derivative function** of function g.
Thus, $f(x) = g'(x)$.

The value of $g'(2)$ is equal to $f(2)$ and can simply be located on the graph of function f. Since the point $(2, 0)$ is on function f,
$$g'(2) = f(2) = 0$$

METHODS OF INTEGRATION AND APPLICATIONS

Fundamental Theorem of Calculus

ANSWERS AND SOLUTIONS

1. $a = 1, b = 3$

2. continuous

3. $F(x) = \dfrac{-1}{x} + C$

4. $-\cos x + C$

5. $-\cos x \big|_0^\pi = -(-1) + (1) = 2$

6. $4x \big|_2^3 = 12 - 8 = 4$

7. $\cos x \, dx$

   $\int (2\cos x) \, dx$
   $= \int (\cos x + \cos x) \, dx$
   $= \int \cos x \, dx + \int \cos x \, dx$

Integration by Substitution

ANSWERS AND SOLUTIONS

1. **a)** $\int \cot x \, dx$

   Look at integrand:
   $\cot x$
   $\dfrac{\cos x}{\sin x}$
   $u = \sin x$
   $du = \cos x \, dx$
   $dx = \dfrac{du}{\cos x}$

   Now, apply this to original integral:
   $\int \dfrac{\cos x}{u} \dfrac{du}{\cos x}$
   $\int \dfrac{1}{u} \, du$
   $\ln |u| + C$
   $\ln |\sin x| + C$

   b) $\int \dfrac{2e^{\sqrt{x}}}{\sqrt{x}} \, dx$

   $u = \sqrt{x}$
   $du = \dfrac{1}{2\sqrt{x}} \, dx$
   $dx = \left(\dfrac{2u}{1} \right) du$
   $\int \dfrac{2e^u}{u} \left(\dfrac{2u}{1} \right) du$
   $\int 4e^u \, du$
   $4e^u + C$
   $4e^{\sqrt{x}} + C$

2. $\dfrac{1}{6}$

   $\int_0^2 \left[\dfrac{x}{\left(2 + x^2\right)^2} \right] dx$

   Let $u = \left(2 + x^2\right)$
   $du = 2x \, dx$

   Determine the new limits of integration.
   When $x = 0$, $u = 2 + 0^2 = 2$.
   When $x = 2$, $u = 2 + 2^2 = 6$.

$$\int_0^2 \left[\frac{x}{\left(2+x^2\right)^2}\right]dx$$

$$=\int_2^6 \left(\frac{x}{u^2}\right)\left(\frac{du}{2x}\right)$$

$$=\frac{1}{2}\int_2^6 \left(u^{-2}\right)du$$

$$=\frac{1}{2}\left(-\frac{1}{u}\right)\Big|_2^6$$

$$=\frac{1}{2}\left(-\frac{1}{6}+\frac{1}{2}\right)$$

$$=\frac{1}{6}$$

3. a) $\ln 4 - \ln 3$

$$\int_3^4 \left(\frac{1}{x-1}\right)dx$$

Let $u = x-1$
$du = dx$
When $x = 3$, $u = 3 - 1 = 2$
When $x = 4$, $u = 4 - 1 = 3$

$$\int_3^4 \left(\frac{1}{x-1}\right)dx$$

$$=\int_2^3 \left(\frac{1}{u}\right)du$$

$$=\left(\ln|u|+C\right)\Big|_2^3$$

$$=\ln 3 - \ln 2$$

$$\doteq 0.405$$

b) $\displaystyle\int_3^4 \left(\frac{1}{x-1}\right)dx$

$$=\left(\ln|x-1|+C\right)\Big|_3^4$$

$$=\ln|4-1|-\ln|3-1|$$

$$=\ln 3 - \ln 4$$

ANSWERS AND SOLUTIONS

1. a)   Divide each term by the denominator.

$$\int\left(\frac{1}{x}+\frac{1}{x^2}\right)dx$$

$$\ln|x|-\frac{1}{x}+C$$

b)   When performing division, set up as follows:
$\dfrac{x^3 - x^2 - 0x - 1}{x+1}$, then divide.

Integrand becomes $\dfrac{x^2-2x+2}{1}-\dfrac{3}{x+1}$ (the quotient and remainder)

Integrate to obtain the final answer:

$$\frac{x^3}{3}-x^2+2x-3\ln|x+1|+C$$

c) $\displaystyle\int\frac{1}{2x^2-2}dx \Rightarrow \frac{1}{2}\int\frac{1}{x^2-1}dx$

Work with integrand:

$$\frac{1}{x^2-1}=\frac{1}{(x+1)(x-1)}$$

$$\frac{A}{x+1}+\frac{B}{x-1}$$

$$A(x-1)+B(x+1)=1$$

$$A+B=0$$

$$-A+B=1$$

$$B=0.5$$

$$A=-0.5$$

So,

$$\frac{1}{2}\int\left(\frac{-1}{2(x+1)}+\frac{1}{2(x-1)}\right)dx$$

$$\frac{1}{2}\left(\frac{1}{2}\right)\left(-\ln|x+1|+\ln|x-1|\right)$$

$$\frac{-\ln|x+1|}{4}+\frac{\ln|x-1|}{4}+C$$

---

d) $\int \dfrac{x+2}{(x+1)^2}\,dx$

Work with integrand:

$\dfrac{A}{x+1}+\dfrac{B}{(x+1)^2}$

$A(x+1)+B = x+2\,(\text{equating numerators})$

This equates to the original, so solve for variables:

$A = 1$

$A + B = 2$

Solve, substitute and complete:

$\int \left(\dfrac{1}{x+1}+\dfrac{1}{(x+1)^2}\right)dx$

$\ln|x+1|-\dfrac{1}{(x+1)}+C$

2. a) We solve this the same way we would an indefinite integral, then apply the upper and lower values of the integral at the end.

Integrand: $\dfrac{-1x-1}{(x-2)(x-1)}$ factoring a negative

1 out of the numerator is optional here. Apply fractions, set up system, and solve. Now, apply given integral parameters:

$\dfrac{A}{x-2}+\dfrac{B}{x-1}$

$A(x-1)+B(x-2)=-1x-1$

$A + B = -1$

$-1A - 2B = -1$

$A = -3$

$B = 2$

$\dfrac{-3}{x-2}+\dfrac{2}{x-1}$

$-3\ln|x-2|+2\ln|x-1|+C$

$-3\ln|x-2|+2\ln|x-1|\ \Big|_3^4$

Now, the constant disappears.

$-3\ln 2+2\ln 3-\left(-3\ln 1+2\ln 2\right)$

$\ln\left(\dfrac{2^{-3}3^2 1^3}{2^2}\right)$

-1.27

b) $\int_3^4 \left(\dfrac{2x-4}{2(x-2)^2}\right)dx$

$=\int_3^4 \left(\dfrac{2(x-2)}{2(x-2)^2}\right)dx$

$=\int_3^4 \left(\dfrac{1}{x-2}\right)dx$

$=\left(\ln|x-2|+C\right)\Big|_3^4$

$=\ln 2-\ln 1$

$=\ln 2$

Integration by Parts

ANSWERS AND SOLUTIONS

1. a) $\int (2x+1)e^{-x}\,dx$

First, write out the integration by parts formula, then apply:

$\int f(x)g'(x)\,dx = f(x)g(x)-\int g(x)f'(x)\,dx$

$f(x)=2x+1$

$f'(x)=2$

$g'(x)=e^{-x}$

$g(x)=-e^{-x}$

Once we identify the separate parts and the left-hand side of the formula is identical to our given integral, we can immediately solve using only the right-hand side of the formula. (In some occasions, as seen in previous examples, we re-arrange the original integral).

$=-(2x+1)e^{-x}-\int -e^{-x}(2)\,dx$

$=-(2x+1)e^{-x}+2\int e^{-x}\,dx$

$=-(2x+1)e^{-x}-2e^{-x}+C$

$=-2xe^{-x}-e^{-x}-2e^{-x}+C$

$=-2xe^{-x}-3e^{-x}+C$

$=-(2x+3)e^{-x}+C$

b) $f(x) = x$
$f'(x) = 1$
$g'(x) = \cos 3x$
$g(x) = \dfrac{1}{3}\sin 3x$

Then, using the formula:

$= \dfrac{1}{3}x\sin 3x - \int (\sin 3x)dx$

$= \dfrac{1}{3}x\sin 3x + \dfrac{1}{9}\cos 3x + C$

c) $f(x) = x$

$f'(x) = 1$
$g'(x) = \sec^2 x$
$g(x) = \tan x$

Now, apply the formula:

$= x\tan x - \int \tan x(1)dx$

$= x\tan x - \left(-\ln|\cos x|\right) + C$

$= x\tan x + \ln|\cos x| + C$

d) $f(x) = \dfrac{x}{2}$

$f'(x) = \dfrac{1}{2}$
$g'(x) = e^x$
$g(x) = e^x$

$= \dfrac{xe^x}{2} - \int \left(\dfrac{1}{2}\right)e^x dx$

$= \dfrac{xe^x}{2} - \dfrac{e^x}{2} + C$

This answer can be combined as a single fraction, if desired.

e) -4

$f(x) = 2$
$f'(x) = 2$
$g'(x) = \cos x$
$g(x) = \sin x$

$f'(x)g(x) - \int g(x)f'(x)dx$

$= 2x\sin x - \int (\sin x)(2)dx$

$= 2x\sin x + 2\cos x + C$

$\int_0^\pi 2x\cos x\,dx$

$= \left(2x\sin x + 2\cos x + C\right)\Big|_0^\pi$

$= \left[2\pi\sin \pi + 2\cos \pi\right] - \left[2(0)\sin 0 + 2\cos 0\right]$

$= \left[0 + 2(-1)\right] - \left[0 + 2(1)\right]$

$= -4$

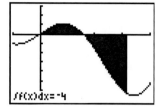

f) $\pi - 2$

Similar to **e)** except the limits of integration are changed, so the answer becomes:

$\int_0^{\frac{\pi}{2}} 2x\cos x\,dx$

$= \left(2x\sin x + 2\cos x + C\right)\Big|_0^{\frac{\pi}{2}}$

$= \left[2\left(\dfrac{\pi}{2}\right)\sin \dfrac{\pi}{2} + 2\cos \dfrac{\pi}{2}\right]$
$\quad - \left[2(0)\sin 0 + 2\cos 0\right]$

$= \left[\pi + 2(0)\right] - \left[0 + 2(1)\right]$

$= \pi - 2$

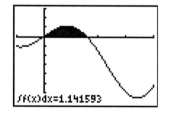

Topic Practice Questions 1

ANSWERS AND SOLUTIONS

1. $\dfrac{\pi^2}{2} \doteq 4.935$

$$\int_0^\pi (x + \cos x)\,dx$$

$$= \left(\frac{1}{2}x^2 + \sin x + C\right)\Big|_0^\pi$$

$$= \left[\frac{1}{2}(\pi)^2 + \sin \pi\right] - \left[\frac{1}{2}(0)^2 + \sin 0\right]$$

$$= \frac{\pi^2}{2}$$

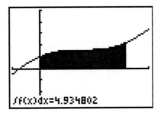

∫f(x)dx=4.934802

2. Change $2\int \tan x\,dx$ to $2\int \dfrac{\sin x}{\cos x}\,dx$.

Let $u = \cos x$

$du = -\sin x\,dx$

$$2\int \frac{\sin x}{u}\frac{du}{-\sin x}$$

$$2\int \frac{-du}{u}$$

$$= -2\ln|\cos x| + C$$

$\cos x \neq 0$

3. First rewrite and simplify the function:

$$\int \frac{(x^2-1)}{(x^2-1)^2(x-1)}\,dx \Rightarrow \int \frac{1}{(x^2-1)(x-1)}\,dx$$

Normally, we would set this up as follows:

$$\frac{Ax+B}{(x^2-1)} + \frac{D}{(x-1)}$$

But if we tried to solve this using a system, we will find it does not work. The reason for this is that the denominator of our integrand must be rewritten as follows before solving:

$$(x^2-1)(x-1)$$
$$(x+1)(x-1)(x-1)$$
$$(x+1)(x-1)^2$$

This is why the hint was necessary.

Properly applied, the rules of partial fractions suggest we break this up as:

$$\frac{A}{x+1} + \frac{B}{(x-1)} + \frac{D}{(x-1)^2}$$

$$A(x-1)^2 + B(x+1)(x-1) + D(x+1) = 1$$
$$A(x^2-2x+1) + B(x^2-1) + D(x+1) = 1$$

$$A + B = 0$$
$$-2A + D = 0$$
$$A - B + D = 1$$

$$A = \frac{1}{4}$$
$$B = -\frac{1}{4}$$
$$D = \frac{1}{2}$$

We can bring a common factor out in front of the integral sign in order to simplify the equation until the final step. We use the rule that says:

$$\int kf(x)\,dx = k\int f(x)\,dx$$

$$\frac{1}{4}\int \left(\frac{1}{x+1} + \frac{-1}{(x-1)} + \frac{2}{(x-1)^2}\right)dx$$

$$\frac{1}{4}\ln|x+1| - \frac{1}{4}\ln|x-1| - \frac{2}{(x-1)} + C$$

4. To solve $\int 2x\cos x\,dx$, apply the formula:

$$\int f(x)g'(x)\,dx = f(x)g(x) - \int g(x)f'(x)\,dx$$

$$f(x) = 2x$$
$$f'(x) = 2$$
$$g'(x) = \cos x$$
$$g(x) = \sin x$$

$$= (2x)\sin x - \int \sin x(2)\,dx$$
$$= 2x\sin x - (-2\cos x) + C$$
$$= 2x\sin x + 2\cos x + C$$

5. $-\ln(e^2-1) + \ln(e-1) \doteq -1.313$

$$\int_1^2 \frac{e^x}{1-e^x}\,dx$$

$$u = (1-e^x)$$
$$du = -e^x\,dx$$

Determine the new limits of integration,
When $x = 1$, $u = 1 - e$.
When $x = 2$, $u = 1 - e^2$.

$$\int_1^2 \frac{e^x}{1-e^x}dx = -\int_{1-e}^{1-e^2} u^{-1}du$$

$$= \left(-\ln|u| + C\right)\Big|_{1-e}^{1-e^2}$$

$$= \left[-\ln\left|1-e^2\right|\right] - \left[-\ln|1-e|\right]$$

$$= -\ln\left(e^2-1\right) + \ln(e-1)$$

$$\doteq -1.313$$

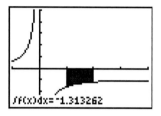

∫f(x)dx=-1.313262

6. $\int\left(4-x^2\right)dx - \int\left(x-x^2\right)dx$

Express as a single integral:
$$\int\left(4-x^2-x+x^2\right)dx$$
$$\int\left(4-x\right)dx$$
$$= 4x - \frac{x^2}{2} + C$$

Volumes of Revolution

ANSWERS AND SOLUTIONS

1. **a)** Use the formula for volume:
$$\int_a^b \pi\left[f(x)\right]^2 dx$$

$$\int_2^3 \pi x^4 dx$$

$$= \frac{\pi x^5}{5}\Big|_2^3$$

$$= \frac{243\pi}{5} - \frac{32\pi}{5}$$

$$= \frac{211}{5}\pi$$

b) The interval in question is from $0 \to \frac{\pi}{4}$.

(Knowing that $180° = \pi$ radians)

$$\int_a^b \pi\left[f(x)\right]^2 dx$$

for $f(x) = y = \sec x$

$$V = \int_0^{\frac{\pi}{4}} \pi \sec^2 xdx$$

$$= \pi \tan x\Big|_0^{\frac{\pi}{4}}$$

$$= \pi(1-0)$$

$$= \pi$$

c) $\int_a^b \pi\left[f(x)\right]^2 dx$

$$V = \int_0^3 \pi(2)^2 dx$$

$$= 4\pi x\Big|_0^3$$

$$= 12\pi$$

Confirm: The original function is just the line at $y = 2$. If we break this up into rectangles, they will all rotate to form a cylinder of radius 2 and a height equal to the interval $0 \to 3$, or 3 units.

The formula for the volume of a cylinder is $\pi r^2 h$.
$$V = \pi r^2 h$$
$$V = \pi(4)(3)$$
$$= 12\pi$$
So, it is confirmed.

d) $y = (x-1)^2$

$$V = \int_0^1 \pi\left(x^2-2x+1\right)^2 dx$$

$$= \pi\left(\frac{x^5}{5} - \frac{x^4}{1} + \frac{2x^3}{1} - 2x^2 + x\right)\Big|_0^1$$

$$= \pi\left(\frac{1}{5} - 1 + 2 - 2 + 1\right) - 0$$

$$= \frac{\pi}{5}$$

e) We can use the preliminary work done in (d) above, and skip to the step where the interval is calculated into the equation.

$$= \pi\left(\frac{x^5}{5} - \frac{x^4}{1} + \frac{2x^3}{1} - 2x^2 + x\right)\Bigg|_1^2$$

$$= \pi\left(\frac{32}{5} - 16 + 16 - 8 + 2\right) - \pi\left(\frac{1}{5} - 1 + 2 - 2 + 1\right)$$

$$= \pi\left(\frac{2}{5}\right) - \pi\left(\frac{1}{5}\right)$$

$$= \frac{\pi}{5}$$

Compare and comment: The value obtained for the volume is equal to **d)**. However, this is not simply because the interval was the same length in each case. The key to this answer lies in the fact that the original function, $y = (x-1)^2$, is a parabola with a vertex at (1, 0). It has a line of symmetry at $x = 1$. So, any volume generated to the left of this line would be the same generated to the right. The interval in **d)** is one unit left of the axis of symmetry. The interval in **e)** is one unit immediately to the right of the axis of symmetry.

f) $y = \sqrt{x}$

$$V = \int_0^a \pi(x)^1 \, dx$$

The square root is removed since the function is being squared.

$$V = \frac{\pi x^2}{2}\Bigg|_0^a$$

$$= \frac{a^2 \pi}{2}$$

If, $a = 2$, then $V = 2\pi$

Topic Practice Questions 2

ANSWERS AND SOLUTIONS

1. $F(b) - F(a)$, F continuous

2. $\int(6x^2 - \sin x) \, dx$

$$= 2x^3 + \cos x + C$$

3. $\int\left[\sqrt{3x^2 - 5}\,(12x)\right] dx$

$u = \sqrt{3x^2 - 5}$

$du = \dfrac{6x}{2u}\,dx$

$$\int u(12x)\frac{2u}{6x}\,du$$

$$\int 4u^2 \, du$$

$$= \frac{4u^3}{3} + C$$

$$= \frac{4}{3}(3x^2 - 5)^{\frac{3}{2}} + C$$

4. $\int 3\sin^5 x \cos x \, dx$

$u = \sin x$

$du = \cos x \, dx$

$$\int 3u^5 \cos x \frac{du}{\cos x}$$

$$\int 3u^5 \, du$$

$$= \frac{u^6}{2} + C$$

$$= \frac{\sin^6 x}{2} + C$$

5. $\int 5x \sin x \, dx$

$f(x) = 5x$

$f'(x) = 5$

$g'(x) = \sin x$

$g(x) = -\cos x$

$$= 5x(-\cos x) - \int(5)(-\cos x)\,dx$$

$$= -5x\cos x + 5\int\cos x \, dx$$

$$= -5x\cos x + 5\sin x + C$$

6. $\int x^2 e^x \, dx$

$f(x) = x^2$

$f'(x) = 2x$

$g'(x) = e^x$

$g(x) = e^x$

$$= x^2 e^x - \int 2x(e^x)\,dx$$

We have to work with the integral again to solve.

$\int 2xe^x dx$

$f(x) = 2x$

$f'(x) = 2$

$g'(x) = e^x$

$g(x) = e^x$

$= 2x(e^x) - \int 2e^x dx$

$= 2xe^x - 2e^x$

Now, put this back into the partially solved original solution.

$x^2 e^x - 2xe^x + 2e^x + C$

$e^x(x^2 - 2x + 2) + C$

We don't need to add the constant until the final step.

7. For question 2, we used basic integration techniques and the final answer (now a definite integral) is $1 + \cos 1$, which is approximately 1.54.

For question 3, we used integration by substitution, but this function has $\sqrt{3x^2 - 5}$ as part of its original function and its integral. This is only defined if $x^2 \geq \dfrac{5}{3}$, so our limits of integration will not give us an answer with real roots. The function is not continuous over the interval.

For question 4, we used integration by substitution, and the final answer is $\dfrac{\sin^6 1}{2}$ or $\doteq 0.1775$.

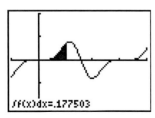

For question 5, we used integration by parts and the final answer is $-5\cos 1 + 5\sin 1$.

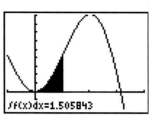

For question 6, we used integration by parts, twice, obtaining a final answer of $e - 2$.

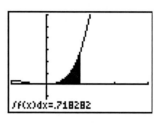

8. $\dfrac{x+2}{(x+4)^2}$

$\dfrac{A}{x+4} + \dfrac{B}{(x+4)^2}$

$A(x+4) + B \Rightarrow x + 2$

$A = 1$

$4A + B = 2$

$B = -2$

$\dfrac{1}{x+4} - \dfrac{2}{(x+4)^2}$

The antiderivative of this would be:

$\ln|x+4| + \dfrac{2}{(x-4)^1} + C$

Here, the points of concern would be $x = -4$ (making the natural logarithm undefined) and $x = 4$ (causing the denominator of the second term to be zero). Any limit of integration for this function would have to avoid these values.

9. a) $\dfrac{Ax+B}{(x^2 - x - 1)} + \dfrac{C}{(x-3)}$

b) $\dfrac{A}{(x-2)} + \dfrac{B}{(x-2)^2} + \dfrac{C}{(x-2)^3} + \dfrac{Dx+E}{(x^2 + x + 1)}$

10. $y = x^2 - 6x + 9$

$$V = \int_3^5 \pi \left(x^2 - 6x + 9 \right)^2 dx$$

$$= \pi \int_3^5 \left(x^4 - 12x^3 + 54x^2 - 108x + 81 \right) dx$$

$$= \pi \left(\frac{x^5}{5} - 3x^4 + 18x^3 - 54x^2 + 81x \right) \Bigg|_3^5$$

$$= \frac{32\pi}{5}$$

Another method involves factoring the original trinomial.

$$x^2 - 6x + 9 = \left(x - 3 \right)^2$$

$$V = \pi \int_3^5 \left[\left(x - 3 \right)^2 \right]^2 dx$$

$$= \pi \int_3^5 \left(x - 3 \right)^4 dx$$

$$= \pi \left(\frac{1}{5} \left(x - 3 \right)^5 + C \right) \Bigg|_3^5$$

$$= \pi \left(\left[\frac{1}{5} \left(5 - 3 \right)^5 \right] - \frac{1}{5} \left(3 - 3 \right)^5 \right)$$

$$= \pi \left(\left[\frac{32}{5} \right] - \left[0 \right] \right)$$

$$= \frac{32\pi}{5}$$

Credits

Every effort has been made to provide proper acknowledgement of the original source and to comply with copyright law. However, some attempts to establish original copyright ownership may have been unsuccessful. If copyright ownership can be identified, please notify Castle Rock Research Corp so that appropriate corrective action can be taken.

ORDERING INFORMATION

SCHOOL ORDERS

Schools and school jurisdictions are eligible for our educational discount rate. Contact Castle Rock Research for more information.

THE KEY **Study Guides** are specifically designed to assist students in preparing for unit tests, final exams, and provincial examinations.

THE KEY **Study Guides**—$29.95 each plus G.S.T.

SENIOR HIGH		JUNIOR HIGH	ELEMENTARY
Biology 30	Biology 20	English Language Arts 9	English Language Arts 6
Chemistry 30	Chemistry 20	Mathematics 9	Mathematics 6
English 30-1	English 20-1	Science 9	Science 6
English 30-2	Mathematics 20-1	Social Studies 9	Social Studies 6
Mathematics 30-1	Physics 20	Mathematics 8	Mathematics 4
Mathematics 30-2	Social Studies 20-1	Mathematics 7	English Language Arts 3
Physics 30	English 10-1		Mathematics 3
Social Studies 30-1	Mathematics 10		
Social Studies 30-2	Combined		
	Science 10		
	Social Studies 10-1		

Student Notes and Problems (SNAP) Workbooks contain complete explanations of curriculum concepts, examples, and exercise questions.

SNAP Workbooks—$29.95 each plus G.S.T.

SENIOR HIGH		JUNIOR HIGH	ELEMENTARY
Biology 30	Biology 20	Mathematics 9	Mathematics 6
Chemistry 30	Chemistry 20	Science 9	Mathematics 5
Mathematics 30-1	Mathematics 20-1	Mathematics 8	Mathematics 4
Mathematics 30-2	Physics 20	Science 8	Mathematics 3
Mathematics 31	Mathematics 10	Mathematics 7	
Physics 30	Combined	Science 7	
	Science 10		

Class Notes and Problem Solved—$19.95 each plus G.S.T.

SENIOR HIGH		JUNIOR HIGH
Biology 30	Biology 20	Mathematics 9
Chemistry 30	Chemistry 20	Science 9
Mathematics 30-1	Mathematics 20-1	Mathematics 8
Mathematics 30-2	Physics 20	Science 8
Mathematics 31	Mathematics 10 Combined	Mathematics 7
Physics 30		Science 7

Visit our website for a tour of resource content and features or order resources online at
www.castlerockresearch.com/store/

#2410, 10180 – 101 Street NW
Edmonton, AB Canada T5J 3S4
e-mail: learn@castlerockresearch.com

Phone: 780.448.9619
Toll-free: 1.800.840.6224
Fax: 780.426.3917

ORDER FORM

THE KEY	QUANTITY
Biology 30	
Chemistry 30	
English 30-1	
English 30-2	
Mathematics 30-1	
Mathematics 30-2	
Physics 30	
Social Studies 30-1	
Social Studies 30-2	
Biology 20	
Chemistry 20	
English 20-1	
Mathematics 20-1	
Physics 20	
Social Studies 20-1	
English 10-1	
Math 10 Combined	
Science 10	
Social Studies 10-1	
Social Studies 9	
English Language Arts 9	
Mathematics 9	
Science 9	
Mathematics 8	
Mathematics 7	
English Language Arts 6	
Mathematics 6	
Science 6	
Social Studies 6	
Mathematics 4	
Mathematics 3	
English Language Arts 3	

Student Notes and Problems Workbooks	QUANTITY SNAP Workbooks
Mathematics 31	
Biology 30	
Chemistry 30	
Mathematics 30-1	
Mathematics 30-2	
Physics 30	
Chemistry 20	
Mathematics 20-1	
Physics 20	
Mathematics 10 Combined	
Science 10	
Mathematics 9	
Science 9	
Mathematics 8	
Science 8	
Mathematics 7	
Mathematics 6	
Mathematics 5	
Mathematics 4	
Mathematics 3	

Problem Solved and Class Notes	QUANTITY Class Notes	QUANTITY Problem Solved
Mathematics 31		
Biology 30		
Chemistry 30		
Mathematics 30-1		
Mathematics 30-2		
Physics 30		
Biology 20		
Chemistry 20		
Mathematics 20-1		
Physics 20		
Mathematics 10		
Combined		
Mathematics 9		
Science 9		
Mathematics 8		
Science 8		
Mathematics 7		
Science 7		

Total Cost

Subtotal 1	
Subtotal 2	
Subtotal 3	
Cost Subtotal	
Shipping and Handling*	
G.S.T	
Order Total	

*(Please call for current rates)

School Discounts

Schools and school jurisdictions are eligible for our educational discount rate. Contact Castle Rock Research for more information.

PAYMENT AND SHIPPING INFORMATION

Name: _____
School _____
Telephone: _____

SHIP TO
School Code: _____
School: _____
Address: _____
City: _____ Postal Code: _____

PAYMENT
☐ By credit card   VISA/MC
Number: _____
Expiry Date: _____
Name on card: _____
☐ Enclosed cheque
☐ Invoice school   P.O. number: _____

RESEARCH CORP

#2410, 10180 – 101 Street NW, Edmonton, AB T5J 3S4   **Phone:** 780.448.9619 **Fax:** 780.426.3917
Email: learn@castlerockresearch.com   **Toll-free:** 1.800.840.6224
www.castlerockresearch.com